Momentum

Chasing the Olympic Dream

Peter Vordenberg

ISBN 1-892590-56-5

Copyright, 2002, by Pete Vordenberg

Library of Congress Control Number: 2002116762

published by Out Your Backdoor Press
Jeff Potter, publisher

order copies for $17.95 + $2.05 post/handl (cash, check, MO) from:

Out Your Backdoor Press
4686 Meridian Rd.
Williamston MI 48895

or with a credit card from: OutYourBackdoor.com

cover photos by Bob Allen
cover graphic design by Owen Neils
copyediting by Joey Harrison
pen-and-ink sketches by Pete Vordenberg

A portion of the chapter "The '94 Olympic Trials" appeared in *VeloNews*.

"It is easy to see," replied Don Quixote, "that you are not used to this business of adventures. Those are giants, and if you are afraid, away with you out of here and betake yourself to prayer, while I engage them in fierce and unequal combat."

"What giants?" said Sancho Panza.

from *Don Quixote* by Miguel de Cervantes

To
Sue and Lloyd

Contents

Working on the Dream

The trick is to leap out of bed as soon as you are aware of consciousness. Up, into motion, no time for doubt, no questions asked. New day. Game on. Eli Brown taught me that. He wakes up awake. His eyes open and he's swinging legs over the bed, popping out from under the covers. Eli attacks from the gun. Then we are out the door and in the van—on our way to work on the dream. On our way to training. This is a mission. Every day is a mission. Some days the mission is to rest, some days it's academics, some days fun, but most days the mission is to work. The planning and thinking have been done. This is the time for doing.

Sten Fjeldheim is driving. He is a person who believes whole-heartedly in the philosophy of doing. Sten looks at us as he drives by turning all the way around in his seat. He is telling a story we have all heard before but to which we listen with rapt interest. The story doesn't matter. The energy and emotion involved make the story. And Sten doesn't just tell stories, he relives them. As the story unfolds, the road flies beneath us, and the van negotiates the corners seemingly without Sten's assistance. He is bouncing around, gesturing with his arms and making faces at us, talking loudly and laughing. Energy and excitement vibrate from the guy. We're going training! Just like yesterday afternoon, and yesterday morning, and the day before, and the day before that. For the past month, year, ten years. Sten can hardly wait to get out there and seriously *do it*.

Training can be fun. A run through sunbeams splintered by tall pines in the cool of evening, feeling fresh and light, skiing in hard tracks, on fast snow, full of life. But today training threatens to be less than fun. Low clouds, dark and cold. We are pushing through a hard ten days of training. No one feels fresh and light. If tall pines and sun exist, I cannot remember having enjoyed running through them. Training right now is nothing more than work, laboring up a gravel road in the light rain and in complete discomfort. It is our last interval. All are head-down, snot and rain dripping off the nose, fully involved in the task. We are a soggy string of runners stretched out up a steep incline deep in the woods. Alone—save for Sten, soaked and shivering, hollering encouragement to us. We are doing it, and even if the act of training itself is less than fun right now, we are working on the dream, and working on the dream is what drives me out of bed each morning. No hesitation, no doubt, up into motion.

***

To commit to something grand, something that may not be possible, to say "I am going to do it," even when you may not be able to: That is dreaming. To actually set about the task of living up to your commitment, to begin doing, to tenaciously pursue what you said you would achieve: That is working on the dream.

Eagle Glacier, Alaska. Training 5 hours a day. (1997)

Route 23

From our house in Boulder, Colorado, my dad, Lloyd, found the Blacks in Trout Lake, Washington, in just two phone calls. It was done in Lloyd's style, which though effective, embarrassed me, for in the interest of clarity no detail was spared. His first call was to the only number we could find in Trout Lake, the general store. The conversation went something like this:

"Lloyd Vordenberg calling," at which point he would have cleared his throat into the phone before continuing, and I imagined the clerk at the register thinking, *Who the hell is Lloyd Vordenberg?*

"My son Pete and four of his teammates from Northern Michigan University would like to live up there in Trout Lake this summer to train." *What the hell?* I imagined the poor clerk thinking, *This guy has to have the wrong number.*

"They are cross-country ski racers," Lloyd continued, "and will be doing a lot of training, so they won't be any trouble to anyone. But they'll be needing somewhere to stay." *Well, they ain't gonna be staying with me, Mister, ah, Wordenberger*—and it must have come as some relief when Lloyd finally arrived at the point. "I was wondering if you might know of anyone there in the Trout Lake area who might have a few rooms for rent or, if not, if you know who I might call?"

The clerk knew.

The summer of '93 was to be our first summer in Trout Lake, and our second in Southern Washington State. It was also our first with the Blacks, a family who took us in, charging us little more than a hundred bucks a month each in rent. They were a conglomerate family of Arkansas country folk and Utah Mormons, all joined in one way or another and relocated to the foothills of Mt. Adams near the southern border of Washington, on the outskirts of a town so small our address was simply: General Delivery, Trout Lake, Washington.

We picked Trout Lake because the terrain was perfect for ski training, living there was cheap, and because it was remote and surrounded by open and wild country. In Trout Lake we could live the life of a ski racer: eat, sleep train...eat, sleep, train...eat, sleep, train.

Roger Black had the demeanor of an old circus bear: friendly and tired, with hands scarred from work and swollen from the herbicide he sprayed along the roads all day for the Washington Department of Transportation. He scratched absently at his wrists and hands, and greeted us every evening when he came home with an honest lopsided smile and a handshake he'd use to leverage you into a gruff hug. "Roger, now," his wife, Connie, would scold in a high drawl, "let them boys go. They got to be tired, all that running, and you all boys are hungry too, ain't you?" And then you'd be in her embrace, as big as Roger's but soft and cool. Sara, their teenage daughter, would wave shyly and return to the TV or her paperback.

Their married daughter, Carmen Grigsby, wasn't shy. "Why hello!" with a lot of power behind the *hello*. "How you boys doing?" she'd ask as she shook hands and pulled you into a careful hug, like she knew she could squeeze you too hard if she didn't watch it. Robert Grigsby was Carmen's husband. He wore the same thing every day—we all did, come to think of it—but his outfit was particularly lean: jean shorts, tennis shoes and a thin mustache. Whatever he said, he said it slow, with sincerity. Robert and Carmen had a happy, squirming, dirt-eating, roly-poly toddler called Bugsy.

Bugsy, Carmen, Sara and Connie were round on all fronts, big and soft. They worked hard and ate American. Roger was big but harder. He had served in Vietnam, and the droop in his eyes showed an ease with life but also a sad knowledge of what the world was capable of dishing out.

The Black-Grigsby house sat across an irrigation ditch from the dirt-strip airport, which was surrounded by cow pastures and tall grass-filled fields. We five skiers pulled up in two Japanese cars, and unloaded ourselves, young and early in the adventure of life, in front of the Black-Grigsby clan.

Kurt Wulff had purple hair, pierced nipples, and wore green leather Doc Martin boots and long baggy shorts. Cory Custer had a topknot of hair tied into a bun: a Samurai warrior in running shorts and T-shirt. I had a buzz cut and a beard matching the length of my hair. There was a momentary standoff as we looked at the Blacks and they looked at us and neither of us was sure what to do next or how this was going to turn out.

Luckily we had Eli Brown, who in any company is at home. While his clothes were standard baggy shorts and T-shirt, and his hair a simple crew cut, something in Eli's uniquely open and slightly goofy manner sets people at ease. He is the son of a jazz-band, tuba-playing preacher from the inner city of Minneapolis, and kids love him at first sight. Bugsy crawled to him like an old friend, stood against Eli's leg and stretched his arms for Eli to lift him. Eli, his lower jaw and big round chin jutting out in an under-bite smile, looked down, scooped the diapered kid up and tossed him four feet into the air. Bugsy let loose a screech of delight, and five minutes after arriving, the odd group of us were home.

The house had plank siding and was constructed with thick beams of roughhewn timber. It was three stories and perfectly square. The Blacks, who owned the house, gave it up to the Grigsbys and slept in a trailer across the pasture. The Grigsbys occupied the second floor, and we skiers the top. The bottom story of the old place was dedicated to communal cooking and the consumption of food. There was a big couch covered with hand-crocheted afghans, Bugsy's toys, and half-devoured magazines. Next to it were two recliners, springy-soft and lumpy with use, that would envelop you when you gave them your weight. The furniture faced a television sprouting bent, hopeless antennas that supplied it with reception so poor that only Donnie Grigsby and Sara Black, the teenagers, could stand to watch it. The basement was dedicated to the storage of consumables, purchased with great glee at the Costco in Portland, or fished with equal glee out of the nearby streams and lakes.

Steep stairs connected the floors. After only a few days, our floor was littered with training clothes, shorts, T-shirts, running shoes, roller-skis, snow skis, poles, boots, duffels, packs, bike tubes, bike pumps, tools, sleeping bags, a tent, a snowboard, a guitar, books and clutter. Next to each of the five mattresses scattered throughout the two small rooms lay a training log. A training log is a calendar outlining the ski season. It contains sections for planning and structuring months, weeks, days, and hours.

A training log is a diary, a journal, a day planner, and a calendar, but it is much more than the sum of these things. It is the map to an Olympic medal. And believing as I did that I could become an Olympic champion, I knew that to accomplish this I had to follow a hard regimen of training. The training plan my coach and I conceived covered, to varying degrees of specificity, days, a month, a year, two years, ten years. The plan took me from Monday to Sunday, from May 1 all the way around to April 30, from junior high to college. And, finally, to the top step of the Olympic podium. It led me into a future that was plotted in ink and carried out by the hour, day, and year, for many years. To meet the future, as it was planned on paper, I had to accomplish a certain amount of training, a certain intensity of training, and all of it in flexible yet prescribed methods and doses. My training log held the plan. My religion was to follow it.

Each night before we fell asleep, we lay on our mattresses in holy silence with our training logs open before us, reviewing our vows of dedication. We did not dream at night. We dreamt during the day, and we chased those dreams with such intensity that at night we slipped into a coma-like slumber.

***

There is a dirt road running west from the Black-Grigsby house. Not long after it passes the Black's trailer, the road Tee's into Washington Route 23, about a half mile from our doorstep. Route 23 is a narrow two-lane road paved smooth with sticky black asphalt. It Y's at the foot of Mt. Adams—the right branch heading directly up the mountain, the left branch rising around and over the foothills. Both branches climb steadily. There is almost no traffic on Route 23 because it turns to dirt and then dives into a hilly, twisty course through logging country on its way toward Mt. Rainier to the north.

Far up Route 23, mile marker 21 pokes its head out of the tall, dry grass at the top of a straight, steep pitch of road. From this crest, the flat-topped volcanic cone of Mt. Adams can be seen to the northeast. There is snow on Mt. Adams all year long. Starting in the fall, the snow line lowers steadily, until in winter even the Black-Grigsby house has snow in the yard. In the summer as the snow melts, the snow-line recedes until it gets just above tree line, by which time it is fall and the high mountain snow is falling again.

A July entry in my training log says: *Classical roller-ski on 23 with Cory, Kurt.* The entry evokes a memory of the event.

It is quiet except for the humming of insects, the tweet of birds, and a peculiar click-clack rhythm of something coming up the road. The birds become quiet, watching from the trees, as the click-clacking chorus ascends the road toward mile marker 21. The origin of this noise comes into sight. It is a line of three skiers ascending the road on wheeled skis—roller-skis. They are one behind another, skiing in rhythm, the sharp carbide-tipped ski poles striking the asphalt in unison. Click. Clack. Click. Clack. Click. They are at the bottom of the straight, steep section and climbing hard toward the mile marker. As the skiers near the marker their tempo increases, the click-clacking loses its synchrony as each skier increases his pace. They lose formation as they spread out across the lane. As one skier pulls ahead, the others speed up, until the speed, which has gone from a relaxed rhythm to a controlled sprint, loses its element of control and all three are pushing all-out for the finish at mile marker 21. With ten feet to go they are side by side; five feet and one skier has pulled ahead. The others fight to regain the lead, but cannot make up the gap. They cross the invisible line, one skier clearly first, then the other two stretching across the line trying to beat each other. They stagger, stop, their heads hang, they lean on their poles panting hard, sucking air, trying to recover from the effort.

The entry in the training log says: *Twelve sprints. Kurt quickest...today.*

Kurt Wulff grew up the biggest fish in his and all neighboring ponds. He was from Minocqua, Wisconsin, the son of a schoolteacher and an artist. His parents were cool, his house was cool, his sister was cool, and back home no one could touch him. He was the fastest skier, fastest bike racer, held a black belt in kenpo karate, and played bass guitar.

Kurt, dubbed the Purple Lupus for his hair color and wolf-like name, carried himself with the confidence supplied by his upbringing. He was smooth, his face was smooth, his muscles were smooth, his hands, skin, walk, speech, even his laugh was smooth. In Minocqua, Kurt was king.

As for Cory, he too had confidence, but rather than believing in his past or the present, he believed in his future. If he wasn't the fastest, he believed that through training and toughness he would be.

My own belief in both how fast I was and how fast I would become combined well with Cory's stubborn drive, Kurt's cool confidence, and everyone's competitiveness, to push us up and down the roads and trails around Trout Lake.

Cory, Kurt, and I stand at the top of Route 23 sucking the last of our sport drinks. Dusk has settled. The air is cool and dry, and in the calm evening the view is clear. From here we can see what's left of Mt. St. Helens to the west, and to the north we can just see Mt. Rainier. But Mt. Adams, east and north, dominates the skyline. Dusk leaves a bright blush on the snow, which stands in contrast to the darkening sky behind it and the miles of shaded evergreens surrounding it. Below us, thirteen miles of Route 23 wind through tall pine down onto the flat Trout Lake basin where the town sits, the Black-Grigsby household waits, and dinner is likely cooking.

When descending on roller-skis there is reason to hope nothing will block your way—because roller-skis have no brakes. Going up, a roller-skier's speed is controlled by the strength of the skier; going down it is all in the hands of gravity and friction. Once in serious motion, there is no stopping, at least not in any kindly fashion. On Route 23, downward-bound,

Route 23   13

serious motion is achieved in about twenty seconds. It takes over an hour and a half to climb what we will descend in half an hour.

A couple of hard pushes with our ski poles and Cory, Kurt and I are flying down the road. We pull into low tucks and glide one behind the other, drafting. The last person in line gains more speed than the first and so comes around and rolls through to the front of the line, and this pattern is repeated so that we are in a constant state of rotation. Most of the descent is done at twenty to thirty miles per hour, but just after mile marker 16 the road drops more steeply around a corner. There is a gap in the trees where a section of the forest has been logged. Through it we get a last look at Mt. Adams before dropping into the fastest mile on Route 23. All three of us hit the start button on our stopwatches, and get lower in our tucks. The breeze is intimate, flapping the edges of your shorts, holding your hair against your scalp or, if you don't have hair, riding over your scalp with a tingle. At dusk the bugs are thick. Bats swoop through the purple night, and even though it's getting dark, to keep bugs out of our eyes we wear sunglasses. This is an informal and unspoken race, where courage, weight, and skill decide the winner.

The trees whip past and the rubber roller-ski wheels hold the asphalt with a sticky hum. The pavement zips along just three inches beneath our feet.

We have timed this mile many times. The record is just over a minute and ten seconds, or a little less than fifty miles per hour. As usual Kurt has pulled a little ahead of Cory and me; the two of us continue to rotate, so as to stay in each other's draft. The tips of Cory's poles, held parallel to the ground and his back, are snug under his arms and less than a foot in front of my face. In his draft I gain speed and pull even closer until I have to lean out and come around him, letting the sharp tips pass a few inches to the side of my face. For a second we are side by side, then I am past and he leans toward me and slips into my draft. The mile marker approaches through the twilight. We are past it in an instant, and hit the stop button on our watches. Legs screaming from holding the low position, we rise slightly from our tucks, and stand up, still ripping down the road.

One minute 12 seconds; Kurt hits 1:10.

It was one afternoon in a hundred just like it. That same morning we had run at an easy pace for an hour and a half on the trails and dirt logging roads behind the house. Mid-day we did general strength training, which is a forty-minute routine of pull-ups, push-ups, sit-ups, and dips. It was one day in a hundred just like it. It was not the one day that mattered, but the hundred; not the one sprint up to mile marker 21, or even the dozen we did that day, but the routine of doing sprints every week all summer, all fall, all winter, all year, for many years.

The first day of one season falls directly after the last day of the previous season. It is a cycle of training that does not end. According to my training log, the last race of the '92-'93 season was at the end of April. The very next day, the first day of the new season, I trained three hours. In my log for that day I wrote: *Only thirty-eight weeks until the '94 Olympic Trials.*

One day amounts to nothing without the following day. One season spills into the next—the days and the seasons are like tributaries combining to form a river. A trickle of snowmelt will never reach the ocean alone, but a river almost inevitably reaches the deep. The ocean my tributaries were combining to reach, my goal, was an Olympic gold medal. I was twenty-two years old, which is young for a cross-country ski racer, and so I did not expect to compete for a medal at the '94 Olympics or even the '98 Olympics. I thought I could do it in 2002, or even at the 2006 Olympics, because then I would be at my athletic peak.

On the first day of the '93-'94 season I was training for the 1994 Olympic Trials, thirty-eight weeks away, but the Trials were only a step toward the 1994 Olympics. At the same time, the '94 Olympics were only a step toward an Olympic medal in 2002, which was then only eight and a half years away. By that early summer of 1993, I had already been building toward the future for over nine years. After the evening roller-ski and a huge dinner, while lying on my bed on the third floor of the Black-Grigsby home, falling quickly into sleep, I felt that I was halfway there.

Coming back from a long training ski at NMU, 1992. Cory Custer, me, Jeff Stasser (left to right).

The Whole Truth

Our summer in Trout Lake ended three days before fall term was to start at Northern Michigan University. NMU is located on the shore of Lake Superior in Michigan's Upper Peninsula, the U.P., or "da you-pee" as it is commonly pronounced up there. NMU was a long two-days drive from Trout Lake—if you only stopped for gas. It was our sophomore year and so we knew what awaited us.

"You're late," spoke Coach Sten Fjeldheim as the last group of recruits came through the weight-room door. The appointed 6:30 a.m. training time had passed by upwards of a minute and a half and a dark-red, almost purple hue had spread like a thunderstorm's shadow over Coach Fjeldheim's forehead.

"All of you," he said. "In the gym. Right now." We scurried down the hall from the weight room, where we had been milling around, into the gym. Sten led the march, a tall, bowlegged man in his early forties. Veins bulged from long, taut muscles through paper-thin skin. His muscled arms hung heavy from bulbous shoulders and his head was large and carved with angular features. Sten's bald forehead sloped back to a shock of blond hair, and from both temples veins wormed their way toward each other across his forehead. One thick vein stuck out prominently right down the center of his scull.

He stood over us, looking down from eyes inset and overhung by blond brows. He was silent, but his mouth moved slightly as if fishing for the right word to start with.

We stood looking at our toes, and though I knew what was going on and was therefore aware of the subtle joy Sten found in the storm he was about to unleash, I could not bear to look up.

For some the onslaught came with such a shock that they jumped with his first bolt of lightning. In a voice that carried throughout NMU's physical education building, Sten let us know that we were not trying out for a sport, that we were not players of a game, that from this day, from this moment forward our lives would be very different.

"You gotta want it!" yelled Sten Fjeldheim, and there was the whole truth. In the first five syllables, in the first few seconds of the first day of school Sten told us all we really had to know about cross-country ski racing or likely anything else. "And if you want it bad enough you can train on the moon. But if you don't want it bad enough you may as well head for the dorms. You show up here five minutes late. What the hell am I supposed to do with that? We *start* training at 6:30. We don't *show up* at 6:30. Show up at 6:35—hell, hit the road, man. I don't have time for that. If you don't have the courtesy to show up on time, I don't need you. If you don't want it bad enough to show up on time, you don't need me."

Back roads are for training. Northern Michigan.

Weeding Out the Weenies Week

In the first week of school, Coach Sten Fjeldheim conducted what came to be called "Weeding Out the Weenies Week."

Though it would become routine, training at 6:30 a.m. was a shock for all during Weeding Out the Weenies Week. On the mornings we didn't lift weights we ran, and afternoon practice began every day at 2 p.m. We did not ease into it. Summers were for preparing for the fall, and fall was for preparing for the season. You came to school ready. Weeding Out the Weenies Week was just one long, steep step in the whole process, a process that could make the ill-prepared feel like the end goal was not an Olympic medal but an early death.

After the first week the team size was reduced considerably.

Sten Fjeldheim was not interested in killing us. He had genuine, fire-hardened, cold-pressed, undefeatable passion. He was in his place, a self-carved niche, a home and an empire of skiing in the Upper Peninsula, where he could focus every volt of his vibrating, electric being on developing cross-country ski racers.

Back in the weight room he made the rounds. "That's it, that's it. Come on Nelson! My grandma can lift more then that!"

After a week of training it became obvious that Sten's grandma was an extraordinary woman. She could out-run, out-lift, and out-ski every one of us, but when praise was due, Sten was not withholding.

"There you go," Sten continued, "Jesus, Sarah, how many of those things can you do? Nelson! Hey, Brad! Are you watching her? Yeah, Brad! Come on Amy! Good! Now we're talking, huh? What did I tell you? Now we're talking! *Awwwooowwww!*" Sten was no less red, the veins were no less distended, but now with the clang of weights and the sound of primal grunts, with the team training, Sten shone—a man in his own perfect place.

After weights we ran across campus to the dorms where we frantically changed, showered, ran to the cafeteria, wolfed breakfast, and then marched to class. It being the first week of school everyone had more to do...and we skiers still had to get to afternoon practice on time.

Afternoon practice began at two, which means you'd better be in the van before two, because come two o'clock Sten jammed the old van into gear and didn't look back.

For most, Marquette Mountain is the local downhill ski area. For us it was the local uphill area. Two o'clock on a U.P. fall day often found us driving there to do uphill ski bounding or ski walking intervals. Ski bounding and ski walking resemble skiing without snow and are a common method of dry-land ski training. It takes around five minutes to bound hard from the bottom of Marquette Mountain to the top, and five minutes to run back down. After about two hours of this Sten is satisfied and ready to go home.

Coach Sten cared, and if *you* didn't, it was an unforgivable insult, a waste of more than just time and effort. Caring is what it took, what it takes—a whole lot of caring. Sten said you had to want it, and he was right.

The Training Weekend
...and a Memory of the
1992 Olympic Trials

At the end of Weeding Out the Weenies Week Sten conducted what he called the "Training Weekend." Of course we trained every weekend, and in the fall that meant a cross-country running race on Saturday of ten kilometers, and an over-distance roller-ski or run on Sunday. A normal Sunday over-distance workout lasted three to four hours during which time we would either run about twenty miles on rolling trails or roller-ski thirty plus miles on hilly terrain. Basically, the Training Weekend was dedicated to extreme over-distance and consisted of two very long over-distance workouts.

The first day of the 1993 Training Weekend was to be a thirty-five-mile combination run and mountain bike. Each of us was to team up with a partner and take turns running and biking through the woods. The idea was that one person would bike ahead, abandon the bike at trailside, and start running. His teammate would find the bike, ride it well past his partner and then leave the bike for him. The partners would leapfrog one another until both reached the end of the trail. Biking provided something of a recovery from running for each partner so that we could stay out longer than if we only ran. The idea with long distance training was not to go hard or fast, but to keep going, to build endurance.

From the Training Weekend until the 1994 Olympic Trials in early January there were sixteen weeks. No one was more aware of this than Cory Custer, who believed more than anyone else that success was won by pure effort alone. This being the case, Cory decided to run the whole thirty-five miles.

Many warm fall afternoons in the U.P. we would jump from a set of cliffs on the coast of Lake Superior into the chilly, clear water. On the best afternoons it was a fun expedition. On the worst of them, Cory Custer would climb to the highest point and jump many silent seconds to the chill water below. That's when you knew with a sickening realization that you were next, and that is why Cory did it. And so when Cory decided he had to run the thirty-five hilly miles, I knew I had to also.

Cory and I were not alone. Randy, a lanky graduate student from Colorado who was our assistant coach, decided to join in. Eli, naturally, was in. Aaron, a freckled, redheaded, slow-talking Oregonian also held Olympic dreams, so he was in. The rest of the team was running and biking. We took off at 7:00 a.m. on Day One of the Training Weekend.

An hour into our run we were giddy with the adventure. The trail that unwound before us was covered in a patchwork of colorful fallen leaves. Groves of dark pine stood out against a backdrop of the white trunks and yellow leaves of birch trees. The trail rolled over hills and through swamps, into meadows thick with tall, dry grass. We ran past beaver dams where tails slapped the water, and through thickets where deer snorted and bounced out of our path.

In the rhythm of running we weren't training, or working, or thinking. We imagined ourselves running through the woods a hundred years ago. Eli Brown, the big red-cheeked son of a minister, started singing in languages of his own design. He would yell a wild singsong chant and we would echo it as best we could. It wasn't long before we had stripped out of our clothes, tied our shirts over our shoulders like capes, and put our shorts on our heads like headdresses. We grabbed sticks, and smeared mud on our faces and in patterns across our chests. We were running through the northern Michigan woods naked, chanting, singing, and waving sticks like they were spears. We ran naked for over two hours, our songs bouncing off ahead of us through the woods—"HiddlyHiddlyHeee"… *hiddlyhiddlyheee*….

We did not notice time or distance passing. There was nothing else in the world but the path and our song and the hypnosis brought on by the repetitive, rhythmic act of running.

We turned a corner in the trail and ran singing, unabashedly naked and carefree, into a large open meadow with a meandering brook, and a beaver pond…and a chatty gaggle of eager bird watchers. There was a moment of stillness as bird watchers clad in tweed and armed with binoculars met skiers clad in mud and armed with sticks. Both stood awkwardly frozen.

We were leaderless. Half the group was inclined to bolt back into the forest, while the others seemed intent on continuing into the meadow. When one group saw where the other group was headed both would change their direction, and so the meadow group turned abruptly and headed for the forest, while the forest group turned back into the meadow. A consensus was eventually reached and we all jogged with as much nonchalance as possible right on into the meadow up to and past the still-frozen bird watchers.

As we ran past the birders our head songster, the always grinning Eli Brown, bid them a hearty greeting: "Nice day for it!"

Sten met us at the halfway point with the van and sandwiches and juice. We'd pulled our shorts on by now, and jogged up to the van.

"You boys run into the president's wife," asked Sten, "and the assistant athletic director out there bird-watching?"

Randy, the assistant coach, answered: "Nope."

Cory was a conundrum to most. He was quick-witted and funny, but didn't go out of his way to make friends. But when he did make friends it was an honest and mutually earned friendship. He was not going to compromise his ideas or ideals in the interest of sharing pleasantries. We had run over 17 miles through rough terrain and had just fueled up with half a peanut-butter sandwich, some apple juice and water. It was pleasantly warm, and I felt like lying down in the grass, closing my eyes, and slipping into unconsciousness, rather than turning around and running back. Those who had run and biked were feeling good about their effort and the day. It was perfectly pleasant and, for Cory, a fine time to disturb the perfection. There was some cheerful banter about the previous race season—who beat whom in what race—and someone mentioned, good naturedly, how they took Cory to school in some race. Cory, who was too competitive to let "being taken to school" pass with a grin, spoke his mind openly on the matter. And it wasn't so much what he said, as the matter-of-fact and confident way he spoke that set the team off. "*Humph*," snorted Cory. "I'll be conducting the classes this year." It wasn't a joke, or a half joke, but in Cory's mind a complete truth, and one he did not hesitate to share.

From Cory's first day training at NMU he was goading the older members of the team for not training hard enough, and while this didn't earn him any quick friends among the old guard, he was more than partially responsible for turning a bunch of skiers comfortable in their mediocrity into a group of guys bent on, at the very least, beating the hell out of Cory in every race and training session they possibly could. Since Cory's arrival at NMU their training days were much less comfortable. But even in their first winter with Cory, they skied faster than they ever had before.

And so those who had taken turns running and biking out to the half-way mark, and who had been happy with that, suddenly became eager to run the whole way home, and also to put some serious hurt on Professor Custer en route.

With seventeen miles to go, Cory led a pack of pissed-off elder team members into the woods toward home. We wove back through the same swamps and meadows, over the same hills and leaf-covered trails, past the same gaggle of now giggling bird watchers. But this time there was no singing, no nudity, only a hard-nosed silence and an ever-increasing pace. There is an undeniable truth to the mental aspect of sport. Behind Cory, a small mob of upper classmen trod directly at his heels.

Cory Custer is built like an Incan wrestler. He is short with a wide, barrel chest with long limbs braided with tight bundles of muscle. I could see their eyes fixed on the back of his thick head, cursing the annoying flop of his feet on the hard earth, his popping little calf muscles—*That arrogant little bastard*, I imagined them thinking. *Oh yeah, we'll see, we'll just see.* But I have a feeling they were afraid he was right. Still, they ran on at Cory's back much faster and much longer than expected. In the end, the one who wanted it more lasted longer, and Cory wanted it more.

The fun had been run out of our adventure. My feet and legs were carrying me along on autopilot, and I was able to retreat into my mind and explore.

Running or skiing or doing anything repetitive and rhythmic can allow you to escape easily into memory. Running through the Northern Michigan woods I drifted back to the 1992 Olympic Trials in Biwabik, Minnesota.

At the Giants Ridge Ski Area the water runs red from the tap. Biwabik, like the U.P. of Michigan where we ran the first day of the Training Weekend, is in what is called the Iron Range, a rusty swath of rolling forest stretching across northern Minnesota, Wisconsin, and the U.P. It is where rivers slide red and orange beneath ice and snow, and jumbled mountains of black and red mine tailings stand above the glacially carved landscape. In Minnesota the locals go ice fishing in Vikings jackets; in Wisconsin and the U.P. they snowmobile in Packers jackets. In both places they drink Wisconsin-brewed beer by the case, and bait deer year-round with apples, so everyone is fat for the November harvest.

In the Iron Range they scrape ore from gaping wounds in the earth every day, all day, all year round. The people hail mostly from Scandinavia

and other northern climes. They say "ya" when they mean "yes" and pro-
nounce their o's, '*ohhh*', and a's, '*ahhh.*' Along with the accent, certain additional aspects of their Scandinavian heritage remain. Among other things,
the Finns brought ski jumping. Scattered across the landscape are rickety
wooden towers topped with small huts. In those huts, the ski jumpers wait,
smoking and praying, before sliding down the steep ramp which hangs like
a tongue from the mouth of a panting dog, and hurl themselves off the
end, flying, or more like falling forward through the air until they land
with a great slap on hard-packed snow. The Norwegians and Swedes
brought cross-country skiing, and each town has a park with groomed ski
trails meandering out through the birch and pine forests. Giants Ridge is
the largest of these Iron Range ski areas. Over the years Giants Ridge has
been home to many U.S. National Championship cross-country ski events
and a number of U.S. Ski Team tryout races, called Trials, and even a few
World Cup events.

In 1992 Giants Ridge hosted the Trials for the '92 Olympic Games in
Albertville, France. It was my first year of college at NMU, and my first
Olympic Trials. I was twenty years old.

I think of this as Cory leads us through the similar U.P. landscape on
our thirty-five-mile run. Logs submerged in beaver ponds are dyed orange, as are the rocks beneath the surface of gurgling streams. Whole ponds
are orange. Even the mud on our shoes has an orange tint. At the '92 Trials
in Biwabik I remember filling my water bottle from the tap. The water was
rusty orange and tasted like blood.

Before the '92 Trials I was viewed as a complete outsider. Despite having won three junior national titles, I was not even considered a long shot
to make the Olympic team. Since I knew all along what I wanted and was
extremely aware of what I was doing to achieve it, it came as a bit of a shock
to me that my performance at the Trials was so unexpected by the American ski world. *Don't they know what I've been doing*, I thought. *Don't they
know what I've been dreaming?* Of course they didn't.

Halfway through the first race, though feeling a little sluggish, I was in
seventh place. The coaches giving me split-times compared to the other
racers were not yelling with great enthusiasm, but were checking their
numbers and scratching their heads in some disbelief. The splits were right.
I was skiing my way onto the Olympic team. Though the coaches were
surprised, even as a freshman I didn't feel out of place skiing with the best
in the country. My goal was to beat them.

I finished the first three races among the top five out of the 100 skiers who had qualified to race in the Olympic Trials. If I finished at least as well in the last race, I would be going to France as a member of the 1992 U.S. Olympic team.

The night before the last race I wandered over to Sten's room to absorb some confidence. I knew what I needed to do in the race the next day. I just wanted to hear from Sten that I *could* do it. There was muffled laughter, music and incoherent shouts coming from within the room. Sten and his assistant, Randy, were in the middle of the hot and smelly job of applying the final key layers of wax to 15 pairs of skis. Because of the noise my knock was unanswered, and so I opened the door. They stood over the wax benches wearing gas masks to protect their lungs from the wax fumes. The hotel room was hazy with smoke and they had plastic bags tied over the smoke detectors. A few beer bottles stood in piles of wax shavings, next to wax irons, vials of wax, scrapers, brushes, and other tools of the waxing trade. Waxing was prohibited in the rooms, as the hotel manager had frequently reminded us, and so when I opened the door, both heads snapped in my direction and stared at me through the haze, from behind their masks, with the guilty expression of children caught by an angry mom.

Randy shouted a muffled "Jesus!" through the waxing mask.

"Vordenberg!" Sten said as he lifted his mask from his mouth, and tilted a beer under it, drinking a few swallows.

"Christ," finished Randy, turning down the music and laughing.

"So," I said, trying to sound unconcerned, "how's it going?" which was met by silence. "So," I continued, "what do you think I have to do tomorrow?" It came out stupid. Sten sat down.

"I was just over at the coaches' meeting," started Sten. "People were walking around wringing their hands. You have them sweating, Vordenberg. You know these guys thought they had it narrowed down, had the score, you know? 'There's so and so, and if I do such and such, and if he beats him.' They have all the numbers, and every night these athletes are walking around up there, puzzling it over in their minds, asking their coaches, 'How's it look coach? How's it looking for me, now?' But you know, Pete, this is the first time you've talked about it," and I'm adding in a few *uh-huhs, yeps, yeahs.* "Hell," continued Sten, "this is the first I've seen of you, really, and that's good. I had Stone come up to me and actually say, 'All I have to do is beat Vordenberg. That is, so long as Koch isn't in the top three and Wadsworth doesn't come around and...' I stopped him right there and said, 'Man, forget all that. You aren't *going* to beat Vordenberg.' You should have seen his jaw drop." Sten let loose a crazy giggle, his eyes peering about maniacally, shooting back and forth between Randy and me.

"Oh, we got 'em, alright," he said. And then, looking at me with a hand on my shoulder, "Let me tell you what you gotta do..."

The thought that my success was something of a surprise to him, and even a source of unexpected stress, hadn't occurred to me, but he was sweating a little now, and thinking.

The Olympics were a dream we shared. A coach feels a pressure to do all he can. He also feels an unavoidable helplessness brought on by the fact that even after he does everything and has done it well, the outcome is largely out of his hands, and is largely in the athletes wanting it enough.

Never one to be slowed for long, Sten gained a huge, crooked grin, and where there had been some consternation, his eyes now shone with adrenaline.

He leaned forward and took me by both my shoulders. "Vordenberg, you just keep doing whatever it is you've been doing, and you're going to the god-damned Olympic Games!"

"*Yeeeeee-hawwwww!*" yelled Randy.

Back in the U.P. we had now been running for almost five hours, and I found myself at the front of the pack. I was reliving the '92 Olympic Trials, and my body was alive with the memory. The mind doesn't always distinguish between something that is imagined and something that is real. The excitement evoked by my memory of the Trials had my mind telling my body it was time to race, time to go, time to make the Olympics.

At the Trials I roomed with Aaron Lish rather than Cory, because Cory, Sten thought, was too tightly wound to do me any good at this potentially stressful time. Aaron was levelheaded, calm, had a story to fit every situation, and a slow, easy way of telling it. Even when rushed, Aaron spoke deliberately, choosing his words with care. Aaron and I would make up huge pots of noodles to share, and then sit around talking. Even though I'm not a fast talker, I felt like I was rattling out sentences compared to Aaron.

The morning of the final race, Aaron and I each choked down a huge bowl of oatmeal, and pulled on our racing gear. We went about our business in jerky, nervous movements.

In his slow, exacting way, Aaron spoke: "I feel like I am...preparing for war."

I was pulling on long underwear and a Lycra racing suit, getting ready to realize a major step of my life's dream, and I could hardly breathe. It was an excited pressure. My life was not at stake, there was no danger, yet my movements were stiff and awkward with nervous anticipation. I needed to move, but felt restrained. Though I hadn't had even a sip of coffee, I had the sensation of being highly caffeinated, but contained, unable to move. I felt like I was being held down and tickled. I itched but could not scratch.

From the parking lot of the Biwabik Inn Hotel our team van's horn sounded. The Northern Michigan University ski team emerged into the cold morning and wobbled into the parking lot like 1950s movie robots called to action. We lurched, veering toward the van as if it were going to carry us to our deaths.

Sten was behind the wheel. He didn't take his caffeine intravenously, but would if he could have. He had a wad of chew under his upper-lip big enough to have put Pete Rose to shame. His third cup of coffee was sitting on the dash steaming up the window, and he was absolutely vibrating.

"*Awwwwoooooooooo!* Load 'em up! Are you ready to kick some ass!" It was not a question. "*Awwooooo! Aw-Aw-Awwwwwooooo!*"

It was too much. Being in that van was like sitting in the electric chair and having the executioner *pretend* to throw the switch—*gotcha*! The van pulled out of the parking lot with reckless energy, and Sten began telling jokes. He was talking about the time he pulled his old VW bug in front of the double doors of Marquette's biggest bar so no one could get out, and then…

Even though we all knew the story, or at least some version of it, we let ourselves get caught up in its telling.

"When I finally did pull away from those doors, a swarm of miners piled out of that bar like ants from an ant hill. And I tell you what, that VW bug and I got all kinds of inspired. I mean, Holy H. Shit! I bet I hit the railroad tracks going sixty. All four wheels were in the air, and when that bug came down there was a bang-like sound, and my car shuttered and continued down the road wobbling like a drunkard, the wheel was jerking my hands around"—and he's jerking the wheel of the van around to illus- trate—"and I could hardly hold on. And that's when I saw the pickup trucks in the rearview mirror—man, they were *coming* for me!"

The robots that had been the Northern Michigan ski team morphed back to their human selves by laughing at this version of Sten's well-worn tale. "How Sten Escaped the Miners" varies each time, but each time it was by a hair, and each time he had to abandon the Bug and flee on foot, and each time he ended up having to kick a little ass along the way.

Listening to the tale, I felt my head slip off the executioner's block. And by the time we reached the racecourse, I was the one holding the ax.

Our team van, now full of racers excited to compete and do well in the last day of the Trials, pulled into the parking lot at the Giants Ridge Ski Area. We scrambled from the van and set into motion, preparing for the race. This was the Olympic Trials after all, and the venue was crawling with people. There were fans, reporters, television cameras, hundreds of keyed-up racers and nervous coaches, excited parents, friends, and representatives from every business in the Nordic ski industry. I was so focused that I did not see a single face. It was the last day, the kind of day where lives change.

Before a race each skier generally waxes two or three pairs of skis. The morning of the race each skier tests his skis, and the fastest pair is chosen. Last minute waxing must be done for those whose skis are not gliding well.

Racers have to make sure they have eaten enough prior to the race, and have had enough water to drink. To run out of energy or become dehydrated is to forfeit a spot on the Olympic team. Rampant food and liquid intake combined with restless nerves make for constant trips to the bathroom. One must have a routine, a task to guide you through the mayhem and distractions.

Most importantly, a racer must warm up well. I picked out my race skis and set them aside, then picked another pair to warm up on and headed out for my warm up. My body did not work. My legs felt heavy and stiff, my arms were cramped, my head floated, banging around with each stride like a helium-filled balloon at the top of a string. I had to go to the bathroom again. My body was resisting what it sensed was coming. It was to be subjected to another race and was understandably reluctant to go through with the ordeal. This was a *good* sign. My nerves knew what was to be demanded of my body, and my body would come around; and when it did, I would be ready.

I skied slowly, letting my muscles warm up gradually, letting my mind come back to earth in its own time. As I skied the first few kilometers of my warm-up, I began to get new signals from my legs. I could breathe deeply and my arms and shoulders became relaxed. My legs lost their rubbery sensation, and I felt like I could control them. I reeled in my helium-filled head, and headed back to the start area in the ski stadium where, in a few minutes, I would blast onto the racecourse, hopefully en route to the Olympic Games.

Cross-country ski racing is called a power-endurance sport. It requires power and speed for periods of seconds to minutes, and it requires endur-

Sten Feldheim. I should be holding him up. This is after winning the 1993 NCAA Championships for Northern Michigan University. As of 2002 no other American male has won. It's time for that streak to end. My NCAA record: 3rd and 10th in 1992, 1st and 5th in 1993, 2nd and 3rd in 1994.

ance because races range from 10 kilometers, or 6.2 miles, to 50 kilometers or 31 miles. It is a sport where one must sprint over short steep hills and, on the longer hills, climb at a hard, steady pace uphill for several kilometers. The hills are separated by fast, twisting descents in which the racer hopes to recover from the hard effort of climbing, or by flat sections where speed is earned by strength. A top skier covers ten kilometers in twenty-three to twenty-seven minutes depending on snow conditions and difficulty of the course. A racer can travel at twenty miles per hour over flat terrain, around fifty mph on steep descents, and as slowly as five to ten mph on steep ascents.

Cross-country skiing places a higher demand on the cardiovascular system than any other sport, bar none. Humans are bipedal creatures—we use only our two legs for locomotion. Our internal energy systems expect to supply energy to the legs for moving and the arms for working, but not both the arms, legs and whole trunk for hauling you across the snow at great speed. Cross-country ski racing uses the whole body all at once, hard, for a long time.

Cross-country skiers have evolved backwards. You can see it in the Cro-Magnon gait, the hunched shoulders. We move like apes—as if on four legs. Our quadrapedal mode of transportation doubles the load on the cardiovascular system and so the investment of time required in years and hours to develop the physiology to be strong enough to support high-level racing is long.

Most Olympic medalists range from twenty-six to thirty-two years old, and all started training in their early teens. At the age of twenty I had not developed the kind of power or endurance it takes to compete well with the best skiers in the world. I had, however, developed enough to compete with the best in the U.S.

Thus, in 1992, in Biwabik, Minnesota, in the last race at the Olympic Trials, I raced past the other Olympic hopefuls, U.S. Ski Team members, the country's best. I passed Bill Koch, America's only Olympic medalist. It seemed almost a sin to catch him, a hero all over the cross-country ski world, and as our only champion, more than a hero among U.S. ski racers.

The sensation was such pure joy, a feeling of power and confidence and unending endurance. I was so comfortable on my skis. Under me they were no more than an extension of my legs, and my poles were extensions of my arms. I could not go too fast, no climb was too long.

I crossed the finish line in third place and made the 1992 U.S. Olympic Team.

As I pulled my warm-ups on in the finish area, a figure approached. "Pete"—it was Koch, reaching for my hand, looking me right in the eyes and smiling widely—"you skied one hell of a race, man."

To me, making the Olympic team at the age of twenty was a sign of things to come, a sign that a gold medal was within my grasp—granted, not for another eight to twelve years—but the notion that I could really do it evolved from distant dream to a real possibility.

Still, the fact that I had actually qualified for the Olympic Games, that I would be racing in them, that very winter in Albertville, France, that I would march into the packed Olympic stadium, and hear "*And now ladies and gentlemen, I am proud to announce the team from the United States of America!*" was just beginning to sink in. It had been a race, a series of races like many others. I had simply done what I could do and skied as fast as I could. Sten had protected me from most of the hype, and now I was dazed by it. After answering questions I couldn't focus on, and giving a number of what were probably mindless and confused interviews, I called home from the pressroom and spoke to my mom, Sue.

"Well," I said, "I'm going to the Olympics."

"Well," she answered, "all right." And then, her throat pinched, grew excited, wobbling, and high pitched, "all right, *All Right! ALL RIGHT!*" After all the fuss and interviews, tight handshakes, backslaps, and words of congratulations, it was the tone of Sue's voice that made it real.

***

Back on our thirty-five-mile run I began, without really trying, to *haul*. I was lost in the memory of the Trials from two seasons ago and the electricity was flowing through me, powering me forward.

After six hours of running we were trucking through the Northern Michigan woods in a state of crazed hypnosis. The core of runners had dwindled. My teammates, who would not let go, must have been in a state similar to my own. Had we given it any thought, we would never have run so fast. It was stupid to raise the intensity above anything but an easy pace, but we were out of control—dreaming and running.

We ran on an old jeep trail. My legs were turning over beneath me; without my looking, my feet avoided rocks and roots, touched the ground, and sent me down the trail. The run was almost over. There were only a few miles left. Eli was at my shoulder, Cory was at my heels. The others were somewhere behind us. We had run almost thirty-five miles over rough and hilly terrain and had been flying during the last half-hour. Like the race, it was a sensation of joy. Much of training is not joyful. It is very obviously difficult and seen only as necessary for the sake of improvement. This run was beyond training for future days. It was everything it needed to be for its own sake, in its own day.

After 35 miles of running we arrived at Sten's cabin, where the team was staying for the training weekend. We stopped running abruptly. The hypnotist had snapped his fingers and we were conscious again, standing bewildered. And like participants of a public hypnosis show, we were herded off the stage feeling half stupid and half disappointed the experience was over. We went directly inside, where each of us consumed bowl after bowl of cereal. The milk went down smooth and cold. We gobbled spoonfuls, letting the milk run off our chins. Tremors shook our legs.

Eli, Cory, and I had just begun to feel the full effect of our thirty-five-mile effort when Sten came striding through the door.

"I'll be damned," he said, beaming. "I can't wait for the 100k roller-ski tomorrow, how 'bout you boys?"

Boulder

I hated cross-country skiing as a kid. Just as the Saturday morning cartoons were starting to crank, my folks, Lloyd and Sue, bundled me into itchy woolen socks and geeky knickers. They loaded me in the backseat of our old Volvo with a mess of skis and our saluki hounds, who had no notion of personal space or oral hygiene. We then drove an hour up a winding canyon road to the windy trailhead for Brainard Lake near the Continental Divide. We joined the granola-crunching cross-country crowd on what I considered a death march on skis from the parking lot to a small cabin set in the snow-filled woods.

It seemed like a wild place, and my imagination made it so. There was a mock-warning sign in the cabin for snotgurgles, the infamous enemy of gnomes, and though I was almost sure they weren't real, I let myself believe in them, and so the treks gained an element of danger. Skiing along at an irritatingly unhurried pace behind my enthusiastically chugging parents I swung my poles at branches knocking the snow off them, and whacked at imaginary snotgurgles.

The trail was rolling and passed almost entirely through thick pine. Occasionally it would pop into a small clearing; and the mountains, hard and gray in the winter light, would open up above and to the west. They held back dark clouds that seemed to be constantly building and boiling up behind them, swirling and fighting against the stone, flinging white fingers over the peaks like a creature trying to climb the Divide. Sometimes the creature made it. Rousing from stillness, the trees would moan and sway. As the wind picked up you'd stop with a kind of ancient anxiety, and bend backwards to squint at the treetops. The light would shrink from the sky, the sky would lower, and the clouds climbed down the high stone, descending upon you. Flakes of snow fell a few at a time, then more, then heavy, and the trees disappeared, until you were in a world of white interrupted by dark trunks and clutching pine bows. Ahead of me in the snow were my two parents sliding merrily along, and behind me, two shivering dogs. It could have been the dogs' fault. I could have learned my distaste for the sport from them. They loved the trip, and ran crazy with delight, right up until the snow between their toes froze and the cold got through their fur. From that point on they didn't hide the fact that for them, the fun was over. They crowded the back of my skis, clicking and clacking at my ski tails with their toenails, stopping, looking back over their shoulder, wondering maybe what chance they had of running all the way home. Then you'd smell the smoke. Not campfire smoke. But a damp, sticky stink that, to this day, makes my head itch, as though I'm wearing a sweaty, too-warm wool hat. You could hardly see the cabin even in clear weather. It was piled over with snow. A path was shoveled down to the front door, the roof was covered, the walls were nearly invisible. We took off our skis, stuck them tail first into the snow alongside the others, and hung our poles from our ski tips. For the dogs, wandering around looking for somewhere to sit, we opened a pouch of dog food. And, finally, shaking snow from our clothes, we crept down the snow stairs to the cabin door. We ate cold sandwiches and drank lukewarm tea. The dogs sat outside on their haunches with one foot in their mouth gnawing ice chunks from between their toes. I had no sympathy for them. They'd spent the whole ride up the canyon trying to take my seat in the car, and would do the same on the way home, only this time they would be wet.

Ski touring had little to offer compared to riding the lifts up and whistling easily back down the alpine slopes, and eating hot hamburgers in the lodge. But for my parents touring stuck, and therefore I was stuck with touring.

Only a few years later it was my cross-country ski races that took up whole weekends of my parents' time. It was an unplanned and unexpected revenge, but I did not know then how much I owed my parents for what I once considered abuse. Nor, while I was cross-country ski racing and loving it, did I realize how much I owed my parents for supporting my dreams in the sport I once hated.

Perfection

There are two types of cross-country ski racing, classical and skating. Each ski race is designated as one or the other. Classical is the old style of skiing, it emulates running but is more fluid and faster. Skating, also called ski-skating or freestyle, is like speed-skating on ice, but with skis and poles on snow over the usual steep terrain of cross-country.

My first Olympic race, the thirty kilometer, classical style race at the 1992 Games, took place on a perfect day for cross-country skiing. It was cold and clear. The cross-country venue in Les Saisies, France, is surrounded by high, rocky, snow-covered mountains. The race started in a stadium that sat in a shallow depression, full of flags and fans, and climbed up through snowy pine forests into bright, open meadows, and wound, climbed and descended through them beneath the mountainous backdrop.

The cold weather made waxing easy. The race was classical style. In classical skiing, a wax is applied to a short section of the ski base right under the foot, which enables the skier to grip the snow when striding forward. The rest of the ski is waxed with glide wax, which enables the skier to glide forward with less friction. The combination of grip and glide yields a sport that is considerably faster than running, even over terrain that is ten times as difficult. When the snow is cold and hard, it is easy to grip; and the tracks, made by machine, are firm and allow for fast glide.

At my best I could run ten kilometers in just under thirty-two minutes. I could cover the same distance in classic style in less than twenty-six and skate-ski it in less than twenty-three.

When touring with my parents the length of a skiing stride was only minutely longer than the length of a walking step. Racing is another matter, another sport. If a running stride takes you five feet, in ski racing the same stride takes you nearly ten. It is human-powered flight across hard-packed snow.

One of a million super-steep uphills in the 30k at the Albertville, France, Olympic Games, 1992.

There is a lot of commercial, shiny, sparkly stuff at the Olympics. The spectacle you see on TV was fun, but for the most part I was not interested in that. I was there to race.

I wasn't going to win for the simple fact that I was not fast enough, and so I had only to go fast as I could. Throughout my career it too often escaped me that this is *all* there *ever* is to do. But it did not escape me in the 30k at the '92 Olympics. That is not to say I was there as a half-assed participant. To race as fast as I could was to give an all-out effort, to be there as a competitor.

I stood at the start with 16 miles of perfect ski tracks and terrain ahead of me, and I held no expectations. I was ready to ski as hard and fast as I could.

"From the United States," said the Olympic announcer, "*Peee-ter Vor-den-berg.*"

This sport is so much a matter of momentum. Keep it and you fly up hills. Lose it and you crawl over them. It is a sport of building and maintaining momentum.

A ski course swoops, dives, climbs, and rolls; and the skier swoops, dives, climbs, and rolls along with it.

They say the engine is the most important thing in skiing. You have to have muscles, and the heart and lungs to feed them, this is true. Skiing is an engine-driven sport, but you need more than that. You have to have a feel for the snow and for the terrain.

It is *cross country* skiing, and in racing the country it crosses is never gentle. The trails are difficult even to hike. It is also held on a dynamic, slick, unstable, and changeable surface—*snow*—and for these reasons economy may be as important as engine size. Economy is technique, which is what you use to propel yourself over the snow. It is also snow-feel, which is the ability to ride the skis and use the terrain to best advantage.

Of course to have both a big engine and perfect economy is best, but often the skier with better economy can beat the skier with a bigger engine, because the skier with better economy is always a master of momentum; and this is a sport of momentum.

For me momentum is a function of enjoyment. In the '92 Olympic 30k, when I found my rhythm and could match it to the terrain, I gained momentum and I flew. I found myself engaged in a sensation of utter enjoyment.

But when my rhythm faltered, I labored. To regain it, I had to let go of the future, of how I was doing, of how the results would look when it was over, and focus on the present moment—on skiing perfectly and on maximizing my economy.

In this state I was at my best. I did everything I could do to cover each section of course as well as I could. To save seconds I hugged the corners, I milked my speed as downhills rose into uphills, I focused on technique, staying forward, and maintaining momentum on the long ups and in powering over the top. In this state I was not exempt from pain, but because I felt myself absorbed in the moment, skiing as well as I could, I was able to accept and even enjoy it.

I recall hiking behind my Grandpa Steve on a backpacking trip in the Rockies when I was quite young. I was suffering from the effort. We were hiking a hill (a hill by Colorado standards) that was many miles long and very steep, and we both carried heavy packs. The day was hot and dry and smelled sharply of pine and sage. My shoulders ached and I was at the upper limit of my ability. But because I respected my grandpa's opinion of me so much, I did not complain. So I suffered hard in silence and looked through the trees above for the glimmer of blue that would tell me we were near the top. When I saw blue through the trees a feeling of elation shot through me but also instant sorrow. I wasn't sure I wanted it to end after all.

At the top I took off my pack and nearly levitated. I seemed to float and could hardly place my feet on the ground as I stepped, spinning dizzy circles and panting.

Nearing the end of my first race at the 1992 Olympics I had the same feeling. I suffered, but when I knew it was almost over I did not want it to end. I wanted to suffer more, wanted to go faster, to be able to have gone faster all along. I went as hard as I could; I could not take in enough of the experience. I crossed the line, and felt so light I could not touch the ground.

Lloyd and Sue

I call my parents Lloyd and Sue, and have never addressed them as Mom and Dad. With no siblings, I never heard them called anything else; and to me they have always been more than just my Mom and Dad.

I grew up in the house my Grandpa Steve built on the corner of 13th and Cascade in Boulder, Colorado. It's the same house my mom grew up in. Lloyd is from Cincinnati, which is another world. I was born in Rota, Spain, but left too soon to remember it. At the time, Lloyd and Sue were in Europe teaching high school for the U.S. Department of Defense schools. We moved to Boulder in time for kindergarten. By that time I'd been from Rota, Spain, through Turkey and lived in Vicenza, Italy, and near Hamburg, Germany. In Boulder I spent my early childhood in the dirt out back under our apple tree with toy cars and plastic army soldiers.

We were an active family of six, including the dogs, who would not be excluded. They were Darji, Raffi and Jehan—saluki hounds with long snouts and long legs. They were thin and fast. You could call them my siblings. We had similar builds and all sat in the backseat of the car. I was the youngest.

One of our favorite outings was to drive to the grasslands of Northeastern Colorado with the salukis and our .22 rifles. Lloyd and I were there to shoot at jackrabbits. The dogs were there to chase jackrabbits. Sue was there to look for arrowheads and to save us from shooting each other—or the dogs—and to try and enjoy the scenery in spite of the gunfire.

Salukis are very fast dogs. Fast enough to catch a deer. Over a long distance they are faster than greyhounds. Jackrabbits are also very fast and even more nimble than salukis. It didn't discourage the salukis though. Each time a jackrabbit started they ran like they knew they'd catch it, and they left swatches of hair on many a barbwire fence trying. Those dogs lived for the chase.

At the same time, since the only jackrabbits we ever saw were doing forty miles per hour across the prairie with two salukis about ten feet back and closing, we shot only one rabbit in five years of trying. We sent hundreds of rounds hurling into the brush and dirt, our tongues cocked into the corner of our mouths, one eye closed, one peering down the barrel.

There are very few humans who can hit a jackrabbit running at full speed with a .22 rifle, but I have done it. When that rabbit tumbled the only one more surprised than I was Lloyd, who shook his head in wonder, and the dogs who stood around the still creature bewildered and disappointed. I haven't shot at another one since.

Most the time the six of us just walked. We walked for hours through the grass not following any trails or heading anywhere in particular, just meandering happily through the wide-open, rolling hills. While we walked we talked. Lloyd often made up stories, to which even the dogs seemed to listen. Sometimes we debated which person in line would get bit if we walked across a rattler. We never could decide, and personally, I think it depends on the particular snake. In all the years we only saw one rattler, and it made no attempt to bite any of us.

Lloyd and I both have veins running the length of our legs, down our arms, pulsing at our temples. Lloyd is strong, especially his hands, which have been conditioned by working on cars for fun and necessity all his life. Most of the time there is grease lining his fingernails, and he doesn't mind eating with grease-stained hands, and neither do I.

It's fortunate that I'm also Sue's son. It's Sue's cardiovascular system I've inherited. Her whole side of the family climbs, hikes, skis, runs, and races.

Saluki and jackrabbit in the grasslands of NE Colorado.

While Lloyd does these things, too, he does them at his own pace and purely for their own sake. Sue likes to win, and I have inherited her competitiveness as well.

Genetic inheritance has its rewards—big lungs, for instance—and its disadvantages—like pattern balding—but what is most important is the inheritance of attitude.

I always wanted to be a cowboy. In third grade Lloyd and Sue bought me a cowboy hat. They also enrolled me in horseback riding lessons—unfortunately they were lessons in the English riding style. English style makes you look perky and prim instead of slouching and tough, and they wouldn't let me wear my hat.

Next I wanted to be a samurai, so I studied kendo, the art of Japanese sword fighting. Beyond getting all hell whacked out of me with a bamboo sword three nights a week, there was little future for a young samurai. I played Little League and basketball and did as well with them as anything I did at the time. I was a starter on all teams, played well and enjoyed them, but I was always drawn to more unusual sports. I wanted to be Pele rather than Pete Rose. I listened to Willie Nelson rather than rock 'n' roll. I played soccer rabidly and didn't watch football.

I also liked to run. In high school, soccer shared the same season with cross-country running, so I couldn't do both. I chose running because there I was the sole owner of each competition's outcome.

My childhood wasn't entirely free of fears and anxieties but I wasn't burdened by a constraining sense of limitations. Lloyd and Sue didn't need to teach me that my dreams were possible. That is a truth we're born with, and a truth that can only be taught away. When I learned to ride a horse my parents didn't warn me that I might fall off. I learned that for myself, and as importantly, I also learned that I could stay on.

There are limits, but I was left to find and define my own, rather than have them handed to me. At the same time, I wasn't pushed to follow any particular career path. My parents may have had specific fears and they may have had specific dreams for me, but I never knew them, and I believe that took great self-restraint on their part. I was encouraged to do my own dreaming, and regardless of the direction of my dreams, Lloyd and Sue offered their support. As for the dogs, so long as the rabbits ran unmolested, they didn't seem to care either way.

Getting the Girl

I was fortunate enough to grow into my nose. In junior high it stood out monumentally, in high school it stood out less, and later, though still hawk-like, it went for days without being noticed. I don't know whether it was my face that filled in around it or my self-consciousness that mellowed out in spite of it, but we came to peace.

During the time that my nose and I were not at peace, I was in love with three girls. The third of the three was Janine O'Neal, who in sixth grade was not only beautiful, redheaded, smart, kind, and perfect, but also had boobs. My infatuation for Janine was no less than that of any of the other boys in my class. It was complete. She was *the one*. The most beautiful and most popular, and for good reason.

I was handicapped with a big nose, but even so, I had to do something. So I slipped anonymous notes into her desk in handwriting so bad and with spelling so poor they were nearly indecipherable.

Mandatory classroom participation had made my dismal scholarly skills no secret, and as the girls poured around Janine's desk to examine one of the scraps of paper and its amorous scribbling, I became the first suspect. While the flock of sixth graders laughed at the notes, the penmanship, and the spelling, I failed to take serious the fact that one of the girls was not laughing, but smiling. My mistake was not in writing the notes, but in denying they were mine. It was Janine who smiled.

Here is the heartbreaking truth: Janine O'Neal actually liked me. Janine O'Neal asked me to go roller-skating, and I did not go. That I was such a damn fool is still exasperating to me today.

The other two girls were different from Janine. One was Sarah Daney. I was infatuated with Janine O'Neal, but Sarah Daney was real. I thought she was just cool, and that I was lucky enough to be a part of her world. I could approach her, and we spoke and it was mostly easy. The fact that her lofty manner and my shyness were a result of an immaturity and self-consciousness that afflicted us both escaped me completely. The important thing was we were both skiers, and so spoke the same language.

My other love was Sarah's next-door neighbor and archrival, Casey Clifford. Both Casey and Sarah were members of our small junior ski team, and Casey was the younger sister of one of my best friends, Ryder. Sarah, Ryder and I were all the same age. Casey was a year younger and a grade lower. A year in elementary school is a long time, and Casey being Ryder's younger sister made her an even more unrealistic target of my affection. On a long car trip during junior high, I held her hand; and even though we sat together hand in hand for hours, the next day I called to apologize. I don't know why.

Back in third grade I had a girlfriend named Penny. To win her I had to fight her boyfriend, Kyle. Kyle and Penny were both tough kids from poor families. But in those days I fought a lot and well. It was Penny who put us up to it and that added a considerable romantic quality to rolling around in the sand trading punches with a kid from the tougher part of town. Penny said she loved me and Kyle equally and couldn't decide between us. I can imagine the giggling discussions Penny and her cohorts had regarding who she should go out with before she finally threw up her hands and had us fight it out. Our first kiss took place on the pitcher's mound behind University Hill Elementary School just hours after the fight. She kissed my cheek and I nearly fainted. I kissed her cheek and she was soft and warm and sweet and close, and when we said goodbye for the day I floated up Cascade Avenue on my way home loving something better than soccer, better than fighting or winning, better than anything. We kissed square on the lips at recess every day for several weeks after that. Her love for me faded, however, and eventually Kyle won her back without a fight. It could have been that I was a better fighter than kisser, but I think it was just because she liked Kyle better. Now, many years later, I don't think love has much to do with being better at anything, or even having a nice nose. Still, there was something intoxicating about winning that fight and getting the girl.

It's not okay to fight. But it's good to win. Come junior high my deficiencies were solidly evident in the classroom, and my talents were equally solid and evident in gym class. I loved gym because I could throw and catch and run. And while little Stevie could shame me in front of the whole class by spelling acidophilus, while I couldn't spell "could" ("kud" still seems reasonable). But in the next period I could knock the glasses right off of little Stevie's face in dodge ball and feel like we were even.

Which is crueler, I don't know. All students suffer humiliation some time, and most score triumphs. I imagine that little Stevie, little Susie, and little Pete probably all had talents both in the gym and in the classroom, but school just wasn't set up to bring them out. I was lucky. In gym I was somebody. Without it, my problems in math might have shaped my identity. The kids who really suffered were the ones whose talents weren't uncovered anywhere at school. Back then more of us were lucky. There was art, music, gym, the whole range of academics, even shop and home economics. Now, as gym is cut, as shop is cut, as art and music programs are cut, more kids lose their chance to shine, and it isn't just the odd-ones-out who suffer.

By seventh grade I thought I was destined to be either a jock or a complete oddball. I loved soccer and played on two teams. I played baseball, basketball, took karate, and I could outrun any junior high kid in town. But I couldn't spell and I couldn't multiply. I was a reluctant reader and I got in mild but frequent trouble. Furthermore, I liked country music. I seldom played video games, or just hung out watching TV. I preferred stalking deer in the woods dressed in full camo or running through my neighborhood to the mountains, only minutes away. I needed a fight to fight, a fight to win. It seemed like I had two choices: I could be either an oddball or a jock. By taking up cross-country ski racing I doomed myself to being both.

Transitioning from a kid who hated skiing to one who loved it was made possible by my friends, my family, and training.

Skiing in high school with Cory Custer and LERT, 1987.

Enablers

Dave Daney, Sarah's dad, started the ski team that I joined in the sixth grade, and which would set the direction of my life for at least the next eighteen years. That first year, Dave was creator, organizer, manager, coach, ski waxer, and driver of the Lake Eldora Racing Team—LERT Nordic, named after the area where we skied. There were four of us.

Sarah Daney, Casey and Ryder Clifford, and I would load into Dave's Honda Civic every day after school and drive forty minutes up Boulder Canyon to Eldora. We skied for an hour and a half, after which Dave drove us forty minutes down, before dragging himself an additional twenty minutes home. On the very best days I would be sandwiched between Sarah and Casey all the way up and all the way down, their thighs squeezed against mine. I sat quiet, staring straight ahead, happy...

It is easy to place the moment my opinion of the sport changed. It was sixth grade, and I had moved to Flatirons Elementary, where my parents, teachers, and administrators thought I might stay out of trouble and learn more. I went from being a member of the Moose Club—a three-person club for troublemakers with a face-punching the only fee for admission—to LERT.

We made the drive to Eldora, a ski area just as windblown and desolate as Brainard Lake, to do what seemed to be the same thing I had done with my parents for so many years. But, in fact, it was a different sport altogether. It was faster and it was with kids my own age—and that was all it took. Right from the start it became apparent that training was the secret. I trained over the summer, which meant adding to my already active life a few hours a week running with ski poles. Before that summer I couldn't really *ski*. I had walked or run on skis—and not quickly. After that summer of training I could finally, truly, ski.

A cross-country ski racer is a skipping stone that picks up speed with each skip. He alternates between explosion and calm. For a second he is floating like a bird with wings outstretched, gliding. And then before his momentum fades he gathers like a cat to pounce, and in an instant, *is* the cat—a coiled-spring unleashed. He is bird, cougar, then bird again in a repetitive rhythm of generating, maintaining and milking momentum.

A racer does not run on skis, but drives and then rides them, is more bounding gazelle than galloping horse. Glide makes this possible. Skis glide on snow, and gliding on snow is where the fun is.

A ski gliding across the snow is like the deer in mid-air—pure momentum. A skier is able to glide by generating and unleashing power quickly and then riding its reward. Look closely and see that a skier is pushing simultaneously with legs, arms, and back, and pulling with the stomach, compressing the entire body, and then exploding forward and gliding, like a hawk riding a high thermal. Upon close inspection it is physics, but in practice it is poetry. It's not easy to learn and it's very hard to master, but it's worth the effort. There is no better sensation.

Combine this with competition, the pure fight-or-flight adrenaline surge of a race, and you have something. I got into it, we all did. Ski racing takes strength, power, and grace; but with even a little training I had gained enough of these things that skiing became fun, and training became satisfying and rewarding. And everything changed.

In all of this I too became something not only different from what I had been but something better. I improved myself. With momentum, I gained confidence. I became a ski racer. I bought a notebook and made it into a training log, and in it made my first entry:

April 28, 1984. Mesa Trail. 12 km not timed.

This first entry in my first training log indicates that I ran 12 kilometers on the Mesa Trail above Boulder.

After that first entry, and for the next 15 years, I recorded every day's training and all other relevant (and many not-so-relevant) things. By logging my training I was able to look back and note what had allowed me the greatest amounts of improvement so that I could better plot my march toward the Olympic podium.

I played soccer, skied, ran, biked, hiked, worked on trails in the mountains, and generally played hard outside; but recording it in a training log took what had been random action and gave it purpose and direction. At the same time it also helped define me. I was twelve years old when I started calling what I did for fun "training," when I turned doing what I simply wanted to do into a goal. I was no longer just dreaming. Now I was working on a dream. In my mind, I was no longer just the kid down the street. I was an athlete and a future Olympic medalist.

The next year our junior race team grew enough to buy a van and hire another coach. LERT had become something. The team grew to eight, then ten. Eventually there would be thirty kids and three coaches. Dave would still be the power behind it, my dad became team mechanic, and the parents contributed in some manner, doing fundraising, preparing news-letters, car pooling, cooking and organizing. The parents were involved at all levels except coaching. This was no drop-your-kid-off-and-come-back-an-hour-later kind of commitment. From November into April most our parents' weekends were dedicated to our ski racing. In addition to that, the rest of the year they spent many hours a week helping us get ready for the following ski season. This was a huge investment of energy and money. My parents were not wealthy. Lloyd taught voc-tech and dropout-preven-tion (among other things) at the public schools, and Sue was an adminis-trator at nearby Front Range Community College. They worked hard so we could live well and so I could pursue my dream. It did not occur to me at the time that their commitment was special or unique. It does now.

LERT too was unique. It was based on other existing race clubs and on the Scandinavian club model, but it was unique in how quickly it grew, and on the number of junior national champions it produced in only a few years. It was the vision and work of Dave Daney that created it and the selfless enthusiasm of the parents that sustained it.

Cory Custer was the fifth member of LERT. He joined in the seventh grade, and until our mid-twenties we trained together year-round. Chad Kipfer—LERT's "Lizard King," our Jim Morrison on skis, a philosopher and poet—was our sixth member. Chad and I explored hidden canyons and whole worlds on runs behind our house.

On the way to Aspen for a race, Jon Finnoff, the eighth member of LERT, put the ear-buds of his Walkman to my ears and pushed play. I had never used a Walkman, never listened to rock, had never heard of the Talk-ing Heads. The sound thundered in my head. I listened to the tape for four hours, from Boulder to Aspen, again and again, non-stop, and I would have on the way home, too, but Jon wanted his Walkman back. Until then music had never gotten into my adrenal system, had never served to fire me up. From then on even the country music I had listened for years to gained access to my emotions.

Also among the first in LERT was Nathan Schultz, with whom I would train almost as much as I did with Cory. And there was Chris Riddle, boy genius, and Eric Sparling and his little brother Brett, who would come down all the way from Fort Collins for practice.

At Eldora, if it isn't tied down, it's gone. The wind blows across Eldora's gravel and ice parking lot at hurricane force, scouring it of anything loose. A dropped mitten—gone; empty ski bag—gone; snow—blown clean away. After the forty-minute van ride from school it would be near dusk by the time we got to Eldora; and at 9,500 feet in mid-winter, it was cold and very windy.

Dave Daney would pull the old LERT van into this maelstrom, and the van would lean away and sway from a strong gust, and I'd swear, *This time, I'm seriously not going out there.*

Before climbing out of the van we'd pull everything on, hat, gloves, mittens, jackets, wind-pants, ski boots, boot covers, and one of us would open the door and a gust would slam it shut. *Forget it, let's go home.*

Bundled up like this we'd run from the van across the parking lot to the trailhead and the sheltering trees, click into our bindings and shoot off down the trail, wind-blown raw.

All workouts started hard. Eldora's parking lot is at the ski area's base, so all trails go up from there. But we pushed for speed simply to get warm.

In Boulder, in midwinter, it was often sunny and, though breezy, relatively warm. School got out at three, and from the school doors students poured onto the lawn which, even in winter was more often grassy than snowy. Students took off giddily across the grass to I-don't-know-where to do I-have-no-idea-what. But I imagined them doing fun things—things they were probably not supposed to do. We skiers were off to live a very different life.

We had an oversized locker for our equipment near the industrial arts classroom, and after school we grabbed our things and hurriedly change into ski clothes.

"Nice pants," says Casey Clifford.

"What?" I answer.

"Nothing," she says.

"What?" I repeat.

"Whatever," she says, giggling now, successfully under my skin.

"What about my pants?" They were pure discount-department-store. I was oblivious to such things as fashion.

"Well," she continued as we strode out to the curb to wait for Dave and the van, "what I said was, those pants you were wearing, are *sure* nice." I imagine she tossed her hair or rolled her eyes or something, but maybe not.

I grew furious with frustration. Despite my pimples, my unruly head of hair, and my big nose, I knew I was in love, was stricken dumb by new chemicals screaming and whispering. And now there was something wrong with my pants. But what? Casey, oh man, Casey, Casey, Casey, leave me alone. Please, Casey, never ever leave me alone.

In junior high, I suffered. That I was not alone made no difference.

While driving up Boulder Canyon, a winding, climbing serpentine stretch of road taking us from Boulder's temperate, sunny 5,000-foot elevation to Eldora's hard 9,500, our load of chemically demented junior high-schoolers ricocheted around the van laughing and yelling and pouting and fighting, all suffering from youth and school and the winding road.

In the parking lot now, I pulled my ski hat over my scraggly head. It was my favorite hat, a reward given to me by our coach for training at the right pace. Its top was adorned with a small pom-pom. Casey lunged for it, ripped off the pom-pom, and threw them out the door into the sucking wind. Chad Kipfer was already out there, and he stomped on the hat and saved it, but the pom-pom was gone. I lunged for Casey's book bag, but she grabbed me by the head. Her thumb slipped into my mouth. She tried to retract it, but I bit down and held it clamped between my teeth and lips.

"Peeeeete!" she screeched.

"Ma fave-rit hat!" I gurgled.

"Let...go..." she said, tugging my ear with each word, "of...my...thumb!" And I did. And she gave my ear a final yank and I lunged again at her books and Casey and I became entangled in combat that was rough and somehow sensual and I couldn't tell if I wanted to hurt or kiss her and she fought against me the same way. I got hold of a chemistry textbook and whipped it far into the parking lot. It landed on its open pages, flipped in the gravel, and came apart. Pages erupted from the book and blew off, tearing across the parking lot, gone.

"*Peeeeete!*" Casey screeched and slugged me hard in the chest. I knew right away I was wrong for doing it—wrong and mixed up—and both ears burned with the fight and the swirling chemicals of growing up and from knowing I'd just ruined Casey's expensive book.

I took off for the trees carrying my skis and my tangled thoughts.

In the wide open, in a gusting wind, in cold weather, there are no smells, just stinging air and hard-blown snow. But in the trees it's calm and the snow is soft rather than scoured, and there is a mellow, tangy smell of pine needles. Though it is still cold, the trees and their soft scent are a real respite from the parking lot—and all other things. Above, the treetops lash and moan, and the wind whistles, but below we are sheltered. The world becomes a trail in the woods and the act of skiing down it and nothing else.

The team is divided in the first few minutes of skiing into the faster and the slower. Cory Custer, who was then a strict vegetarian, weighed a hundred pounds and stood just five-seven. There was Chad, big and smiling, and Jon Finnoff, who was several years older and like an older brother to me. There was also Chris Riddle, the Sparling brothers, Matt Sobey, and my close friend Ryder Clifford, Casey's brother, who was always first to get his skis on and take off up the trail. Ryder was driven to be the fastest and believed he already was. The rest of us were always in pursuit: Chad behind me, Chris and Eric behind Chad, with Brett and Matt slowly falling behind. Skinny Cory hung on for all he was worth at the tail of the group.

Bundled up and working hard we go from chattering to sweaty in a few kilometers. On skis there is a transformation—in action, a calming. The chemicals leave me alone for a moment. We reach the top of the trail system, an intersection of trails, where we stop and strip off extra clothes, throw them on tree branches, hang them up, or toss them in the snow. There, in the middle of the forest, our colorful clothes are scattered like a tangle of tattered Tibetan prayer flags, and off we go again.

I won the hat, now pom-pom-free, and better for it, for supposedly skiing slowly. Over the years our coaches spent much of the time trying to get us to slow down in easy training. Training requires balance; if you go too fast on your easy days you're likely to go too slow on your hard ones. So our coach would stop us in the middle of practice and put a finger on our necks to find our pulse. More than a hundred and forty beats a minute on an easy day of training, your name was removed from the hat-contest, under one-forty and your name stayed in. To a degree I could control my pulse. Once stopped, even after skiing too fast, I could lower it by willpower. I wanted the hat bad, but didn't like to ski too slowly.

Even in the quickly fading afternoon light we had time to ski all the trails at Eldora, and then in the twilight venture onto the alpine hill for a downhill race—fear training. We skied the trails as a train. A crew of kids skiing together, but each engaged in some individual battle. Cory worked to hold on—and did. Ryder worked to win, to stay in front, and often did. I was into perfecting my technique. I watched old tapes of my ski heroes, and copied their style while skiing. I knew how each skier skied and took from each what I thought their strong points were. I tried to feel while skiing how they looked in the tapes. I learned by watching and doing and feeling what enabled me to move well over the snow—to flow. For me that was fun, to ski as fast as possible, smooth and strong, adapted to the terrain. We stopped every 20 minutes to drink from our water bottles and laugh and talk. We flew along cocky as kings.

"Imagine a LERT Olympic team. All LERT skiers."

"Winning the Olympic relay, as LERT!"

We believed it would happen.

We were different on skis than off them. The group of us boys met up with Sarah and Casey out on the trails; and in spite of our earlier spat, I didn't look away from Casey, or her away from me. In the van we were junior high kids. Skiing had a civilizing effect. *Howsitgoing?* asks Casey. *Hi, good,* I answer. And then we're off again, skiing.

We neared the crest of the backside of "17th Avenue"—one of Eldora's infamous climbs. We were all skating on skis, one right after the other, looking like a centipede, legs and arms going on both sides, moving steadily, pushing the collective body up the long hill. Then the centipede starts to come apart, a segment at a time. Ryder is pushing over the top and stretching us out. Cory comes detached from the back—the centipede's tail is going it alone, determined to rejoin the body. A few more strides and we were over the top—head, middle, then tail—and onto the downhill. And we *always* race the downhills. On all the hills we know where the jumps are and where the tough corners are, and as we crest the top, right on Ryder's tails, we pole hard and skate furiously. We drop into a tuck, still skating one right behind the other, grinning all the way. Looking for room to pass, we skate hard and fall into a low tuck. We try to grab each other's poles, yank the other person back, bang into each other. Chad is leaning against me. There is a steep drop to one side and a steep uphill bank on the other, but we are comfortable, at home on our skis. Ahead, Ryder is looking back under his arm. Chad and I are tangled and falling behind. Chris comes around. Chad pulls away and snatches Chris's pole as he goes by. It cocks Chris back and off-balance. Now he's on one ski, his arms windmilling, close to taking a tremendous spill. But he pulls himself together, and we continue the wrestling, high-speed descent. At the bottom there is a big jump, and at full speed it launches you high and far. Sadly, the landing is flat and nearly impossible to land and is lined closely with trees. You can avoid it by hanging a hard left, or hit it and fly. We flew off it, one after the other, all landing hard and all falling in a heap. We rarely landed this jump upright, and we strutted if we did, and strutted when we didn't. Either way, we always hit the snow hard. *Dude, you okay?*

Then we were all back up, wiping snow from each other, skiing up the next hill. On skis there was a transformation each time and every time: from the insanity of the early teens to being a skier, and not just a skier but a skier training toward Olympic medals. It was a savage pursuit, but compared to junior high it was a peaceful escape. The peace lasted an hour-fifteen to two hours. With fifteen minutes left before we had to leave, there was just time enough to hit the alpine slope.

We ran on our skis up, up, up, panting all the way, to the top of a high, straight, smooth, and steep run that shot back down to the base. In the near dark the slope shone dull-white between the walls of dark trees. It seemed to narrow as it fell away, but compared to the cross-country trails it was wide open, so we lined up to race side-by-side. We waited for Cory to catch up, for Matt to catch up, for everyone else to get there. Ten kids perched atop a downhill run all of it hardly visible. We all eyeball each other, looking to see no one jumps the gun. *Ready, set*—Ryder takes off early, as usual—*GO!* We pick up speed fast.

Cross-country skis are narrow, and back then less forgiving. They would clatter at high speed and were hard to control. Early in the descent you began to have doubts. There is always a point of no return, a speed where you could safely stand up, turn the skis sideways and slide to a stop. Beyond that point, standing up, throwing the skis sideways, any big move at all, would end in ugly self-destruction.

Matt crashed early. One ski shot out from under him heading left, the other went right, and Matt barreled straight forward, head first. He fought to stay up—*No!*—and then he gave in, going down hard. Then a chaos of skis and poles and another body tumbling—*Ohhhh, that wasn't good*. After gaining serious speed, falling was dangerous. Eric nearly poked his eye out once with the tip of his ski. He had to go to the hospital, and wore an eye patch for a month.

We tucked straight down, tears streaming from wide eyes, feet struggling to hold skis flat, legs burning and working to keep feet together. The trees were just a dark wall. Too dark to measure our speed against. There was only the sensation of rushing along, the chattering skis, the wind, and the shrill sound of clothing flapping insanely. We skipped over the hard, snow, the air sucking past our ears in a horrible racket.

Going downhill there's little you can do to go faster—just get lower and *will* yourself to greater speed. In a real cross-country race, there is so *much* you can do. With each uphill it's obvious: go harder, ski better, hurt more. Downhill you crouch low and chant to yourself, *come on, come on, come on*.

We worked on both ups and downs as a form of play, pretending to be the Olympic champions we dreamed of becoming.

Equipment was purposefully a minor part of the game. We learned to take care of our skis as the very important tools they were, and nothing more. For many years I raced on a used pair of Fischer junior race skis mounted with three-pin touring bindings. I was self-conscious about my old touring boots—right up until the race started—then they were forgotten.

Too many skiers seek success through equipment, and many use it for excuses. Of this phenomenon Bjorn Sætroy, one of our first coaches, said: "Idolatry! They worship skis and pray to wax. It is the skier that matters, and training makes the skier." He was right. That is the way it was then and the way it is now. In its first years of existence LERT scored seven junior national titles among five of its skiers. That is no accident.

The wind generally died at dark, and we took our time climbing into the van. Other than the calm of evening, the world was as we left it. And the same teenage shells climbed into the van as earlier climbed out. But now, climbing back into the van we were different people, better skiers for sure, but also different. On the way home Casey and I could sit side-by-side in peace and relative calm. The next day however it would only take another morning in junior high to undo the peace we had achieved on skis the previous evening. Then, every day at three in the afternoon we set off on skis to remake ourselves in Eldora's howling wind.

Andrew Hooker was another of the first members of LERT. The summer before our senior year in high school Andy and I drove together from Boulder to Bend, Oregon, for a ski camp. The camp was run by a guy named Jon Underwood. Jon subsisted on Rainer Beer and hotdogs. He had maybe two percent body fat and could run a mile in a few seconds over four minutes. Jon was training young skiers to win at the Olympic Games. Few U.S. coaches were doing that then. Most trained skiers to have fun, to feel good about themselves, or maybe to win the state meet. Their training was not adequate, and more importantly, they dreamed too small, if at all.

We trained hard with Jon. Future Olympians and Olympic medalists find fun in effort above all else. Those who couldn't hack it packed up and went home. Many left. Some took offense. But no insult was intended. No one was singled out. It wasn't like choosing teams in gym class where the unpopular kids were last to be picked. Ski racing is self-selecting.

After a few weeks Jon pulled me aside. "Vorde," he said, "you can do this, man."

Pele rather than Pete Rose.

I started out hating the sport I ended up dedicating the next fifteen years to…and counting.

Lloyd, Sue and Pete.

Grandpa Steve, leading the way—as he did all his life.

Lloyd, at the Colorado Mountain Club's cabin near Brainard Lake in the Colorado Rockies—early '80s.

Grandpa Steve—still rollerskiing at age 85.

*Post-race at the Bolder
Boulder 10k, 1983. Lloyd, Uncle
Mike Romine and Pete, age 11.*

*Andy Hooker and I in the
Steeplechase, high school, (1988).*

*High School cross country running.
This course had hills, giving a skier the
advantage—I won this one.*

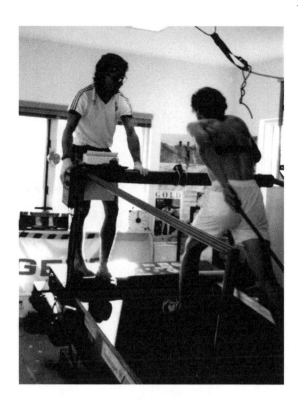

"Vorde, you can do this, man!"
Jon Underwood yelling;
me on the treadmill, (1988).

Right after graduating from high school, Cory Custer and I
find ourselves at Holmenkollen stadium, Oslo, Norway.

The Dream Awakens
Something Like This...

The dream awakens something like this. As a kid, after dinner one evening you take a seat on the floor directly in front of the television set. You see your dark and convex reflection in the blank, black screen. You push the button and *blip*: the Olympics appear.

From my training logs:

12 years old *(1984)*
March. 6:06 mile.
May. 5k run. 3k run. Run on track. One-mile race, 5:39, first place
June. Playing a lot of soccer. First roller-ski. Hard to come down hills.
   Crashed, but okay. Ran by myself. Five times, one lap around the
   track. Kendo practice.

13 years old *(1985)*
March. 5:15 mile.
May. Ran my sixth Bolder Boulder 10k race in 38:47.
June. Playing on two soccer teams.
July. Saturday: 3k cross-country run, 10:51. Sunday: 100-mile bike
   ride with parents.
October. Hard intervals with Bjorn. 6x45-second double-pole intervals.
   3x30-second single-pole intervals. 10k roller-ski time trial. Chicken
   pox. Kendo. Specific strength. Circuit. Speed. Qualified to run at
   nationals in California—didn't go. Instead, ski race! Snow Mt.
   Ranch, third place.

True to almost anything transmitted to the young mind over the television, the images of the Olympic Games pull at your mind until the outside world fades, blurs, disappears and you are one with the images and absorbed in the sound. After a few moments of watching, you think: This Olympic thing certainly appears to be a big deal.

14 years old *(1986)*
March. 4:47 mile: ninth grade city record. Ski race 10k, 29 minutes, second overall. 7x400 on track. Easy run. Distance roller-ski. Going out with Kasha, totally dig her, but she's driving me crazy.

For some, the "Star Spangled Banner" is the national anthem. For others it postpones the first pitch of the big game. For those of us who sat half a foot from the TV dreaming of the Olympics, the "Star Spangled Banner" is the gold-medal theme song. For us the song accompanies heroic images of an athlete on the highest step of the biggest podium, wearing the most sought-after medal in the world.

15 years old *(1987)*
High School! Training five to eight hours a week. Cory and my team won the AAU cross-country running National Championship! Aspen Jr. National ski qualifier, First place. I must train hard to race as fast as I need to at Nationals. Steamboat qualifier, fifth, what the hell? National Championship, Lake Placid, New York. 10k skate, Yes! Eighth. Bjorn says I have to pick my true sport in the next year.

We watched it on TV. Images of the flag, the sound of the anthem, a person on the podium. We let the image evolve. The stranger, the idol on the top step of the podium, becomes a more familiar figure. The smiling face, tears and all, turned into a picture of ourselves.

16 years old *(1988)*
March. 1200 meter leg, 3:22 = 4:30 mile pace. 13x400, 65 to 68 pace. Man, I like Jessica. Ski, skate. Boulder relays, I can do it! Shit! Ripped the cartilage in my knee walking with Jessica. She likes me! Surgery. Weights every day alternating muscle groups. Out with Jessica! Yee-Haw! Week 10, post-surgery, first roller-ski! Knee weak. Things going awesome with Jess. Start work with Jr. Rangers. Knee hurts. Double-pole training on roller-skis. In love, really. Will double-pole up to NCAR once a week. Must beat old record of 16:30. Awesome time with Jess
September. 30-mile running week. Man, Jessica has gone to college. 8 x 3:30-minute intervals. New NCAR record—15 minutes. Crap, 38th at the state meet. Training 11-14 hours a week. Miss Jessica.

December. Sweden! Race, second place. Surprised some Swedes today. Shouldn't have any trouble getting into a school here now. Sweet! Back to Colorado to kick ass. Trained 14 hours, even with all the travel from Sweden. I feel unbeatable. Frisco, first. Copper Mt., first. Mt. Sopras, first. I will not be beaten. Leadville, shit, fifth. Eldora, second. Durango, got ass kicked. Hard intervals. Long distance skiing. Yes. Yes. Yes. Junior National Championship, first! Whoa, getting together with Amanda. Don't think I really like her, but hell. Fourth, in third race, very pleased. I am setting out to make the 1990 Junior World Team!

When the transformation was complete, when in our minds we became the one on the podium, at that moment we reached out little hands to punch little television knobs, and the blue light blipped into blackness. In the dull, dark reflection of the TV glass a little face stared back at itself, different already, and at that moment, took up the dream.

17 years old *(1989)*

Long bike ride with Andy. Lloyd bought me a heart-rate monitor! Heart-rate monitor is driving me crazy. Training camp in Bend, Oregon. Summer skiing! Fifteen-hour training week on snow. Back home. Start working for Junior Rangers. Training 9-10 hours a week and doing hard work outside all day. Training camp in Alamosa and Sand Dunes National Monument. Morning run, two hours. Noon run, 6x2-minute intervals, hard and fast. Afternoon run up to the tallest sand dune. Evening run, four miles back to the campground.

October. Ran over an hour to Andrea's house with a rose, dropped it off and ran like hell home. Training twice a day, once before school, once with the team after school. Visualizing every night for the race. I can see the win. Sharla likes me for sure. Not too sure if Andrea does any more, but I like her—I think. Won! And it happened just as I visualized it. Seventeen-hour week. Going out with Sharla, not too sure about it though. Seventh place at State, 15:57 5k, pleased, but should have run 15:30. West Yellowstone ski training camp. Seventeen-hour week. Must work, work, work: Junior World Trials in five weeks!

December. Putting in some hours now. Awesome race, third behind two Norwegians. Visualizing 30k in Alaska Junior World Trials! I can make it! No. Not even close. Got ass kicked. Must work on speed, endurance and strength. Must relax at race speeds. Trained 435 hours last year. Must hit 500 next year, then up to 600 the year after that— and must be smart doing it. Going out with Amaraja. Cool.

With the Olympic image freshly burned on the retina and a few bars of the anthem playing through the mind, the magnitude of the dream is quite remote. But out on the trails, alone and wilting, or halfway through a small-time race, a thousand miles and many years from the Olympics, in agony, in tenth place, at the furthest distance from the realization of the dream, where heroic images on television will not sustain you, that is when you know you have really embarked upon something.

My training log for December 6, 1989 reads:

> *Here is a commitment to begin to ski. Starting now I will try to ski for a living. Maybe I can't be the best in the world. Maybe I can't ski at all, but I will try. I must try to know if I can do it. I cannot stand wondering.*

How many chances do you get to really do something? One? None? You might get ten, but you can't know that. How many chances do you get to be great? Maybe one. So there better be some urgency, some serious one-shot intensity, because this is it.

As a kid in LERT getting up in the morning to ski, to run, to work, was no sacrifice to becoming great—it was what I wanted to do. I wanted to win and I wanted to train. My family supported me. My friends enabled me. Momentum was with me. I took my one shot and ran with it for all I was worth.

"Ladies and gentlemen...the Team...from the United States of America."
(Athlete's-eye view of the Opening of the Lillehammer Games.)

Training Experiments

In the early nineties the International Olympic Committee decided to alternate Summer and Winter Games so they wouldn't fall in the same year. From 1992 forward, the Summer Games and Winter Games alternated every two years. To make the transition they held Winter Games in both '92 and '94. After making the 1992 team, the 1994 Games were the next step.

To rise to a new level I knew I would have to have a bigger engine, and better economy. To get them, I was willing to take risks, try new things.

We're back in Trout Lake, the summer of '93—the summer before the 1994 Games. Morning comes to the Black-Grigsby house in stages. Roger is up first, out the door and on the highway spraying weeds for the state before anyone else has cracked an eyelid. Connie is up next, and she's out the door in time to drive twenty-five miles and have breakfast ready for the patients at the Hood River Hospital by 7 a.m.—the same time we skiers woke up.

I developed a plan to get the jump on my friends and fellow competitors, but it worked only once. Before falling asleep I set my alarm for 4:45 a.m. I knew I would awaken just before it went off—something I inherited from my early-rising dad. 4:30 a.m. my eyes opened and I was up and pulling on my shorts before I even knew I was awake. I quietly gathered my roller-skis, and tiptoed downstairs. My watch alarm went off a few minutes later as I roller-skied toward Hood River.

It was still dark and cold, and I was training, alone, in secret. I was certain that no one was doing this. I imagined myself training while the Norwegians mumbled in their sleep, while the Swedes drooled on their pillows, and the Russians *dreamt* of training. While Cory slept, Kurt snored, and Eli rolled, I was training. Before I knew it I was flying along, the tips of my poles striking the pavement with great force, and the only sound in the dim light was my breathing, the hum of my wheels, and the steady click, click, click of my poles.

The sun was coming up as I neared home again. It didn't seem like the trees were casting shadows, but rather that the sun was casting light. In the early morning, light intrudes on darkness; in the evening, shadow intrudes on day.

When I got home Cory was furious. The next morning no one slept past 4:45. We woke with surprising ease. We were always in a state of trying to take our effort to the next level. It didn't always pay off directly, but with each mistake we learned a new limit, and we got tougher all the while. That morning Cory, Eli, Kurt and I double-poled on the road from Hood River—this time together— when light began to intrude on darkness.

"Well," said Connie Black one evening as we discussed places to run, "I wouldn't go running up there if Guy says not to." Guy is the local mushroom hunter. His entire, and supposedly considerable, income is derived from picking and selling top-quality mushrooms to distributors in Portland. He is bearded and wild-haired.

"Yeah, man," Robert is shaking his head slowly, "I'm telling you, those guys are crazy, man, crazy. *Whew!*" making steady, sincere eye contact with me. "Those guys have guns, man."

"Hell, you know how much Guy makes picking them mushrooms? He makes"—and Connie is nodding her head, then shaking it, trying to decide if she should give us the figure—"he makes a lot, *a lot*, of money. Lots of folks coming around here to pick mushrooms, lots of Vietnamese. They certainly know their mushrooms. They got their plots all secret and they guard 'em this time of year, like Robert says. There's someone gets killed every now and then."

Racing is *not* touring. Elite racers ski distances of more than thirty miles in less than two hours—that's an average of over fifteen miles per hour, or four minutes per mile— for mile after mile. Ski racing demands endurance, strength, speed, power, persistence, skill, toughness and, as it turned out, brains.

In the quest for Olympic glory we tried many unusual methods, and abandoned most of them. For two weeks straight we took a dip in the irrigation ditch behind the Black-Grigsby-Skier home at first light. It was supposed to be a spiritual awakening —something Cory and Kurt dreamed up, but the water was recently melted snow from Mt. Adams, and so it was nothing more than a ritual submersion in freezing cold water. We would shiver all the way through breakfast. We abandoned that, and we abandoned the 4:45 a.m. training session as well. We had to abandon the weekly pull-up contest, too. We were so competitive we'd be sore for days afterward; so sore we could hardly lift our arms. We would alternate doing ten pull-ups at a time until someone cracked. In the end, after well over a hundred each, we all cracked. For a while we tied logs around our waists with long ropes and dragged them for hours while running over dirt roads.

Dragging logs was a trick of the great Gunde Svan. He tied a rope around his waist and to the rope he tied a log, and with the log in tow he would set off running across the Swedish countryside. His reasoning was that he had to add an element of power to his long-distance runs because the terrain where he lived wasn't hilly enough.

Just prior to the dawn of my life as a ski racer, sometime in the sixth grade, Lloyd found an old poster of a skier racing in the Sarajevo Olympics. He was serene and relaxed, but his body was poised and his muscles taut like an oversized, European Bruce Lee. I didn't know cross-country skiing was a sport like that. I though it was a trudge, a family outing, something best done alone, deep in the woods. The bottom of the poster read "Gunde Svan, Sweden, Olympic Champion." The world of skiing began to open up. It was many years later that Cory, Kurt, Eli, and I began dragging logs behind us through the forests of Southern Washington. It was Gunde who got us there.

While dragging logs definitely made us stronger, it definitely didn't make us faster. We didn't live in the rolling swampland of Sweden; we lived at the base of a mountain, where the terrain alone had enough to challenge us. So eventually we abandoned log dragging as well. Before we did, though, we had an encounter with the mushroom hunters, just as Guy warned us we would.

We were spread across one of the area's million dirt logging roads running home and chatting happily. We passed a few cars parked on the road, which was odd, but the connection to Robert's and Connie's warning didn't cross our minds.

We'd dragged our logs for an hour, straining mightily, continually adjusting the ropes around our waists to ease the pressure on our hips. It was sweat-in-the-eyes hot, and the dust was sticking to our perspiring legs, turning them dark brown and fuzzy. Marking the gravel road we had just ascended were four shallow trenches stretching down the road and out of sight. They were the trenches dug by the logs we dragged. The road was marked in this way for five miles. The log-dragging workout was over. We untied the logs and were running home free of their burden, which felt real fine, like taking off a backpack after a long hike, and we were light and talkative.

Ke-rack! Shit! *Ke-rack! Ke-rack!* Then ringing silence. Eyes wide on the forest and over our shoulders, hair on end, blood pounding in the ears, we took off like startled deer, scattering down the road, into the trees, and finally coming together half a mile downhill, still panting and looking around anxiously.

"You boys done got warned off," said Guy that night, still picking twigs from his beard. "Most of them fellas have been doing some drinking, too, probably."

We tried many things, and kept doing only what we believed we needed to do to be the best. We axed log dragging, and from then on always ran with our eyes and ears open.

Over the summer in Trout Lake we trained hard, and in the fall, when we returned to NMU, we trained harder. That is what we believed had to be done, and we reasoned that, in the end, regardless of outcome, if we had done what we believed, if we could not have done more, then we had to be satisfied, even if we failed.

Even so, I did not believe at the time in the Olympic motto. It reads: "The most important thing in the Olympic Games is not to win but to take part, just as the most important thing in life is not the triumph but the struggle." In the summer of 1993 I would have told you that the Olympic motto was complete bullshit. I would have told you that to race in an Olympic event without the expectation of winning is to go as merely a participant, not as a competitor. Imagine a boxer stepping into the ring with anything on his mind but winning. Such a boxer would invite a broken nose and a pounding headache. To step on the starting line of the Olympic Games with the attitude of a *participant* is to invite defeat. I would have told you that participating in the Games was worthy only as a step toward winning. My dream was to win. Today, I can tell you that the Olympic motto is not bullshit, but I can also tell you that, as a dreamer and a racer, as someone training to win, I believed that the Olympic motto was written only as solace to those who lost.

Devouring the Dream

The best thing I ever did was to chase a dream. I chased it through junior and senior high, to Sweden, Austria, and Estonia, caught a glimpse of it in France, and saw it disappear over a hill in Norway. I chased it up volcanoes in Oregon, over mountains in Colorado, and on trails from Mexico to Canada; I followed it on roads from Rumford, Maine, to Zakopane, Poland and Nove Mesto in the Czech Republic, but the strangest place I ever chased it was into the Northern Michigan University cafeteria.

It sits at the bottom of the campus in Marquette, Michigan. Marquette stands against the storm-blasted southern shore of Lake Superior in the Upper Peninsula of Michigan. The U.P.'s northern, storm-prone location meant snow, and snow was vital to the chase. I followed the snow to the U.P., and once there found I wasn't the only one chasing dreams of Olympic medals. College-aged ski racers from all over the United States migrated to NMU to race for the university ski team over the boundless snow of the U.P., under the tutelage of Coach Sten Fjeldheim. We dreamed of winning Olympic medals, Sten dreamed of coaching an Olympic champion, and we all imagined that the copious U.P. snow furthered our dream.

Snow doesn't *fall* on the Upper Peninsula of Michigan. The wind sucks water off the top of Lake Superior, carries it up into the frozen sky, then spits it back frozen, sharp, and stinging as snow. The snow hurls across the glacially carved landscape, piles into the pine and birch woods, covers, blankets, drifts, and devours town, lake, and forest.

The core of the NMU cross-country ski team was as driven as the snow. We had come from all over the States to the winter bounty of the U.P. so we could train for skiing in the quantity and intensity demanded by our Olympic dreams. The snow piled up in feet; we piled up training in hours. Snow relentlessly raced across the U.P. on the wind. Daily, we drove each other to exhaustion in our training. To replenish its stock of water for snowmaking, the wind dug into Lake Superior. To replenish our stock of energy for training, we went to the NMU cafeteria.

Sten believed that as long as there was water in Lake Superior there would be snow in the U.P., and so long as there was food in the bellies of his skiers, there was energy enough in their bodies to complete the training he demanded. This meant a constant cycle of training and eating, training and eating, in no small quantities of either.

Toward the end of a workout, the sensation of fatigue would often give way to a sensation of hunger. Instead of thinking, *Man, I'm tired*, you start thinking, *Pizza*. Next, a giddy lightheadedness merges with the hunger, and, oddly, fatigue is totally replaced by food fixation. We often ended our training sessions in dreamy conversations about what we would eat right then if we could:

"Man, I'd eat a whole chocolate cake."

"I could eat a pig. A whole barbecued pig."

"No, no. Doughnuts."

"Yeah, doughnuts. You think Sten'll stop at Dunkin' Donuts on the way home if we ask?"

"No, man, just wait 'til we get to the Caf!"

The NMU cafeteria—the Caf, as we called it—was an all-you-could-eat establishment, and we ate all we could for breakfast, lunch, and dinner—every day. Our feasting had to keep pace with our training, and our training did not relent.

It was the fall prior to the 1994 Olympic Games. We were training like a sled dog pulls at the start of the Iditarod—with great enthusiasm, but with little anticipation of the miles ahead.

Each of the NMU dorms had a name. Most of the skiers lived in a dorm named Payne—I couldn't have invented a more apt name. Each dorm was broken into sections, and named something that college dorm advisors consider quirky and fun. Ours was called Tarawa. Each dorm room was built for two, and was connected as a suite to another room through the bathroom. Cory and I were roommates. Kurt and Eli were our suitemates.

It was a morning without weights, and so, we were to run. I arose early, but not as early or with the enthusiasm of Eli Brown. My eyes were open when I heard his shout.

"*Aiggh!*" Eli said, jumping from bed.

"Eli!" scolded Kurt in mock exasperation. Eli was in his clothes and running shoes and was moving fast. The Caf wasn't our only source of energy. Eli was throwing things into his blender, grinding away at some secret potion. A yellow sludge made of ginger, ginseng, carbo drink, protein mix, y;:east, a banana, some orange juice, and whatever was at hand or left in it from yesterday was being tossed against the walls of the blender.

Eli took a long pull and lowered the blender from his lips.

"*Sha-zam!*" he shouted with a dramatic forward thrust of his hips.

"Give me some of that shazam, Eli," Kurt said, reaching out from bed.

"Eli!…Yuck!" said Kurt sliding out of bed. The blender made its rounds, each of us taking a pull on the thick morning mix until it was gone.

We started our run, away from the dorms, over the large lawn, angling across a network of sidewalks, toward the trees, each of us trying to steady the up and down motion of our stride in order to limit the discomfort of our shazam-induced side-aches.

It was 6 a.m. The run out Big Bay Road to Sugarloaf Mountain was five miles out—five back. Most often we branched off the road onto a trail into the woods, but sometimes it was more fun to pick a destination and stay on the pavement where we could just settle into a pace and motor. The ill effects of shazam wore off quickly, and the reputed *good* effects supposedly kicked in. We eased into a comfortable cruise, too fast for the easy pace Sten advised, but more fun. It was fast enough to act like a drug yet still allowed for conversation and a bit of mind wandering. In ten miles—a few minutes over an hour on this particular morning—we covered it all.

On this particular day the conversation started with shazam and, as usual, wound its way to women, and in this case went on from there.

"Feel it?" asked Eli.

"Not any more," answered Cory.

"He means the ginseng, not the side-ache," I say.

"Yeah, right. Aren't you the kid that got drunk on O'Doul's, Eli? 'Oh, man, I'm *sooo* wasted,' " blurts Kurt. Eli had a powerful imagination.

"*Birkerswerstser*"—an Eli reply, meaning, in this case: *maybe, probably, who's asking?*

"Hey, Eli," Kurt says with a sly grin.

"Anyways," says Eli, knowing what story Kurt is about to share, and not being eager for him to share it.

"Anyway," corrects Cory who is always trying to correct Eli's grammar.

"Anyways," repeats Eli who has made it a mission to ignore Cory's grammatical suggestions.

"Eli, it's anyway," repeats Cory.

"Anyways," says Kurt. "I was asking Eli a question."

We all stare at Eli who is quiet and red-cheeked.

"Come on Eli," prods Kurt, "you want to tell the story or should I?"

"Sha-*ZAM!*" answers Eli, who can make as much or little sense as is in his best interest.

"Ah, Eli, what's the use doing it if you can't tell your friends about it?" I ask, but Eli just gives me a glance meant to suggest I'm being immature.

"Well," starts Kurt, "Eli left the room at about eleven after tossing and turning for an hour."

"Aaigh!" yells Eli, increasing the pace to keep Kurt from telling the story.

"Uh-huh," Cory and I say in unison, keeping up with Kurt's tale.

"Before he goes," continues Kurt, "he says 'Kurt?' and I say, 'Eli?' and he says 'What do you think about Maryel?' and I say, 'What about her?' and he says, 'You know, what do you think about Maryel,' and I say, 'Ummm? You mean in a romantic way? I'd say you'd probably better roll over and go to bed' but instead Eli rolls around a while more, gets out of bed, the door cracks open, I see him leave."

"Maryel?" scolds Cory.

"Eli?" I ask.

"Sha-*ZAM!*" answers Eli now with a huge grin spread across his face.

"I don't know," says Kurt. "He slinked back in, like five minutes later."

"Eli!" scolds Cory.

"Check it out," Kurt says and gestures at our surroundings with an outstretched hand.

The trees are bent over the road. Fall leaves—red, yellow, orange—drop, swing, veer in mid-air, and dance their way to the road where passing cars and trucks pick them up, spin them around, and shoot them off, leaving the ditches full of color and sweet decay. Big Bay Road is narrow, no shoulder, no centerline, no white lines. The pavement is dark, stretches up a rise, and curves around out of sight. We rise with it, un-curve it, discover another rise, another curve, descend, climb, and float on our feet, self propelled, in tune, disengaged, carefree, completely free.

"Anyone ever have Babcock?" I ask.

"Oh, hell yeah. The professor that wears moccasins?"

"Dude is into it, chalk flying, I mean he digs his math."

"I had him for calculus," says Cory.

"He was too smart for my class," I say. "Dummy math. We'd all be scratching our heads. Of course, I'm still scratching my head from last week, and almost everyone else is scratching their heads from this week—everyone except my math buddy." I have their half-hearted attention. "You know, the slow kids kind of seek each other out, make each other feel better. My pal is always saying, 'Just get through it, man, just get through it.'"

"Is that the guy, when we're walking—" asks Cory.

"Yeah, that's him. Says hello now and then?"

"Yeah."

"Yeah. We don't know each other's name. We're just math buddies."

"You have an environmental science buddy, too," Eli teases me.

"Well, there is this lady in our class, who Eli is calling my buddy. Well, her serious solution to smog in L.A. is to blast a hole in the mountains," I explain.

"What?" says Cory.

"Yeah, '*What*,' is exactly what Pete said, except," Eli says at full volume, "except Pete says, '*What the fuck?!*'"

"What was she thinking?" Cory can't get over it.

"I don't know, man," I say, "she suggests blowing up the mountains. I mean...it's an environmental science class. Anyway, if I could go back, I wouldn't have blurted anything out at her, not in front of the whole class like that. She was so embarrassed."

"Pete's the teacher's pet."

"Whatever. I will say, that class is the first time I've ever gotten a hundred percent on a test in my life."

"Come on," says Cory. Cory had always gotten hundreds.

"Have you seen Eli take a test?" asks Kurt.

"What?" says Eli in fake indignation, increasing his pace again to avoid being chastised for his test-taking habits.

"Yeah, so Eli, are you a little too fast at everything?" Cory asks, earning a glance from Eli that says *Come off it.*

"Oh, yeah. I have Eli in half my classes," I say. "He always tries for the speed record. This is how it goes. It's ten minutes into the test, people are still getting themselves settled in, and Eli has his head down, his pencil going like this," I gesture wildly as if killing a big snake with a small stick. "And then, Eli gets up, I'd say ten minutes after getting the test, whaps his pencil down and strides over to the professor. Normal huge grin on his face, plops the test down in front of the prof who is looking at him like maybe he has a question or something, and then Eli spins around and walks out of the class like a matador or something, proud as hell"

"I won," says Eli.

"Eli!" scolds Cory.

"I got an A,"

"Eli?"

"Well, B-plus. Okay, B," Eli admits.

"They have special classes for cases like you two," says Cory, panting from the effort of the run.

"No, no. Those classes focus too much on your dumbness," I answer.

"Jesus, I got a *B*," Eli reminds us.

"I didn't start doing well until *after* I got out of those classes," I continue.

"Yeah, because they caught you up," suggests Cory.

"Oh, no. They stole any notion I might have had that I was at least as smart as the average seventh grader."

"That's aiming high," jokes Kurt.

"I was in seventh grade at the time, numb-nuts."

"What should they have done, let you fail?"

"I don't know. All I know was that I lost all academic confidence. In their mind and eventually in my own mind, I wasn't good at anything in school, not writing, or social studies or art, even though I was at least average at those things. The focus was, 'Pete is dumb in math.' Period."

"Yeah, but..." begins Cory.

"Yeah, but what? How can someone in your shoes, Cory, all A's from the start through the present, know what it's like to be in dummy math? It's funny. If a smart kid gets a D in something, the focus remains on the *smart*. When an average kid gets a D in something the focus is on the *dumb*."

"If in skiing all that your coaches focused on since you were a kid were your weaknesses, how long would you last? There has to be some kind of victory or hope, at least, to keep you going. Maybe for every dumb class a kid gets put in they should stick him in one advanced class, give him something to be proud of, give him a victory."

"I sucked at skiing for the longest time," begins Cory.

"You still suck," teases Kurt.

"We'll see," says Cory trying not to sound too serious.

"Anyway, without gym I wouldn't have had anything at school to bolster my self-esteem. Without skiing I'd still be fighting and losing and..." I say.

"...Smoking crack," teases Kurt.

"Yeah, whatever."

"Hurray for dodge-ball," says Kurt. "Time to build up confidence by pelting the shit out of your smarter, slower classmates."

"Amen."

"You get good grades now. Could have been those dummy math classes," suggests Cory.

"A D is not a good grade in math." I tell him.

"You're getting a D?" Cory is confounded by such things.

"Really, my math confidence is so low I freeze. I silently beg that moccasined math freak not to call on me. 'Not me, not me, not me.' It's like my math buddy says, 'Just get through it, man, just get through it.' "

"*Humph,*" grunts Cory, not sold on my point of view.

"He doesn't even wait to be called on in environmental science," says Eli, then imitating me: "*What the fuck?!*"

"I was sorry for saying it."

"She was the dumb one," says Cory.

"It didn't need to be pointed out," I say.

Even leaving at 6 a.m. for the run cut it close for class, so at the Caf we had to wolf our food.

Lunch preceded the afternoon's training and so was as light as possible. While the rest of the school, excepting the football players and maybe the hockey team, tried in vain to keep the pounds off, we were looking for energy, and trying to keep the pounds on. The upper-Midwest, home of the deep-fat-fried cheese curd, is not a light-lunch kind of place. With any luck a nap could be squeezed between lunch and training, and so it was common, come training time, to see a few skiers running across campus for the team van, groggy, wearing miss-matched socks, carrying an assortment of training equipment and clothes and the hope that Sten was in a forgiving mood.

Food conversation began an hour into the afternoon's roller-ski, and for the next forty minutes we batted the names of fat- and sugar-filled goodies about as we cruised over the northern Michigan roads. The fun faded with the sunset, and like the day, our conversation came to an end before our training session did.

Our morning run, as it turned out, had been too fast, and we paid for it that afternoon. We no longer cruised, we trudged. We no longer spoke of food, only hungered for it. The empty feeling you get when your body's energy stores are depleted can induce the sort of frustration and panic a baby feels when sucking an empty bottle.

We made it through the double-wide doors of the Caf, picked up our trays, fumbled for utensils, grabbed a couple desserts each, and ate the first one in the five feet separating desserts from entrees. The evening's main entree was potatoes, pasties, and boiled vegetables. The pasty (as in "nasty") is an Upper Michigan specialty, the U.P. version of an Italian calzone, only heavier. It's a mess of greasy beef, potatoes, and vegetables wrapped in pastry, and baked. An entree plate consisted of one pasty, a lump of mashed potatoes, and a few limp vegetables—all covered in thick, hot, brown gravy.

Stopping to pick up more supplies—juice, milk, a salad, and the like—

we made our way to our usual table by the window and sat down before our steaming trays. We did not speak, but set upon our food. In silence we at first inhaled, then plowed, then powered away the food.

"Jesus" was the first word spoken.

"Dude" was the second.

Frosty Whitworth had four empty entree plates stacked on his tray. Cory, Eli, and I had three. Addison Whitworth three and a half. Each plate was evidence of an entree, a meal in itself, devoured. Frosty had eaten four meals for dinner so far—the rest of us were not far behind.

I was extremely drowsy; my eyes were half closed, and I was all kinds of uncomfortable. Eli got up with an "*umph*," steadied himself, and walked off toward the entree line. At the counter he extended his arms toward the cafeteria worker without looking up. The Caf worker, shaking her head, placed a full plate in his hands.

"That's gonna go right to your love handles," she warned him. "Freshman fifteen, ya know?"

Eli gave her his wide under-bite smile and burped. He turned and, with eyes back on the floor, started back toward our table.

Frosty Whitworth was a big kid. He was about the same weight as Eli, about 175 pounds. But while Eli was about six feet, Frosty was taller. Both Frosty and his younger but even bigger brother Addison took great pride in the amount they could eat.

"Well," Frosty said, pushing back from the table and trying to hide the fact that he almost puked with the effort, "I'm just about ready to get serious about this eating stuff."

"Yep, me too," Addison said, following his brother to the food line. Where there was one Whitworth there were two.

We all rose and filed toward the entrees. We passed Eli without a word, grabbed an entree each, and returned to the table.

I do not recall the actual act of eating, but I remember having eaten. I remember hauling my tray bowed with dirty silverware, glasses, bowl, and empty entree plates, to the dish room. I remember the evil looks cast our way by the already over-burdened student-dishwashers. I remember my friends and I trudging from the Caf through the blustery U.P. night to our dorm, of being uncomfortably full, tired, and sleepy, but I cannot recall ever being happier.

The Upper Peninsula

It was cold in Marquette, Michigan, more than it was warm, and it was warm more than it was hot, and when it was hot, it was also humid. More often than not the wind was blowing in off Lake Superior, which in the winter, when added to the normal temperature and the falling snow, turned things arctic. A parking lot in Marquette can look like a village of truck-sized white tents from one angle and a field of truck-sized rust heaps from another. Even though the parking lot lines are hidden under a foot of snow and ice, parking outside the lines will earn you a ticket. It's only a slight exaggeration to say everyone at NMU drove a rusty truck, and so it is fair to say that the bright orange parking tickets flapping from the snow-covered rust heaps is all that distinguishes an NMU parking lot from an arctic junkyard.

I liked it very much in the U.P. I don't own a rusty truck, and quite often I didn't get along with those who did, but I liked them anyway. I understood them, or believed I did. The U.P. is a place of freedom, as are most places of rugged beauty, harsh winters, and buggy summers. Where there is a price to pay for the right to shoot guns and drive snowmobiles drunk, there are people who are willing to pay it. The U.P. is just such a place.

In the fall, the rolling hills are shades of bright orange, yellow, and red. In the winter the lake is tossed against the shore in wind-driven waves. Huge wave-created ice chalets adorned with wild icicles are made, destroyed and rebuilt by the storm-tossed water. The bare trees and pines are laden with snow, the ground is white, and the rivers gurgle iron-orange beneath ice. Summers find the U.P. in every shade of green. The big lake is rimmed with rocky coves, high cliffs, and sand or pebble beaches. The lake itself is clear and full of fish.

It's not this beauty that attracts the truck and gun people, and it's a romantic notion to think it's the freedom. In reality it is the mines. It is work. People with any kind of mining heritage—mostly Finns, Italians, and the Cornish—came here to work the iron and copper mines. I don't know if there was such a thing as an Iron Rush, but at one point they came here to work, and generations later they are still here. I don't think they came to get rich—and with the exception of the mine owners, they didn't. They just came to make a living. But they stayed to shoot deer out of season, to drink beer, and to ride snowmobiles for more than half the year.

I didn't shoot deer in any season, and I don't ride a snowmobile, but I understand and appreciate those desires. Yoopers want to do what they want to do, and if they have to endure certain climactic hardships to do it, so be it. I was not so different—only I was there to train.

***

At the end of autumn, in cold climes around the world, there's a cult that prays to a god most people aren't aware of. There's no signal and no communication, but when the leaves have fallen, the air is crisp, and the ground is freezing, they appear like leprechauns in March, ghosts in October, and bearded, bell-ringing, fat men in December. They dance and sing and even make sacrifices. They peer out their windows at night and tilt their heads toward heaven by day. They beg the gods to show mercy. The ski team at NMU was a particularly zealous sect of this cult—the snow cult.

Frosty Whitworth starts watching the Weather Channel in mid-September for hints of snow. Every warm day in October is to him a depressing forecast for a late winter. With every cold day he starts getting excited. He is not alone.

Well, Frosty, this is it—the real stuff. I'm sitting in my room watching the first snow of the year fall through the triangular shaft of light under a street lamp. It's wet, sticky snow. The temperature is just a degree or two on the right side of rain.

I am watching the snow gather on the hood of a car parked under the street light. It's my first encounter with snow after a long separation, and I'm giddy and absurdly poetic. The car's color is like that of a distant forest fire at dusk, the color of the harvest moon in a Dakota dust storm, the color of redwood bark. Snow is mounding on its hood, and I am in love with snow.

This is real snow, snow that stays and gets deep. Skiing snow. Snow that puts out the forest fire, conceals the moon, sticks to the bark of trees. The car is white. The sky is white. The ski season is walking up the steps to the porch.

My training log reports snow fell the night of October 24. We skied the morning of the twenty-fifth for two hours. To be back on skis, back in the cold air of winter is like returning home after a long, hard trip to a place you know and love. It's good to be back—it's *great* to be back—sliding across the snow on skis. Ski racers build themselves over the summer with training. But they are born every fall with the first snow when they take their first breath of the only air really worth breathing. Cold and clean, you can feel it fill your lungs. It's an inhalation of energy. On skis they emerge into the only world they regard as real to do what they spend spring, summer and fall preparing to do: *ski*.

By noon the snow had melted, and we silently cursed the snow gods as we roller-skied that afternoon. It isn't just that we are impatient for snow, or that we are plain sick of dry-land training after a long summer's worth—though both of those things are true. In Colorado it's illegal to roller-ski on some public roads. More than once I've ridden back to my car in the back seat of a police cruiser, my roller-skis in the trunk. "Thanks," I always say, and "Have a nice day." That kind of thing doesn't happen in the Upper Peninsula.

An Upper Peninsula trail.

It's not illegal to roller-ski in the U.P., but like so many places, people in cars there hate to slow down and give up a valuable second of their day to avoid killing a pedestrian, or cyclist, or roller-skier. Sealed inside their cars they lose perspective and see other people only as obstacles to their progress. Even outside their cars too many believe the roads are theirs alone, when in reality they are for *everyone*.

Last year a man came out of his house with a shotgun and said he didn't want us roller-skiing on his road any more. It was a public road, but we didn't go back. One elderly lady routinely uses a snow shovel to toss gravel on the road as we pass by. Most people just toss glances, but some people throw things at us from their cars as they pass by. I always get out of the way—way over on the shoulder. I'm polite. I keep my ears open and my eyes keen, but it doesn't always help.

One particularly fine day I was roller-skiing along a deserted road, enjoying the workout, when I caught sight of a heavyset wolf-like creature charging the road from the yard of an old house. A man stood on the porch of the house nonchalantly watering his lawn. He looked on silently as his unchained beast closed in on me. The wolf-dog was going full speed, tail down, ears flat against his back, not barking, all business. I slowed myself down, stopped, wound up like a Samurai with my sturdy training pole in my right arm and assumed a low fighting position. The beast went for me and I let him have it, swinging only once, but hard and accurately. The pole cracked the dog in the chops. The man on the porch yelled, and the beast yelped and whimpered as it hobbled back to the yard, more shamed than pained. Then the man started yelling at me for roller-skiing in front of his house and for viciously attacking his pet.

The snow came for good on October 31. There were ten weeks until the '94 Olympic Trials. I had a training plan leading up to the Trials modeled on the preparation that was so successful in '92; only, since I was older and stronger, Sten and I increased both the volume and the intensity. In my training log we counted down the weeks and created a plan for each week, which we believed contained the proper balance of work and rest to take me to the Trials in top shape. If I trained too much I would be too tired to perform optimally. If I trained too little I would arrive at the Trials unaccustomed to the intensity and speed of each race and too weak to compete at full speed in all four back-to-back races. The key to everything is balance: balance in training and balance in everyday life.

Beating Back the Training Blues

Early one fall day at the NMU Caf, Kurt, Cory, Eli, and I sat down to lunch, as we did every day, and as usual we picked through the pile of fliers touting campus activities that were left on the tables. Kurt picked up one and read it.

"Comedian!"

We all decided to go.

It was a devious plot devised by the student organization Campus Crusade for Christ to attract a crowd for a sermon. The comedian was a decoy. His jokes were thin, the sermon was thick. We'd been tricked.

On Halloween day we found another of their fliers.

"*What is this?!*" Kurt said, holding up the piece of paper. "Listen to this: 'Halloween is Satan's holiday. Come celebrate tonight with Campus Crusade for Christ. Don't let the Devil into your life by taking part in customary Halloween trickery. Remember God loves you, and so do we.' "

"Halloween? It's fun!"

"Is Crusade a good word for a Christian organization to use?"

"Good point."

He read us the time and location, and we began plotting the defense of America's greatest holiday, and our revenge for the fraudulent comedian.

Jamarich Hall is an octagonal building containing NMU's largest lecture halls. They are one hundred- to four hundred-capacity rooms built like amphitheaters, wide at the rear, and narrowing toward the stage. They're positioned like slices of a pie. An elevated circular hallway connects the back of each room. Another smaller hallway at a lower level connects the rooms at the lecturer's end. One can run around the top level or the bottom level, and pass through each hall uninterrupted. The Crusaders had reserved Jamarich's largest hall, Room 101. Evidently they expected a large crowd.

Our plan was to run naked and screaming into the lecture hall and onto the stage, whirl around, yell and dance a bit, and then run back out. Genius.

From Room 102, where we staged our attack, we could hear the lecture in 101: Halloween was under attack as a destroyer of America's youth. Ghosts were a problem, costumes not created in the glory of God were a problem, candy was a problem, trick or treating obviously leads to thievery and beggary, and drug peddlers poison candy to hook youths.

Our fight was not with organized religion. It was with the organization that tricked us into attending something that wasn't what it was advertised to be. Our fight was with the organization that would smugly stand against something as innocent as Halloween. But mostly it would be fun—which, after all, was the whole point.

Cressy, a ski team member and Eli's girlfriend, checked out the show for us. She reported that there wasn't room to sit, so people were standing. It was packed beyond capacity. She took our clothes, promising to leave them for us under Cory's Oldsmobile Delta 88 parked across a wide field a few blocks away. In Room 102 we drew 666's on our chests and upside-down crosses on our thighs and arms with the lipstick. We piled our heads high with shaving cream. As gifts for the audience, we had all sorts of Halloween paraphernalia—skull rings, small pumpkins, and candy. We stood ready at the door. We turned out the lights in 102. All we could see were the thin lines of light outlining the double doors leading into 101. Kurt and Eli stood against the doors, with Cory and me right behind them. We were four naked guys standing in the dark, adrenal glands revving, listening to a sermon from beyond the doors we would momentarily burst through. Except for devil masks, sunglasses, shaving cream and running shoes, we were white-butt naked, and crazy with anticipation. We peered through the cracks of light into the next room. There was one man on stage, a projector, and plenty of room for dancing and carrying on.

Eli started to count down. "On three. One. Two." And then he freaked out, "No, no, I can't do it."

"Come on Eli," said Kurt. And he started pushing us against the doors. I was vibrating and blind with the moment, intoxicated by it. My chest was hollow and my heart pounded.

"OK," says Eli. "Ready? On three. One..."

"*Aiiiighhhhh!*" Kurt howled and we burst through the doors, throwing them open so hard that they banged back against the walls. And then we jumped from the dark of Room 102 into the light of Room 101. The crowd first heard the scream and looked toward its source in time to see the double

Kurt Wulff, Eli Brown and I (left to right), in our dorm room suite after surprising the anti-Halloween zealots.

doors leap open and four naked, painted, screaming demons run on stage. The lecturer jumped backward, knocking into his overhead projector and plastered himself against a large blackboard. His face was contorted in surprise and fear as Kurt ran before him wiggling his hips, jumping up and down, and shouting incoherently. Eli, naturally round, rosy-cheeked, and big, can *dance*. He was center stage, jumping, twisting, shaking, and gyrating, an African shaman caught in the body of a deranged Irish bartender. The crowd was delightfully horrified and silent, witnessing this naked spectacle that was Eli Brown convulsing to some wild beat playing in his head. Cory, not much for dancing, ran in circles, waving his arms as if trying to lift off, a big, plucked turkey running and screeching—in the throws of death. I have no idea what I was doing, do not recall, was in a state of intense and frantic...*being*, like a car crash, hallucinatory and warped, too fast to understand, but slow enough to watch.

We tossed our Halloween goodies at them and never stopped screaming. There were angry sounds coming from the wings. As we dashed for the exit, a large angry-looking man moved to block our escape. Kurt leveled him with a forearm to the chest. As we barreled from the room, I saw a quizzical look on his face saying: *I have just been knocked flat by a naked man.*

More men were heading toward us. Hands clutched at me, but the shaving cream made me too slick to hold. I could hear sounds of pursuit, but I didn't look back. The door we exited through led right into the campus movie. I could hardly see through the twisted eyeholes of my mask and sunglasses. The appearance from nowhere of four naked men in front of the screen, covered with the projected images of the movie, caused the room to explode in cheers, whistles, and applause. We jumped from in front of the screen and sprinted up the aisle toward the top level and the outside hall, the exit doors, and freedom. As we sprinted across the field I looked back to see a small posse of the Crusaders falling behind, fading, returning to the theater to contact security. Cory's Delta 88 roared to life and we were away.

The ensuing Halloween party was laden with debauchery, and raging with music, laughter and loud stories. There were clever costumes, blacklights, and strobe lights. The night resonated with hilarity. People were having fun—just as they are meant to on Halloween.

There is a saying that you can go out drinking with the boys so long as you wake up and train with the men. The next morning we left for training at 7 a.m. Sten took the driver's seat, looked in the rearview mirror, and broke into laughter. Faint whiskers still stood out on last night's pussycats, red noses on last night's clowns. There was lingering hair sparkle, faded fake blood, fang bites, and the whole team shone a pale green. But our fatigued faces also expressed joy. The stories started immediately.

"No!" Sten laughed, as he captained the van to our training grounds for the morning. "Oh god!" he was pounding the wheel and shaking his head with laughter.

Day after day of single-minded determination can lead to the training blues. Without the many extra-curricular adventures we took part in, training could have weighed heavily on our minds. It can make you obsessive, stale, boring, and bored. But with classes to study for, girls to worry about, and trouble always nearby, we were able to make skiing the number one focus and keep it that way. Balance was the key.

***

Balance in life, balance in training. In my training log I recorded not only what I did for training, the amount I trained, and how I felt, but also exactly how much time I trained at which intensity. For instance, on a normal easy-distance ski outing I would spend much of my time training at an easy intensity: level one or level two. Levels one and two mean training with a heart rate around 130 to 165 beats per minute. Both level one and level two are done at an easy pace, but are difficult because of the duration. Level three is faster and therefore harder. Like levels one and two, level three helps condition the cardiovascular system while building strength and endurance. It also increases your ability to work steadily at a high intensity over a long period of time. A skier races at an intensity of level four or even five, which for me is a heart rate between 180 and 200. Level four is a near maximal effort but one which can be maintained for the duration of a race. Level five *is* maximal effort and can only be done for short periods. It is level four training that makes the racer, but it is the lower levels that make a racer strong and fit enough to ski at level four and five on a regular basis.

November 3, 1993. Morning: ski, one hour thirty minutes, levels one and two. Afternoon: level three run, heart rate 175, forty minutes, plus one hour level one/two.

November 4. Morning: didn't want to wake up this morning, did though. Classic ski one hour thirty minutes with some speed, level four. Afternoon: skate one hour thirty minutes, level one and two. Technique feels good.

November 10. Afternoon: level four intervals, three minutes work, two minutes rest, ten times. Very hard, felt strong for the middle six. First few sucked, last few just plain hurt, but good over all.

Recording each day in my training log made it count. When I look back in my log, I seldom look at a single day. The amount of training I did in each level for each day of each week was added up and became a part of the whole. In my training log and in my body I was accumulating a total, a combined effort all of which was aimed solely at making me stronger, faster.

A very hard effort, one that takes you beyond your upper aerobic fitness, is not unlike drowning. Your muscles burn so much they hardly work, your lungs feel wrenched and raw, and you taste iron, see blurred images and stars. Your heart wrestles against your ribs. It's like drowning, but when you're tumbled under the ocean, kept from oxygen by the surf, the only "out" rests with the power of the wave itself. You come up for air when it lets you. In a race, when the pace increases beyond your ability, you must hold yourself under. In reality, this is not an ideal performance state. The heart is not pumping its maximum volume of blood. The muscles are not firing fully. The lungs are not absorbing as much oxygen as they can. You cannot think right. You *are* drowning. You are in a state of oxygen debt. You owe and you cannot pay. And for this you suffer.

If you don't know what I mean, try it sometime. Run one time around the track as fast as you can. That is one-quarter mile. Most likely you will round the first corner feeling strong and fast. You might make it down the next straightaway feeling good, too, but at some point discomfort will overtake you. Soon you will want to "come up for air." And you can at any time. You have only to slow down, walk, stop, and see that you have covered maybe three quarters of one lap. You gave up.

Another option, since it is an option, since you are not being held under or made to do this, is to keep going. Call it an experiment, just to see what happens. You don't ever have to do it again, if you don't want to, but see it through all the way to the end just this once. Extreme discomfort is around the next corner, if not sooner. My advice is to try to stay relaxed without easing up. Relax your face, let your shoulders loosen, but don't slow down. You are going to hurt anyway, but this might help you keep your speed and not tie up. At some point all efforts to stay relaxed will fail and you will have no choice but to give in and run like all hell, squinting and weaving and grimacing and panting down the home stretch in such a state of agony that—well, you'll see. Once over the line you will stagger and bend over and stand up and fall down, and it won't feel any better no matter what you do. You're in debt and you will be paying for several minutes. I suggest— though it goes against instinct—that you walk around.

After it's over and the debt has been paid and you're flush and feeling fine, if a little woozy, you might find that you liked it. There is probably something wrong with you, like there is with me. You missed your calling, and for that you might thank someone and turn your back on the track and return to the normal world. Or you might not. It's better here, pushing yourself sometimes well beyond comfort. I'm convinced of it.

You were running fastest before you started to really hurt, before you were in debt, while you still had credit to spend. Remember, that was just one lap, all out. A mile is four laps. The best runners in the world do those four laps in 55 seconds each. If you trained you would be able to run as fast in oxygen debt as you would with an oxygen surplus. More importantly, with training you would be able to run faster and longer in that pre-oxygen-debt state, when all cylinders are pumping optimally. You still won't be able to run all four laps in 55 seconds each, but don't let that get you down.

Training improves the heart's ability to pump blood by up to 60%, and, with training, the peripheral muscles can increase their ability to consume oxygen by up to 1000%.

Rather than focus your training on that super hard effort, it is more important to improve your pre-oxygen debt fitness, your aerobic fitness. That is how you raise your ability to withstand a higher pace without going over your limit, without having to hold yourself under. To do this you never have to taste iron or fall over with fatigue. For extremely good aerobic fitness, that just isn't necessary. But try the all-out quarter mile anyway. I think you'll like it.

With training you will feel something that you might recall from child-hood. Sensations of excitement and energy will flood over you—if you let them. Don't be afraid, that is energy and strength you are gaining. Fitness, or at least activity, is tied closely with your emotional state. Ski and you will be happier.

The time around Thanksgiving is, for all Americans, a time of overin-dulgence. The same is true for cross-country skiers. But for us it is a time to train at the limits—not of what is possible, but right at the limits of what is wise. It is possible to ski *all* day every day, but the result of such training would not be a faster skier. At the same time it is possible to ski *hard* every-day, but again, the end result would not be a faster skier. The stress of training breaks down the body. The intensity and duration and type of training stresses and breaks down the body in fairly specific ways. Rest builds the body back up. It is rest that makes you fast. To achieve optimal strength and fitness, to be as fast as you can be, you need to find a balance between stress and rest. At certain points throughout the year this balance should be tested. Running thirty-five miles and then roller-skiing a hun-dred kilometers the next day, as we did at the training weekend, is just such a test. Doing thirty kilometers of plyometric-like (explosive bounding) level four ski-bounding intervals, as we did earlier in the fall, is such a test. Rest-ing for three days straight is also a test. In all cases you hope to come out of it stronger. But the idea is to learn about yourself so that you can plan your path toward the future—and arrive there rested, fit and ready.

Johnson's Ski Trails are a short three-hour drive from Marquette. Over Thanksgiving break, Cory, Kurt, Eli, and I pulled into Mickey Johnson's parking lot on Tuesday, November 23, and left seven days later. The first afternoon we skied for three hours. The next morning we skied two and a half, and that afternoon one and a half; three hours the next morning, and two that afternoon, and so it went. At an easy, level one or two pace we covered over 20k in an hour and a half. A three-hour ski took us over 40k. By week's end, we had accumulated over thirty hours of training, and con-servatively 500k, or 350 miles. For the month of November I had trained over eighty-five hours. I was getting close. It was getting close. The '94 Olympic Trials were starting five weeks away, on the first of December.

Two weeks before the Trials, Cory, Kurt, and I traveled to Alaska, where the Olympic Trials were to be held. Funds were always quite limited, and so, whenever possible, it was our custom to stay with friends, or friends of friends, or basically any random person we could recruit. Sometimes we camped out. Sometimes we slept on the floor in a back room of a ski lodge and we often crammed six people into a small hotel room—two guys to a bed, and two on the floor. We cooked oatmeal for breakfast on a camping stove, ate peanut-butter sandwiches for lunch, and cooked spaghetti on the camping stove for dinner. Often, though, we were more fortunate or at least more willing to push the limits of connections and hospitality. On one occasion, Cory, and a great skier named Sara Kylander, and I stayed with Sara's sister's volleyball coach's parents for a week straight. I sometimes wondered if these folks asked themselves as they drifted off to sleep: *Now, who are these people again?*

I once borrowed a car from a friend's friend's ex-mother-in-law, while she was in Florida. I drove the car six hours one way to see a girlfriend who I then discovered was no longer my girlfriend. I drove six hours back, returned the car to my friend's friend, who assured me that his ex-mother-in-law wouldn't mind it a bit that I had accidentally ripped the rear portion of her tail pipe off by sliding into a snow bank. The car's un-muffled engine could be heard for blocks around.

The '94 Trials were close. They were my second Olympic Trials and, I hoped, my second Olympic team. To think about them was to leak a little adrenaline into the system, which feels fine just prior to a race. But when sitting on the plane, or walking through the airport in Anchorage, Alaska— the site of the 1994 Olympic Trials—it feels half good and half wrong—a bit like peeing in your wetsuit when surfing.

In Alaska, prior to the Trials, Cory, Kurt and I were very fortunate: We stayed with our friend Robyn Egloff's parents, who ran a German restaurant and bakery in nearby Girdwood. Every night we were treated to homemade German cooking, and we fell asleep under piles of thick blankets. The hospitality kept the race jitters at bay, and when the rest of the team showed up three days prior to the races we were reluctant to move into the hotel with them.

The '94 Olympic Trials

Picture yourself straddling the centerline of a long, perfectly straight road. You are looking up the road, which steadily climbs toward the distant horizon. As the road stretches away from you, distance gives the illusion that the road becomes narrower. Where the seemingly pencil-thin road meets the horizon, there is the bright glow of the sun. Now picture the road suspended, narrowing as it stretches into the distance through space toward the brightly glowing sun.

With the sun as your goal, start walking down that road. As you walk toward the sun, notice that the road actually *is* getting narrower, that this narrowing is not an illusion. Ten years is a long time to dedicate to a single road, and it is not an easy road to walk. In spite of the difficulty, that's how long you have been walking up it. The road is no wider than the centerline used to be, and the sun lies within your reach.

As you move along this balance beam of a road, you glance down through space on either side of you. Through that space, down below, is a new sight, a new possibility. It is frightening. Seeing it, you feel faint and sick to your stomach.

It is failure.

Don't look down!

This is the first day of the '94 Olympic Trials. My life up to this point has been aimed at an Olympic medal, and making the U.S. Olympic team will justify or deny the validity of my life's direction.

I feel like I am going to throw up. I rise from my tangle of sweat-soaked hotel room sheets. My sleep has been troubled by contradictory dreams of grand success and terrible failure. Shining between the drapes, a streetlight barely makes visible the two pairs of skis I will choose from to race on today. Catching a glimpse of them elicits a tickle of nervous excitement.

My feet are simultaneously cold and sweating. I feel faint, like I am standing with the shaking, spindly legs of a newborn giraffe. I know that the sensation is only psychological, and that my legs are strong and ready to race. I am not faint with sickness, nor am I weak. It is failure calling. And I will not fail.

There are about a hundred male and a hundred female skiers who have qualified for the Trials. Of those, maybe half feel they have a shot at the team. Twenty guys actually have a legitimate chance. Out there in various Anchorage hotels there are a handful of people thinking they will win the race, or at least ski fast enough to make the Olympic team. Only six of each sex will go to the Olympics. The rest will have to face their failure.

Two hours and twenty-five minutes until race start.

This is the worst time. The final few hours before the event. Outside it is dawn, but inside my room it's still dark and dank. I plop down, try to get control of myself. We all have to deal with the pressure. At the same time, we all have our own stories and our own training background. The stories differ greatly, but they are all the same in one respect: We have all invested a lifetime of energy, sacrifice, and emotion into this sport.

Today we see whose lifetime investment pays off.

In Trout Lake and in Marquette, there were so many times I woke up sore and sleepy. No matter how I felt, I had to get up and train. I would repeat my morning mantra, one I stole from The Doors: "The killer awoke before dawn. He put his boots on." Even back in June, I would wake Cory by telling him I was going out to make the Olympic team. It would take him only a moment before the thought of me training while he slept drove him up and into his training clothes. When he came downstairs ready to train, looking as beat and sleepy as I felt, I gave him my line: "The killer awoke before dawn."

Today my teammates and I load up the van and climb sullenly aboard. We exchange quiet greetings. Sten tries a few jokes that bring forced but welcome laughter.

One hour to race start.

As is the case before each race, my body tries to rebel. As at the '92 Trials, I start my warm-up feeling like death. Having done well the last time around, and having competed in the 1992 Games, I was now better prepared to handle the pressure I put on myself.

My routine is set, and I follow it confident that the games my brain plays on my body will be worked out. As in '92 my legs are stiff and my lungs reluctant to pull in air as I begin my warm up. I ski slowly, offering quiet greetings to some competitors and ignoring others. Soon all systems are working in my favor, my legs feel strong, my lungs able to take in any amount of air. I am gliding confidently along.

The feelings that shoot through me, tossing my stomach, are feelings of positive anticipation. I can hardly wait to get the race started and begin the culmination of the last ten years of work.

Ten minutes.

I am in the start area now, surrounded by the other Olympic dreamers. There is a little nervous laughter, a few friendly words. Each is absorbed in a last-minute warm-up. Stretching lightly and bouncing around, staying warm, loose, concentrating on being relaxed, I'm in my own world.

One minute.

On the start line, I can hear the blood coursing through my ears. My chest feels hollow, and my heart beats hard and fast. I am ready. I know what to do, and that is all there is.

The starter gives the thirty-second warning.

I am conscious only of my breathing and the sensation of contained power pulsing through me. I breathe deep and fast, swaying with the count of seconds ticking. I am one step from the sun.

Ten seconds.

I can do it.

Five seconds.

"The killer awoke before dawn." What a strange thought.

Three.

Two.

One.

I'm gone.

At its worst, ski racing is cerebral and introverted. You think. You think about the time you're losing to your competitors, your pain, and your miserable, sorry-ass little, hurting self.

That doesn't mean the best ski racing is totally mindless. Throughout the early part of the race you monitor your intensity, are respectful of the distance, gauge how you will go fastest for the duration. You're conniving, scheming, plotting, assessing so that you can win. Even this becomes automatic and is conditioned into you by years of training and racing. Then, at some point in the race you are able to let go even of that and just *go*. Ski racing, at its best is not really a brains kind of operation; it's more a vicious joy. Picture the giggling-grin on a hyena muzzle deep in wildebeest intestine. That hyena, ripping and giggling in its dinner with pure, deep-down animal joy is cross-country ski racing at its very best.

At least that is how I felt.

They named the Olympic team on the night of the last race. My name was called. I stood, steadied myself, and stepped forward. I tasted blood. I felt I could accomplish it, that I was another giant step toward the ultimate goal, a gold medal. It was my second Olympic team and would be my second Olympics, and so this time it was much different. Where as before I had only to make it, this time I had to improve on my past results. My dream was coming true. A great portion of it had come true.

This nearness I felt to the realization of something big made me think of Dan Ray the Bigfoot hunter, and of Dan's dream.

At the Albertville, France, Olympics, 1992.

Clipping from the Minneapolis Star Tribune, 2000: "Pete Vordenberg won the men's 58K…"

Viceroy of the Vasaloppet

Star Tribune photo by Richard Tsong-Taatarii

Pete Vordenberg won the men's 58K cross-country ski race by two seconds Sunday at the Mora (Minn.) Vasaloppet. "I knew it would come down to a sprint," Vordenberg said. The women's 58K winner, Laura McCabe, won by almost six minutes. *Turn to C8*

*Just like NASCAR.
Victorious at the North
American VASA, Traverse
City, Michigan, 1996.*

*NCAA Championships 1993. I'm skiing behind Luke Bodensteiner,
in front of Marcus Nash. I won this one.*

Vordenberg, skating.

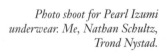

Vordenberg, classical skiing.

Photo shoot for Pearl Izumi underwear. Me, Nathan Schultz, Trond Nystad.

(All photos this spread courtesy Bob Allen.)

The Factory Team's custom Subaru Outback, with photo-ized exterior featuring Barb Jones, Pete Vordenberg.

The Factory Team, 2002. Back row: (left to right) Pat Casey, Dave Stewart, Unni Odegard, Phil Bowen, Magnus Eriksson. Front row: (left to right) Scott Loomis, and Olympians Barb Jones, Kristina Joder, Tessa Benoit, Pete Vordenberg, and Erich Wilbrecht.

Barb (skating) and me (classical). Bohart Ranch; Bozeman, Montana.

Bigfoot

Dan Ray leaves you with two options. Either Bigfoot exists or Dan is a lunatic. The summer prior to the '94 Games, Cory and I were back in Trout Lake, training as usual. Dan Ray lived by chasing dreams as well. He was living on the road, mostly in the Pacific Northwest, searching for Bigfoot.

Cory and I knew Dan from our first year at Northern Michigan University. Dan was a legend, not just in northern Michigan, but wherever he went, and his legend was due mostly to his enthusiasm for the bizarre. He was known to watch entire kung-fu movies in slow motion, for lugging heavy logs around on his shoulders, and for searching with a startling earnestness for Bigfoot. When someone met Dan for the first time, Dan would set in on them with a Bigfoot story. They would listen to the story with the light-hearted enthusiasm one would think appropriate for a Bigfoot tale. But about halfway through, something about Dan's storytelling would alert listeners to the fact that there was nothing light-hearted or, in Dan's mind, fictional about the tale—Dan was in complete earnest. From that point on the listener would eye him dubiously. Dan gave no sign he was aware of the effect his Bigfoot stories had on people, and continued with earnest enthusiasm.

We knew Dan was living out West somewhere, so we were only mildly surprised when, early one morning, a car riding low with gear pulled up in front of the Black-Grigsby house, and Dan got out. He walked two loops around the car, taking his normal long, lunging strides, arms swinging loose in their sockets, his face fixed in a wide grin. From the window we saw him stride up to our door as if to kick it in, only to knock lightly. It was the way of Dan Ray.

"Hello, Dan."

"Gosh, can you believe it?" He grinned, strode forward, filling the door, then the house, walking and looking around as he talked. "I knew you guys were up here, but where? And I just stopped at the gas station and asked for you, and they knew right where you were. Small town, huh? And here you are, eating—what—oatmeal? Gosh, you have any more of that?"

He shared stories as he ate, and when Cory and I said we were heading out for training after breakfast, Dan, who had quit ski racing a few years before, decided to join us. For the rest of the week he trained with us two or three times a day, every day, which is impressive for someone who hadn't trained recently. He was easily assimilated into the household. The Blacks and Grigsbys loved his passionate stories, broad smile, and cherry disposition. They even had a few Bigfoot tales of their own to share.

After four days, however, Dan was wearing on us. Early Saturday morning Cory, Dan, and I piled into my Subaru and drove to a footrace in Portland about an hour away. The Bigfoot talk never stopped. He was obsessed. We drove and Dan talked Bigfoot. We jogged our warm-up and Dan talked Bigfoot.

"Bigfoot, they say—"

Blam! The starter's gun went off and I broke from the line into the first moment of silence I'd enjoyed since Dan arrived. I pushed myself through the first 5k in 15:30, a personal best. As the finish neared I slowed slightly with fatigue, but still came in under 32 minutes for 10k. About a minute later, while I was still dazed from the effort, Dan crosses the line.

"What they say is, Bigfoot is so smelly..."

He picked up right where he left off, half an hour and a whole 10k race earlier.

Through it all, the really impressive thing is that, for a week straight, Dan did not stop talking, and his topic never wavered. Dan talked about Bigfoot for seven unrelenting days, and his storytelling was so impassioned and sincere I couldn't decide if he had lost it or if Bigfoot really was out there.

Sunday morning, Cory, Dan, and I woke up groaning from the race. It was our first real hard run on pavement for the summer, and we were unbelievably sore. Just lowering myself onto the toilet I had to support myself with my arms so as not to crash down on the seat. But because Dan was leaving the next day we decided to go for a long run up Mt. Adams, where we could scout around for Bigfoot.

Mt. Adams stands so big that even though Trout Lake sits at its base, we drove straight uphill for an hour just to make some progress toward Adam's higher reaches—where Bigfoot might be found. Even then the peak looked just as distant as it did from the house. We all complained of sore legs as we started stiffly up through the pines toward the high country and Bigfoot.

"Night's really the only time to see Bigfoot," Dan announced. "I've got night-vision goggles in the car, but we can just look for signs, tracks, and stuff. This one time I thought for sure he saw a Bigfoot during the day, up on Mt. Bachelor. I was skiing, not thinking of much. I looked up and saw this head. Bigfoot has a pointy-head, kind of small for its body, and I see this pointy, not-rock-looking thing poking out from behind these rocks. Oh, jeez, I got so scared. They're so strong and fast, and you just don't want to mess with 'em. It didn't move or nothing."

We hiked until our muscles loosened up and then started running. We ran upward until we were among the small wind-twisted and weather-stunted trees just below the summer snow line. An hour from our car, and running steadily uphill at about 8,000 feet elevation, Dan still did not stop talking even to breathe, or, that I could tell, to look for tracks.

"They're usually about seven feet tall, covered with hair, and do they smell, oh jeez. This one time I was camping and smelled this smell. I was so scared I could hardly move, and I could hear this noise, like mumbling, *gerbergergleberbabagre*. I don't remember falling asleep, but when I woke up my tent-fly was gone. Well, not gone, but off. Not really off, but definitely detached. Ain't no way the wind did that."

After a week of Bigfoot stories I was starting to tune Dan out. Cory was completely fed up and would run ahead, trying to get out of range, but Dan would just run faster, talk louder, and Cory, like a caribou driven mad by spring mosquitoes, would run harder. I silently concluded that Bigfoot could very well exist, but Dan was definitely crazy.

***

Then again, maybe not. The Olympics were my Bigfoot. Since the seventh grade, I had done little that did not connect in some way to my quest to make the Olympic team. I trained and dreamed, traveled to races, raced, won a few, lost a lot, and trained more. Now, ten years of training and dreaming later, I was headed for my second Olympics with the belief that I was one very important step closer to my ultimate goal. I have years of training in my muscles, the support of family, friends, and Coach Sten.

At the ceremony in Anchorage where the teams selected to compete are announced, I am standing on a stage in front of the press, my teammates, my coach, and my friends. The loudspeaker rumbles: "And these are the members of the 1994 U.S. Olympic team to Lillehammer, Norway!" I found myself stiff with fear—for it is one thing to say you are looking for a Bigfoot and another to actually find one.

***

Mt. Adams is but one in a widely spaced string of volcanoes. The whole string is covered in deep snow year round. With the warm summer days and cold nights, the snow goes through a daily freeze-thaw cycle and so is rock hard in the morning until the sun can melt the top layer and loosen it up. So Dan, Cory and I had to kick steps in the hard snow on the steeper pitches, which is a toe-busting proposition in running shoes. But we made Adams' summit, and for once, Dan shut up.

Transparent chunks of ice cover Adams' almost totally flat summit. It was like walking through an ankle-deep pile of beer bottles. The pieces of ice clinked and clunked against each other and our ankles as they shifted under our steps.

"No Bigfoot up here, Dan." It was about the first thing Cory had said all day.

"Nothing much they could eat," answered Dan.

Dan didn't seem to hear the tone of Cory's statement. "I'd say there's little reason to come up here, except to call to a mate, like to lunch or something. From up here a Bigfoot could be heard from a long way off. They make a scream-like sound, real loud, just one loud scream. I've never heard it, but I've been told that it can give you a heart attack. Scariest sound ever." And Dan set off talking again.

"Dan. Please. Leave it alone," Cory begged. "I just want to hike down in quiet, okay?"

"Okay," he said, momentarily disappointed. "Anyway, we're more likely to see something if we're quiet."

And so, except for the wind and the clunking ice chunks, all was quiet. We reached the edge of Adams' flat summit and began the descent using the steps we had kicked in the snow earlier. It was like walking down a steep stairway, and all three of us immediately realized our legs were in for it.

"Aww, jeez you guys. My thighs are killing me," said Dan.

"I am way too sore to walk down forward like this," Cory said. He turned himself around and began to step down backwards, like a person descending a ladder. It was slow going and only a little easier on the legs, but we agreed it was too steep to just glissade down without ice axes to control our speed. So down we went, backwards, one tender step at a time. Cory hiked last in line, just above Dan who down-stepped just above me. Dan remained quiet, as promised, but Cory hardly seemed more at ease, and I felt a little anxious as well. Dan had filled our heads with non-stop Bigfoot talk for a week straight, and I couldn't help but dwell on the possibility, slight as it was, that Bigfoot was out there, hungry and territorial and fast, seven feet tall, and stronger than any man.

We were tired, and the severity of the pitch put the adrenal gland at the ready. This, combined with Dan's persistent storytelling and Cory's steadfast refusal to believe a word of it, put us on edge. So when we heard the scream—and we *did* hear a scream—we froze. And I swear my heart shuddered at the inhuman sound. Right about then we decided it would be okay to glissade without ice axes. Cory launched himself sideways, spun around in mid-air, took two very long steps downhill and commenced sliding. I only got a glance at Cory's face, but he looked genuinely inspired. Dan knocked me down, and I slid on my back until, like a first-time waterskier yanked vertical by the boat, I regained my feet and took off after Cory and Dan. All I could see were the rooster tails of snow kicked up behind them. We didn't stop where the snow ran out; we just kept running all the way back to the car.

In spite of Dan's success in locating Bigfoot, he got in his car that afternoon and disappeared. Cory and I watched and waved good-bye. There was an unmistakable look of fear on Dan's face—his dream had come true.

***

In France, in the '92 Olympics, I had participated and done as well as I could have. Having made it was a success, but this time I was going with firmer goals. In '92 I raced as hard as I could, but I had no expectations. I was pleased—not with my place, but with my race. This time I had to show improvement. I had to prove to myself that I was nearer my ultimate goal. Two years ago in the 30k I had placed in the forties. This time I felt I had to make the Top 20, equivalent to making the Final Four in college basketball, and at least as good as any American had finished in recent history.

At the wax bench.

The 1994 Lillehammer Olympic Fifty Kilometers

An Olympic cross-country ski stadium is a box canyon of screaming fans. In Lillehammer, the Norwegians had their faces painted; they carried flags, horns, cowbells, and had an energy and excitement that emanated from a love for the sport they had invented thousands of years ago. In the stadium and around the course there were more than 100,000 spectators—supposedly the largest crowd ever to attend an Olympic event. It didn't matter that the temperature was 15 degrees. The sun was out and it was the last day of the 1994 Olympics. It was the fifty-kilometer classic event. Norwegians had dominated nearly all the previous cross-country races, and the crowds were there to see it happen again.

The clock must have counted down, and the starter must have taken his hand off my shoulder. I must have pushed myself with all my strength onto the racecourse. I must have skied as hard as I could. Until I left the Olympic stadium, in the first kilometer, I didn't realize how much I relied on the sound of my own breathing as an indicator of the intensity at which I was skiing. I could not hear the sound of my poles in the cold, squeaky snow or my skis lightly slapping the hard tracks. I could not hear my breathing; I could not control my intensity. I do not remember skiing out of the box canyon that was the Olympic stadium, out on my first of three 16.8-kilometer loops, out onto the course packed with even more screaming fans, clanging bells, and blasting air horns. I remember the sensation of my back and hamstrings tightening up, and my breathing getting shallower until I grimaced with the effort. The possibility that I had totally blown it entered my thoughts. I remember that vividly. I remember hearing the bark of the skier behind me, and watching him pass me. I could not hang onto him. I tried, but couldn't do it. My whole body was tight. I was a knot. My vision narrowed; I was squinting; I was nearly blind. It was like I was looking through binoculars the wrong way. I held my shoulders tight against my neck. My strides became short and choppy. Even though my skis had good wax, I slipped every other stride. Another skier passed me, and I had only skied seven kilometers. "*Shit!*" I yelled. I couldn't believe it. I didn't understand it. And I couldn't admit it, but I was ruining my second Olympics. I was watching my dreams escape through a pair of squinting, tear-filled eyes. *SHIIIIIT!*

I came into the stadium after one lap so tight and sore and slow and miserable that I didn't think I could make it back out again. But I still had two more laps to do—33.5 more kilometers. My breathing was shallow, and I was near stumbling.

I pushed on knowing that I would finish the race and thinking that I would quit the sport as soon as I crossed the finish line.

Somehow, by giving up, my body started to relax. I was letting my skis work now, and I was breathing deeply. The self-induced panic and pressure of this single event—the event I believed to be the culmination of a lifetime of work—was heightened by the crowd noise. But giving up, if only for a moment, offered a kind of release. As the race wore on, the noise died down. Even the spectators got tired. The course was the most difficult I had ever skied. Just to keep moving I had to work, but now that I had released myself from the noose of pressure I had tightened around my own neck, I was skiing well. No one was passing me.

I was skiing in a pack of five skiers. The first was Andrus Veerpalu from Estonia. As juniors we had raced each other over several races one spring in Finland, Norway, and Sweden in what was called the Polar Cup. In one Polar Cup relay race, Cory, Veerpalu, and I teamed up and won the event over several top Norwegian and Swedish teams. In all but one of the other races he beat me, but never by a great margin.

Cross-country ski races are run in two ways. There are mass start events, where everyone starts together, and individual start time-Trials, where skiers start one at a time with half a minute between them. The Olympic 50k was an individual start race. To be caught by another skier meant you were behind them by at least half a minute. Andrus Veerpalu had caught me from many people back, and so I was actually skiing many minutes behind him.

So far, in the Olympic 50k Andrus Veerpalu was in tenth place; I was in sixty-fifth—way behind—but working hard to make up as many places as I could. My dream had escaped me momentarily, but I was racing hard now and skiing fast. My focus returned, my face relaxed, my shoulders dropped, and my stride lengthened. The five of us were ski tip to ski tail, and moving in a rhythm like a rowing scull. Veerpalu set the pace. Besides Veerpalu the rest of us were totally out of the race. We would finish in the thirties or forties at best. There were no TV cameras waiting for us at the finish to validate our efforts. The press doesn't care about anyone but the top three, and why should they?

There is no prize and no money for sixtieth place or fortieth place, and there is plenty of pain between them. But I was willing to accept that pain just to be *one* place better, let alone ten or twenty. I was now in sixty-first place and moving up through the field, which was no great feat. I was racing through skiers, by the clock, who I should have been ahead of anyway. I knew I was a better skier than sixtieth, but results do not lie.

We came through the stadium and headed out for our last lap. After 34k I was feeling much better than I felt just one kilometer into the race. The fact that I blew my Olympic chance in the first few kilometers was something I had to force out of my head. I had to race as well as I could from where I was to the top of the next hill, to the next kilometer marker, to the corner—one stride, one pole at a time. I had to forget everything but staying in the rhythm of the skier ahead of me, of keeping up, staying smooth, and skiing efficiently. I had to concentrate on the fundamentals of the sport, moving as fast as I could, as efficiently as possible. Still, the thought that I was racing for a place in the forties—if I was lucky—instead of a place in the Top 20, gnawed at my insides. The disappointment was intense. It was frustrating to be skiing fast, now that it was too late. And it was far too late. If only I had skied well in the beginning. Still I hung on and pushed myself as hard as I could.

The four of us behind Veerpalu were racing for something the press would not be interested in. Those who are in the hunt for a medal, race hard for those medals. We had no earthly reason to work hard, but prior to the event we had promised ourselves we would do all we could. At this point it made little difference that when we made those promises to ourselves we had a goal in mind. Now we were simply working hard. We were skiing as fast as we could because this, *this race*, was the Olympics.

Though we were hurting now and working very hard, we had all worked much harder and put up with even more pain just to get here. These thoughts were not on my mind during the race, but they must have existed somewhere in my subconscious. What an insult to so many years of work, to all those tough days training on Route 23, and to all the sweat-caked runs dragging logs along dusty dirt roads. What an insult to the process and the lifestyle, to roller-skiing before five in the morning, to skiing five hours a day on Johnson's trails fueled by peanut butter sandwiches, to my friends who shared the pain and the dream but did not get to share the Olympics.

If I could have seen into the future during all those tough days of preparation, and seen myself give up in this race, *the* race, the very dream that propelled me would have vanished in an instant.

So, I finished the race as fast as I could. My split times over the last 20k were encouraging, but I finished the 50k in fifty-fourth place. I remember telling myself at Trout Lake that if I trained as well and as hard as I needed to, that I would be satisfied regardless of the outcome. But I sure wasn't satisfied with fifty-fourth place. To have performed so poorly in the race meant I had made mistakes in training.

But, at that point, I didn't care anymore.

"Man, what the hell are you down about? Huh? Jesus, man." Sten had his arm around my shoulder. I felt very, very small. He cared. He wanted it for me, and I couldn't do it. I *didn't* do it.

We were on the bus from Lillehammer to Oslo. I had finished the Olympic 50k only hours before and now we were on our way home, via Oslo. I was ready to quit.

"Man," began Sten, "I never raced in the Olympics. You know how many people make it to the Olympics?" I knew he was just trying to make me feel better, but making it to the Games was only a part of the goal. Winning was the real aim, and I felt very far from ever achieving it.

Rolling countryside sailed past the windows, pine forests and farms, all white and crisp, but the scene was spoiled by the partial reflection of my face. I could pretend to be looking out, but I was looking at myself.

"Hey, you know what? Next time you can do it," Sten assured me. "You know that? Next time. That's 1998. Lookit here." He pulled out a legal pad and sketched out a time line. "Spring 1994, you'll be NCAA champion. That's in three weeks. Then, we rest here, and start training here. Now look at this…"

Two hours later we arrived in Oslo with a rough outline of the next four years of training. Still, something was missing. I felt drained, and I felt as though Sten had doubts, but I was willing to pull myself together. The last twenty kilometers of the race gave me an ounce of confidence, and I knew that the dream would be resurrected, but I wasn't sure anymore that I could achieve it.

Two weeks later I was outsprinted for what would have been my second

NCAA national title. Then, several weeks later, I raced in the pre-World Championship World Cup in Thunder Bay, Canada. It was the Olympic fiasco all over again. I tried to hide. I was supposed to wait around in Thunder Bay for an extra day and then fly back to Marquette, Michigan. It would have been a short and easy day on the plane, but I couldn't stand being there. I was embarrassed about my race and my confidence was destroyed so instead of flying, I jumped in a car with some friends who had driven up to the races, and rode home with them. It was a long, all-night drive, and I was stiff and sore, and miserable, but at least I was on the move. Jumping in that car was an escape for me. To move ahead I had to face and overcome this sort of setback, but at the time all I wanted to do was hide. In my training log I wrote: *I don't think I can be a ski racer anymore.*

I felt as though the future, the last train, had come and gone, and I arrived at the station late, baggage in hand, too out of breath to even shout *Wait*. Instantly, my idealism, my belief, the dream itself, escaped with the train, sucked down the tracks like newspapers and sandwich wrappers swirling in the draft of the departing train. I imagined some bastard waving at me from the caboose: *So long sucker, so long.*

The days of confidently marching toward what I believed to be my destiny were gone. What was to be, wasn't; and I was left wondering, now what? There was a time when I knew where I was going, when destination dictated action, when I measured myself by my progress toward that destination, and even defined myself by the process. Then at the Olympics, at the World Cup, after so many years, I was left standing by the tracks wondering, *What now?* And even scarier, *Who am I now?*

An Afternoon with Bill Koch

In 1995 I was on my way home from my grandparent's house in Edmonds, Washington, and I stopped to visit Bill Koch. We had become friends after the Olympics in '92, where we had been teammates, and we'd kept in occasional contact since then.

Bill was studying neurolinguistic programming at the time and was eager to expose me to the practice. He told me to lie down and gestured toward this faux polar bearskin rug. He said he'd take me back in time, maybe to a previous life. It was an exercise of consciousness and a voyage into motivation, he said, and the subconscious demands reward. He asked me if I liked Red Vine licorice sticks and when I told him I did, he laughed and said they would do the trick. For each picture or story released by the subconscious I was given a Red Vine. The truth was, he said, that it didn't matter if what we found was true or not; it came from somewhere, from the subconscious, and it was, therefore, true enough.

This visit was a return of some kind to the first week of the first summer I spent in southern Washington State training for ski racing, where I stayed at Bill Koch's house.

That was the summer after the '92 Games. I called Bill and asked if my friends and I could crash with him for a few days until we found our own place. Accompanying me were Eli Brown, Cory Custer and Jimmy Defoe, a teammate and friend of ours from Northern Michigan University.

Bill Koch was a God to us. We were silly with awe, living in the house of a multiple World Cup winner and America's only Olympic cross-country medal winner.

Bill lived by his own rules and on his own time. He was into windsurfing and so though he was training for the 1994 Games, most of his time was spent in pursuit of this other passion. He lived not only by his own schedule, but by the wind. When it blew, he drove to the Columbia River Gorge to surf. Wind-surfing was training, but not very ski-specific training. When he felt like doing more ski-specific training, he did, otherwise he did what his heart told him was right. For example, he didn't like to run, and so in spite of the fact that every single ski coach in America said skiers must run, Bill Koch never ran.

Bill Koch is one of the strongest human beings I've ever seen, but he was not interested in strength for strength's sake. He lived for speed. He loved zooming over snow, flying across water on a sailboard, and buzzing the peaks of mountains in his small airplane. He could spend all afternoon jumping on the trampoline with his daughters, or all day on his windsurfer. Bill Koch did what Bill Koch felt like doing. He was, it seemed to us, above judgment and beyond judging, not without care, but past worry, beyond fret, above meaningless distraction. He exuded a passion for the activities and people he loved, and paid no mind to the rest.

This was the summer of the poison oak. We itched like hell all season. Poor Eli Brown wiped with it and suffered inhumanly. The woman at the medical center thought he was kidding when he told her what he'd done. There is something genuine and Midwest-earnest about Eli, but his manner is also highly comical. Immediately, he makes you smile. Eli explained that he had been running in the woods and had to stop and drop trou for a poop break, and had chosen his butt-wipe poorly. The unfortunate woman didn't know what to do. She wavered between laughter and anger, for she couldn't quite believe anyone would ever really wipe with poison oak. In the end she gave Eli some medicine, which made him screech in pain through gritted teeth.

It was also the summer we went to the Snoqualmie Family Nudist Park for the Bare Buns Fun Run. Jimmy Defoe didn't go. By then his life had already turned in what Cory and I thought was the wrong direction. He had a real job; he was making real money working at the John Day Dam on the Columbia River making sure a few salmon made it upstream. We were into saving the salmon, but Jim worked all day, and didn't have time to train right. He was a smart kid, but at the time I saw his forsaking training for work as a sin and a shame.

From my vantage point in 1995, while laying on the faux polar bear rug in Bill Koch's house, our probing of my subconscious suggested that I took Jim's abandonment of ski racing as an attack on the lifestyle I loved. For that, says Bill, reward the subconscious: one Red Vine.

Andy Hooker, a longtime skiing friend of Cory's and mine, came with us to the Bare Buns Fun Run. He would be the next to commit the sin of abandoning ski racing. Cory and I grew up with Andy in Boulder, Colorado, at just about the same time Boulder itself really grew up, or at least outgrew itself. Cory had always wanted to beat Andy, and now that he could, Andy wasn't trying anymore. Cory demanded that Andy be the skier he could be, and Andy wasn't interested. Andy wasn't really out in Washington to train with us, he was there for the adventure, and the Bare Buns was bound to be one.

Andy, Eli, Cory and I drove up the dirt road to the Snoqualmie Nudist Park for their 5k naked foot race—the first annual. I drove, hoping we'd get lost, hoping we'd all chicken out, but we weren't lost and we didn't chicken out. The first person we saw at the nudist park wore a leather biker vest, had long, greasy hair held back with a sweat-stained headband and nothing else. We made a point to maintain eye contact with him. The race was on an out-and-back course—one-and-a-half miles out, then back. There were almost five hundred runners, all of us, except for shoes and socks, in a state of utter nudity. I was in second place at the turnaround. On the way out I had only a solitary naked man fleeing before me, but upon turning around I found myself faced with an amazing view of humankind: 498 naked people running hard right at me. A running race in itself can be very revealing. Competition reveals something about you, not least of all to yourself. Some cheat, others whine, laugh, shout, pant, groan, quit, struggle, fly, flow, die or cry. In all cases some hidden part of you is revealed at least for that inevitable part of a race where the fun wears thin and you have to dig deep. In a naked race there is that, and a whole lot more, exposed by the event.

In one respect the Bare Buns Run was no different from any other race. At the sound of the starting gun, self-consciousness evaporated. It was a race, but different. Coming back along the racecourse, I saw runners who ran, walked, chugged, dashed, darted, plodded, flopped, spun, bounced, jiggled, jangled, shook, rippled, quivered, quavered, convulsed, twitched, shivered, shuffled, staggered, waggled, wagged, wriggled, and labored past in one tremulous herd of naked humanity. It seemed like there was a sense of communion among us. Naked, we all had in common more than we didn't. Though some were fast and others slow, we shared an experience of inescapable honesty.

The kinship was similar to what I experienced in dummy math in junior high, or like an intensive Spanish class I took in college where we all suffered endless mistakes or, as was often the case, the same mistake endlessly—we felt like we were all in it together. We laughed with each other, but we never laughed *at* each other. In a sense in those classes, we were as naked as our fellow runners in the Bare Buns Run.

Cory, Eli, Andy and I received the award for fastest team, and we stood naked and beaming in front of the whole crowd. We had risen above ourselves. The rest of the day we spent playing naked volleyball and lying in the grass talking to naked girls. We were dizzy with joy.

We left before the feeling escaped and drove home elated and boiling with confidence.

From the faux bearskin I related images of my youth and more recent memories, like the Bare Buns Run, to Bill Koch who rewarded me with Red Vines. He ate them too. And why not, it was a mutual journey.

My parents married in Italy, I told him. The wedding was performed by the mayor; the bellhop bore the ring. Lloyd and Sue were both overseas teachers. They were adventurers. I grew up in a backpack, traversing Europe on my parents' backs. There are photos of me at the Danube, on the plains in Turkey, skiing in Spain. I don't remember much, but a particular story from Italy merited a Red Vine reward.

In our village near Vicenza, Italy, I attended a nursery school run by two nuns. The two nuns dressed in bulky black, and strode along on invisible feet, hardly ruffling the layers of robes. There were two of the same nun, as indistinguishable to me then in person and as they are now in memory.

The students dressed in a white knee-length tunic with a blue collar and their street pants underneath. Each morning we greeted the two head nuns and received two suffocating black hugs. The two nuns were kind ladies most of the time, and the Catholic nursery school was a good place. But it was in this Catholic nursery school that my best friend Marco ratted on me.

One day at school we students were all gathered before the nuns with our little heads tilted up toward them, when all of a sudden small hands began to shoot to small noses, and little eyes began to look about. A rich stench filled the room and bodies started to squirm under their white tunic tents. Eventually the smell reached the nuns, and they rightly reasoned it could be traced to one of us. We squirmed and giggled and, though the nuns demanded we tell them who pooped in their pants, no one owned up to it. Then came the order. We were to sniff the person next to us. Marco's hand shot into the air.

One nun took me by the hand while another rolled up her sleeves. I was taken outside in clear view of my classmates, who stood pressed against the windows watching. My shoes came off, socks, pants, and underpants. My underpants were unburdened and taken away. Then my butt was scrubbed. Re-clothed and red-faced I rejoined the still-staring class. Marco was the only one not looking at me.

"Well," said Koch thoughtfully, and I looked at him expecting a guru-esque pronouncement, *"that sucks!"* and we burst into laughter.

Relentless

Since junior high, Cory and I had trained together, working toward the Olympics together. Though he was very fast, Cory was never fast enough to make it. But I would not have made it without him. I recall roller-ski races with Cory that took place many times over our junior and senior high school years on the road up to the National Center for Atmospheric Research above Boulder. In the late evening the steep road to NCAR ("*En-Car*") was free of the usual squall of cars and trucks, leaving Cory and me to our roller-ski races.

It is a steep and unrelenting road. As we race there is a battle between my ears, and the only noise I'm aware of is inside my head. One side of my brain wants to stop; one side wants to win. Not only are there no spectators, there is only one other racer. No prizes await the victor. In fact, I'm sure no victor will be named or spoken of, but we will both know who won.

Every month Cory and I have an uphill double-pole race. It is less than 15 minutes give or take. It is the "give or take" part with which my brain battles. Give or take the exact time no one will know how fast we went but Cory and I. Give or take I beat him or he me no one will know who won but Cory and I. Still we go as fast as we can, we strive to beat each other, and I do not relent, the grade does not relent, and Cory will never relent.

Many years before today and this particular roller-ski race, Cory fell thirty feet while rock climbing. The landing broke him up pretty good. The doctors said he was lucky to have lived. Many months after his fall, after a long time in a wheelchair with arms in slings and legs in casts, months of rehab, training, and hard work, Cory was on the verge of making the Junior National Ski Team. He had made an incredible recovery. Cory had shattered both arms, destroyed his ankle, and had his elbow rebuilt. But he recovered and we were again en route to our dreams.

One day Cory and I were on our way home after skiing at Eldora. Cory was only recently recovered enough to train. I was driving. Our mood was good. The road down Boulder Canyon from the ski area twists tightly as it drops down the canyon. Our teammates Chad Kipfer and Espen Kardel (who we called Head-spin) were with us. Going fast—too fast—the car lost traction on a corner. I lost control of the car, and we rolled three times landing, finally, on four flat tires. The car, a sturdy 1979 Saab, looked like a pup tent erected in the dark by Cub Scouts. Chad had smashed the window with his head and, as the car flipped, smacked the pavement with it as well. When the ambulance arrived, the EMT asked him if he was allergic to anything.

"Country and western," he said. Looking very concerned they loaded him quickly into the ambulance. Espen broke his collarbone, and was loaded up with Chad and driven away.

As it turned out, Chad suffered only a concussion and Espen's collarbone healed fine. I was completely uninjured, but miserable from having injured and almost killed my friends.

Three of Cory's ribs were broken in the crash, but only three weeks later he managed to make the Junior National Ski Team.

It was years before today's double-pole race that I broke Cory's ribs in the car crash, and none of this history is consciously among my thoughts as Cory and I race up the last, most painful portion of our course. But the battle in my head rages, and the history of his accidents and his tenacity matters because I want to stop, but I cannot. If I do, I will be prone to stop again, next time. If I stop I will learn to relent when what I need is to be like Cory—relentless.

The train—my dream—had departed, but I picked up my luggage, and instead of walking home, I started off down the track on foot. I was determined to reenergize my pursuit of Olympic gold yet again.

That summer, the summer of 1994, I returned to Trout Lake with Cory, Kurt, and Eli. The dream was the same, and in Trout Lake, training with my friends and living with the Black-Grigsbys, I found the joy again in work and in pursuing the dream. There were only three and a half years until the '98 Olympics.

Remember Kuusamo!

After the summer of '94 in Trout Lake I did not return to Northern Michigan University. I dropped out of college in order to return to Sweden, where I had lived and trained for a year as a teenager and had made great progress as a skier. My thinking was clear: The next step required another level of dedication, and school, I thought, was getting in the way.

When I first began ski racing, I knew that the best place to ski race was Scandinavia. Consequently, in 1990, when they called my name at the Boulder High School graduation ceremony, I strode across the stage, grabbed my diploma, shook whatever hands were thrust toward me, and got on a plane to Europe. Without hesitation I left my family, girlfriend, hometown, and all but one of my friends. There had never been a moment of doubt in my mind as to what lay in my future. Nor was there any doubt in Cory's mind as to what lay in his.

In high school I worked summers building and maintaining hiking trails all over Boulder County. It was a minimum-wage job that kept me outside working hard all day. It was training without training. It built power, strength, and endurance all while designing and constructing creative solutions for erosion control for Boulder's rocky, dry, and heavily-trodden hiking trails. I loved it.

It was my plan to use my accumulated savings to finance a summer in Europe. This worked only briefly. I quickly tapped out my resources became dependent on support from my parents and others.

Cory and I got off the plane in Zurich. We bought train passes and started our journey. Sightseeing was not on the agenda. Old buildings and statues shrouded in pigeon poop were for the wonder of others. We were in Europe to make ourselves into skiers. From Zurich we traveled to Ramsau, Austria. Less than two weeks later, we had lost a third of our belongings and sent most of what was left ahead to Berlin where, because of the contamination from a single pair of wet socks (ownership debatable), much of it had to be discarded. In the meantime, Ramsau was everything we desired.

We stayed in a room lent to us by a family of farmers. They went out of their way to make us feel at home. On one occasion we gathered enough courage and German vocabulary to ask for oatmeal for breakfast and while trying to explain that we would be happy to cook it ourselves, they somehow concluded that we wanted to kill one of their chickens and cook it for ourselves for breakfast. They angrily declined to let us do this and we couldn't understand what had inspired the sudden and remarkable change in the tone of our conversation or why they so detested the thought of oatmeal for breakfast. Somehow Cory managed to settle them down, and eventually we decided to just go without oats.

We skied every morning on the Dachstein glacier, and in the afternoon we ran in the mountains right out our back door or roller-skied on the local roller-ski track. Up on the glacier, Cory and I skied with some of the world's best. Harri Kirvesniemi from Finland, an Olympic gold medalist, was there. Giorgio Vanzetta, one of the best Italians and a medalist at the World Championships, was there. Silvio Fauner, also from Italy, was there. And Russians Mikhail Botvinov and Aleksey Prokurorov were there too. These were our heroes, and these were exciting, innocent days for us—long before a few of these skiers were exposed for using illegal performance-enhancing drugs.

We weren't just watching them train, we actually trained on the same snow, in the same tracks. In a single month we had graduated from high school, escaped from home, and went from watching our heroes on ski videos to skiing with them.

We began each day with a jolt of strong, hot tea and burst out the door into our new lives, free and doing exactly what we had dreamed. We were kids on our way to being kings.

Up on the glacier Cory and I would glue ourselves behind a Swede, Norwegian, Italian, or Finn, and ski behind them trying to match their speed, rhythm, and technique for hours nonstop. By the end of the morning we would ride the tram down from the glacier in utter exhaustion and complete contentment.

One of our first days on the glacier I spotted a Finnish skier skiing shirtless and in shorts. I was completely psyched to be on the glacier, in the sun, living my dream. Without consideration or sun block, I stripped down to wind-briefs and roared off in pursuit of the Finn. For two hours I skied behind him, in my underwear, in the hot summer sun, in a world of highly reflective snow at almost 10,000 feet. When Cory and I returned to our guesthouse, my whole body, including the skin under my nose, under my arms, and on my previously white butt-cheeks, radiated a brilliant burning-pink. That afternoon I lay in bed with mild heat stroke, a severe burn, and a huge grin reflecting my contentment in a life lived just as one expected life should be lived.

In spite of my condition, that evening we headed out to the insanely steep and twisting Ramsau roller-ski course for more training. We had outdated and extremely unstable roller-ski equipment. Each downhill ended in a sharp corner and, having no brakes, we had no choice but to just grit our teeth and go for it. Our descents were not marked with great skill or even with great courage. We flew down the hills with fear on our faces, dragging our poles in an attempt to slow down, and in a desperate crouching stance. Still surviving the experience gave us courage and we returned to the track the next afternoon only to put ourselves through the same psychological trauma all over again. *This is how elite skiers train*, we reasoned, *and we are elite skiers.* Cory and I were training a lot compared to what we were used to, and we envisioned ourselves becoming the skiers we had dreamed of being. In reality we had a long way to go, but the upcoming fall and winter in Scandinavia would put us on the right track. In the meantime, we had to get ourselves up there.

Fortunately, we had Eurail passes, which assured us of train transportation anywhere anytime. Or so we thought. It was 1990, the Berlin Wall had come down, communism had fallen, and Cory and I boarded the train bound for Berlin through what used to be the Eastern Bloc. As it turned out, it still was the Eastern Bloc.

The train rolled through a field on the outskirts of Prague. I was rolling through a newly-freed country with my head out the window feeling all kinds of fine. It was very loud out there with my ears in the wind, and when we rolled into a field of sunflowers my heart became light with freedom and motion and beauty. I stuck my face partway into the train and shouted, "Sunflowers! Hey, Cory, sunflowers!" Every tired, pale, work-beaten face in our crowded train compartment stared at me with humorless wonder, except Cory, who pretended not to know me.

We rolled along, matched in pace and elevation by a flock of ducks. Their wings a blur of motion and their necks outstretched, they looked like flying bowling pins.

The East German soldiers came aboard with dogs at the checkpoint between Czechoslovakia and Germany. It was night, and they shone flashlights under the train, used mirrors to check under the seats, and checked each passenger's ticket and passport. Cory and I handed over our papers with a smile.

"No ticket. Must buy."

"Yes," we said, showing him the Eurail pass, "we have tickets."

"No ticket. Must buy." He shifted the gun slung from his shoulder, and his German shepherd, which stood low and wide, rattled its chain in seeming annoyance. We paid in U.S. dollars. Even the dog seemed pleased. We, on the other hand, were running out of money.

The train picked up speed, for about half a mile, then it stopped. An entire East German village got on, and they brought cigarettes. There were no seats, but we made room. The train picked up speed, for about half a mile, then it stopped again. A second village got aboard, and this village brought booze. The train became a disturbed party. There was no joy, only shouting. Our compartment filled with cheap cigarette smoke. Cory and I gave up our seats for a place in the hallway near a small window. We took turns breathing the comparatively fresh, coal smoke-laden air through which the train clack-clunked. We were elbow-to-ass with everyone else in a writhing mass of drunkenness. There was no space to move, but everyone was moving anyway. There was no water in the bathroom, nothing to drink but booze, and no fresh air inside or outside the train. For eight hours we fought for space and air.

A huge man had passed out shirtless on the floor. Some people stepped over and around him, but most didn't make the effort. Some kicked at him and shouted for him to move. At times he would grunt and growl and try to get up. His flesh made a sticky sucking sound as he tried to rise from the alcohol, cigarette butts, puke, and general slime on the floor. He couldn't do it. Night's end found the train rolling quietly along, full of drunk passengers. Cory and I sat against the wall on our backpacks wedged next to the snoring man on the floor.

We reached Norway two days later tired and cranky, looking and smelling like we'd spent fifteen hours straight fighting and losing and rolling around in vomit—which was close to the truth. In Oslo we sat around the train station for a couple hours gawking at the girls and wasting coins in the pay phones on a few Norwegian friends who lived there. Unfortunately we happened to arrive during a national holiday, and the whole country had gone away for the week. Dragging an impossible amount of stuff, we took another train, a bus, and then walked to a youth hostel. We smelled like the homeless, but they allowed us in. For days we ate yogurt and bread, the only thing we could afford, for every meal, and trained at a lackluster, dragging pace.

Finally one of our Norwegian friends arrived home and found our messages awaiting him on his answering machine. He invited us over for a while. We stayed for a month.

Our trip through Eastern Europe had left us shaken, but in the green, rolling hills above Oslo we regained our spirits and set back upon the task.

Cory and I split up in Norway. He went off to a small school in the Norwegian countryside where he was to train as a skier and take some classes, and I rode the summer's final train to a small school in Mora, Sweden. I was to be a student at the Mora Folkhogskolan for one school year. The closest thing we have to a Folkhogskola in the U.S. is a community college, but the two are vastly different. A Folkhogskola caters to those just out of high school who are unsure of what they want to do next. It also caters to the elderly who don't know what to do next, housewives and out-of-work pre-college students who don't know what to do next, and to cross-country ski racers who are *really sure* what they want to do next. School is free in socialist Sweden, and if you had no idea what you wanted to do with your days, it would be a shame to pass up a year or two honing your basket-weaving skills at the expense of your countrymen.

I had been planning to come to Mora for two years. One Christmas when I was in high school Lloyd and Sue and I took a week-long trip to Sweden. It was a huge undertaking for us, and the point, besides visiting the country, was to see if it was possible for me to attend a school in Sweden after graduating high school—and to convince them to accept me. There are so many good skiers in Sweden, that, we reasoned, for me to attend the school I would have to prove myself worthy.

On that trip I raced in a relay race called the Annandagsstaffeten. It was a big nationally televised event and all the best Swedes would be there. The local team, IFK Mora let me race on one of their junior squads. The team's expectations for me were low, so they put me in their worst squad to keep me from screwing up their chances at winning. I was the lead-off man, and when the starting gun went off I jumped into the lead and pulled away from the field skiing faster than I ever had before. As I neared the finish, one skier snuck past me, and I tagged off in second place. Had I been on IFK Mora's top team, they would have won. My spot at the school in Mora was sealed.

My fellow students were laid back in the extreme. The Mora Folkhogskolan was a peaceful, friendly, and good place. The school had many fields of specialized study. Cooking was one, art another, as well as science and the humanities and cross-country ski racing. Any country where one can major in skiing is bound to breed some top-notch skiers. I majored in skiing—which they called being in the ski-line.

Even though I was a member of the ski-line, I also took a few regular classes, one of which was birch-bark basket weaving. It is the only class in

An autumn morning in Mora, Sweden, (1990).

all my years to bring me to actual tears. To have many days' work of carefully woven birch-bark spring apart and unravel redefines frustration. In skiing, the process is as great or greater than the reward; in basket weaving, the reward was all that mattered. In the end I made a beautiful backpack out of birch-bark and leather, and it just barely made up for the maddening process of creating it.

All classes were held in Swedish, and though most Swedes are excellent in English, learning the language was vital to having a social life and to simply surviving. Along with basket weaving I studied Swedish, took a cooking class and a leisurely physics class.

There was another American skier, Bruce Bauer, at the school at the same time. Bruce and I lived the good life together on our Swedish adventure. Most of life at the school was mellow and pleasant and Bruce and I loved to engage each other in epic battles at the ping-pong table.

Training, on the other hand, was far from leisurely. Until my time in the Folkhogskolan's ski-line I didn't know what hard training was. Part of the difficulty lay in the fact that for the first month and a half there, my Swedish was nearer to nonexistent than poor, and so each morning Bruce and I would load into the ski-line van with little idea what was going to happen to us that day. Typically the coach would drive us out into the rolling, wooded Swedish countryside and drop the whole ski-line off, at which time we all made our way home. In the fall, when there was no snow, we ran or roller-skied home. In the winter, since there were ski trails all over the Mora area, we skied back to school. Over time I gathered that there was some plan to these outings, for we would run, roller-ski, or ski at paces varying from moderate to extremely fast. Since Bruce and I were totally new to the country, let alone the Mora area, our only plan was to stay with the group so as not to get lost.

There was very little coaching here of the sort I knew from the States. The ski-line coach's name was Suna Aasp, and he looked exactly like GI Joe. He was tall, tan and had a stern, angular face and a close-cropped white head of hair matched by a white close-cropped beard. He came from the old-school method of training and didn't speak a word of English. After training hard every day for the first week I felt I had to ask, as best I could, how we would train the rest of the year. It took me an hour to look up all the words.

His answer took less than half a minute, "On Tuesday we train hard, on Wednesday we train hard, Thursday hard, Friday hard, on Saturday we race, and Sunday we race."

"And on Monday?" I asked.

"On Monday, we don't train."

We didn't work on technique, didn't analyze specifics, and didn't waste time talking. But, as promised, we trained hard. And when it came time to race, we raced fast.

In the first race of the year I almost beat the World Junior Champion-to-be. His name was Mathias Fredriksson. He was the best junior in Sweden, the best junior in the best ski country in the world, and later that year he would be crowned the best junior in the world.

He won the first race of the year, but only by two seconds. I was second. The race was held on a loop in a town called Idre. Early in November I accompanied a group of skiers from my school up to Idre for a training camp. There wasn't much snow, but they were grooming an 8k loop. I skied with my schoolmates for about five days, around and around and around. Though we had trained together all fall, testing each other, pushing and proving ourselves, my schoolmates were especially intent on showing me their superiority on snow. I was especially intent on showing them mine.

We were friendly and even friends, but when we trained we did not speak. That was the way it had been all fall. People talked and laughed with each other at school and in the van on the way to practice, but one step into training and it was silent.

We ate lunch in a cafeteria at the ski area. My friends patiently tried to keep me a part of the conversation. They spoke slowly and repeated themselves when I gave them bewildered looks.

On the third day Gunde Svan showed up. Everyone in the place took two looks. At that time he was the best cross-county skier the world had ever known. He'd won everything—Olympic medals, World Championship medals, more World Cup races than anyone ever had. He was a national hero, an international hero. My friends spoke excitedly among themselves, all stealing glances at him.

Growing up in Boulder the real world of ski racing was so remote as to be pure fiction. Gunde Svan was a fictional character out of worn videotapes and dog-eared ski magazines. He won races I only read about months after they happened. He wasn't any more real or any less heroic than a comic book superhero, and now he was eating Falu-sausage and rice alone at a table ten feet away. Gunde, who couldn't have been oblivious to the attention, ate slowly, didn't look around, cleared his dishes, and walked out.

The first race of the season was upon us. I was comfortable in the knowledge that I was as fast as anyone in my school, but I didn't know what that meant compared to the rest of the country.

Mathias Fredriksson wanted to be the best in the world. I would later see his photo in national newspapers and magazines with the subtitle: "The Next Gunde?" Like Mathias, I wanted to be the best, but for me, ski racing was still in another world. That meant I could proceed with complete ignorance and confidence.

In the first race in my first year in Sweden I skied the loop I already knew so well from twenty hours of skiing around it. I flew. I knew I was flying. I beat everyone by half a minute, except for Mathias Fredriksson, who beat me by two seconds. Next time, I thought; I'll get him next time.

I would never be within a minute of him again, but my season was still simply awesome. One of the biggest races in Sweden was the Svenska Skidspelen, the Swedish Ski Games. I was racing and in good shape. Gunde was there, as were a few others on the Swedish National Team. It was only five days before the World Championships in Italy, which I would watch on TV, and in which Gunde would win the final World Championship gold medal of his career.

After the interval start I was skiing fast and doing well in the junior class, Top 10 at the midpoint. It was a big event in Falun, which is a big ski city in Sweden—which is a huge ski country. There were thousands of fans out on the course cheering. Mostly they were there to cheer for their national heroes prior to their leaving for Italy. The cheering was loud, and getting louder. I felt good, I was doing well, but I could not imagine that the cheering was for me. I absorbed the noise and charged forward having one of my best races of the year. Then I heard the cheers—*Gunde!*

Nearing the finish of the 1991 Mora Vasaloppet, Sweden—90km classic. 19 years old, 25th place.

Gunde! Gunde! I chanced a glance behind me and there he was, bearing down on me. I put my head down and hammered to the top of the hill and over, and fell into a tuck.

Gunde Svan came even with me and passed. The hill leveled out and then popped up over a small rise. I was rested from the short descent and became determined to stay with Gunde until I died. He did not gain a step on me up the hill. The course took a sharp left and descended a long gradual hill. The cheering was thick now, and I was skiing in Gunde's wake. The corner was lined with fans, screaming and blowing horns, pounding drums. I skated for all I was worth. I slipped up alongside Gunde, and we fell into a tuck to ride the long, straight downhill. He gave me a slight glance, but it was one of mild astonishment: "You? Are you still there?" I was. My lungs swelled. I had seen him win races on old race videotapes. Now I was side by side, racing with Gunde.

The trail dropped steeply over a bridge and dove down toward the crowded ski stadium. But instead of heading to the finish it cut back into the woods for one final climb. This final climb at the Falun ski stadium is famous. Here is where the world's biggest races are won and lost by the biggest names in the sport. I had Gunde's ski tails at my ski tips starting the climb. I did not look up, but kept them in front of me. If they eased away, I tried to answer; if they eased away farther, I tried not to let them go; when they pulled away for real, I looked up. He wasn't doing it without effort. He was flying. His head hung between his shoulder blades, his arms drove his poles, and his legs stomped up the hill. He moved away from me—but slowly. The crowd was thickest here and I hung on as best I could, but he was leaving. There were shouts of encouragement for me. "Hang with him!" "Come on now." But it was the encouragement offered almost in jest. *This is Gunde*, they must have thought, *and who are you?*

Who was I? *I am on the rise. You'll know me someday.*

By the top of the big hill I could hardly stand, but Gunde had crested it only seconds before me. I poled my way over the top and remained standing as I slid down the hill, trying to recover before collapsing into a tuck that I rode all the way into the stadium.

I finished well among the juniors, but that wasn't important, what was important was that when Gunde passed me I tried to stay with him and believed I could. My greatest strength was that I had no fear of losing and that I saw myself as a first-rate ski racer. While I was growing up dreaming of an Olympic medal American skiers were struggling to finish in the top quarter of the field in major international competitions. As a result American ski moral in general was low. We were treated as second-tier racers or worse, and as a ski community, we thought of ourselves that way as well.

I was only 19, a young skier who on paper shouldn't have been able to ski with Gunde, the best skier in the world, for even a kilometer, but that isn't how I saw it. Even though Gunde eventually pulled away from me, I stayed with him as long as I did because I believed I could.

The Swedish Vasaloppet gave me another chance to ski with the world's best. The Vasaloppet is an epic 90k classic ski marathon from Salen to Mora. Over 10,000 people race it, including many of the world's top racers.

You might think that a 90k event would start at a reasonable pace, but it doesn't. With the explosion of the starting gun, ten thousand skiers take off with a bolt as though the finish were only a kilometer away. I was frightened. I pictured myself falling and being trampled by the stampede of 10,000 skiers. Falling isn't normally a concern while racing, but with hundreds of skiers thrashing around wildly, knocking into me, and stepping on my skis and poles, falling seemed entirely possible.

The course took a sharp turn and headed up a hill about five kilometers long. Still the pack did not thin and the frenzy did not subside. After we reached the top I could see the front of the pack. There was fresh snow, which made the going tougher even though the tracks were well-groomed. To avoid having to break trail in the fresh snow the skiers pushed into two lanes. I was in maybe 300th place.

After 35 kilometers I was feeling strong. I pushed hard and moved into the top 50. As I made my way through the pack, someone nearly ripped off my arm by stepping on my pole. I kept the arm, but lost the pole. I hesitated and looked back at a swarm of charging skiers. The pole was gone. I gulped and kept going, screaming at spectators and race volunteers to give me a pole. It was nearly five kilometers before I got one, and the one I got was five centimeters shorter than my other pole and twice as heavy.

Prior to the race I began a carbohydrate-loading program. The program started six days prior to the race. For three days straight I refrained from eating any carbohydrates, and ate only protein. During that time I trained as much as I could in order to completely deplete my carbohydrate stores. It is a painful and uncomfortable process that leaves you constantly hungry—which is the idea. After three days of training without carbohydrates the body is starved for them and willing to over-absorb carbs for the next time it runs into a carb-drought. For the second three days of the six-day program, with three days to the race, I stopped training and ate nothing but carbohydrates. For the first day, pasta never tasted so good. I shoveled it in and my body soaked it up. It was a process that was the opposite of dieting. What I ate, my body stored. By the third day I felt so bloated and ill I wasn't sure I could bend over to buckle my bindings without vomiting.

Now, after 50k of the Vasaloppet, I was still in 300th place, but I felt more energetic than when I started. On the starting line I felt stuffed—grotesquely stuffed—but now the carb-loading was working. While my competitors ran lower and lower on energy, I had fuel to spare. My racing plan was simple but sound. Pass on the uphills and don't let anyone pass me back. With thirty kilometers to go I was in twentieth place; nineteen kilometers to go, sixth place. I was told later that the radio and TV announcers reasoned that there must be someone else skiing in my race number, because in a race like the Vasaloppet such a young skier, and an American at that, could not be skiing this fast.

With fifteen kilometers to go, in the greatest moment of my skiing life up to that point, I moved into second place. The eventual winner, Jan Ottosson, was already minutes ahead, but I was second and pulling away from all but one of the other skiers. Maurilio De Zolt, an Olympic gold medalist and a skiing legend, stuck with me as we motored away from the rest, in second and third place.

The greatest moment of my skiing life came to a close with six kilometers to go. Despite my carb-loading program I began to feel extremely bad. My arms ached and cramped, energy left me with every exhalation, and my stomach turned inside out. My arms gave out and so I used my stomach almost exclusively, jack-knifing at the waist, and then after one double-pole motion my gut collapsed and a completely involuntary sound emanated from me like *huck!* I immediately stopped poling, in surprise and fright, and stuck a hand on what I was sure would be a hole, but my midsection was still there, just severely cramped.

I pushed hard and fought off as many skiers as I could, but the general sensation was one of extraordinary ill-being.

I crossed the line in 25th place. De Zolt finished 113th.

That winter a coach by the name of Sten Fjeldheim called me in Sweden all the way from Marquette, Michigan. He asked me if I wanted to go to Northern Michigan University the next year on scholarship. I told him I'd think about it. An hour later I received a call from Lloyd and Sue, who congratulated me on my scholarship and my decision to attend NMU. Sten, it seemed, had called them and told them I had accepted. Such was Sten's style—he wanted me at NMU, and he wasn't above applying a gentle shove to make it happen.

Four years later, I dropped out of college—giving up the best situation I ever had. I had a full-ride scholarship that allowed me to focus on school and skiing, free of worry. And I was leaving Sten—the best coach I'd ever had. The reason was good. To get better I had to race against better skiers, and there were no better skiers in the world than could be found in Scandinavia. But there was more to it than that. It isn't just about being in the right place, it is about having the right state of mind, and the right support system.

I returned to Sweden, this time as a member of the U.S. Ski Team. The idea was that I would train and race in Scandinavia and all over Europe with the best in the world. While the idea was sound, it turned out to be the worst year of my career. This time there was no birch-bark weaving, no Swedish lessons, no GI Joe to keep me in line, and nothing to keep my mind occupied. There was no balance. I was a ski racer, and little else. I did nothing but ski race, thought about nothing but ski racing, and I ended up having exactly one good ski race all year. I was not chosen to race in the 1995 World Championships, and I was kicked off the U.S. Ski Team.

If there was anything redeeming in that year, it was living with Carl Swenson.

Like Bill Koch, Carl Swenson is extremely good at doing what Carl Swenson needs to do. And like Sten Fjeldheim, who has created for himself the perfect life in Marquette, Carl has created for himself his own ideal life on the road. Carl races year-round. He is a professional mountain bike racer in the summer and U.S. Ski Team racer in the winter. He has no off-season because he loves to race too much, because he loves to train too much. And so he races all year-round and doesn't let anything prevent him from doing it.

Carl is home. He has run full speed from the Swedish disco about three miles away. It is about 2:30 a.m. I'm in bed. I know he has run home at full speed because I have been out with him before, and even though he was soaked with sweat, fuzzy with alcohol, and suffering from ringing ears, he set off for home at a dead run. It took me half a mile to catch up, and when I did we didn't say a word—couldn't for lack of breath—and we got home some twenty minutes later, panting and ready for bed. Come morning, we were up for training, and we felt surprisingly good.

Running home from the disco is the best way to go. You don't have to wait or pay for a taxi, you stay warm, and you burn off your buzz before bed. When you get home you're thirsty enough to gulp the glasses of water you need after a night out drinking.

"Come on Vorde," he said on his way to the disco one evening, "this is good stuff. There is a time for this, and this is that time."

It's true, too. Every top athlete, from every country in the ski world, has this trait in common: They are athletes first and always—24-hour athletes—but that doesn't mean they live in a cellar. It means their actions are in line with their goals, and their goals dictate their actions; and to go out at night, drink some beers, and maybe flail around on the dance floor is fine and universally practiced by ski racers. But only when it doesn't interfere with the grand picture. Balancing this is something Carl is extremely good at. It's not something many of the other athletes on the team were good at, and it slowed them down, while Carl only got faster.

Carl is home now, and I am in bed giggling at his antics. He's doing the dishes, singing Bob Dylan tunes at top volume. *"Those not being born...are busy dying."* Carl actually likes washing dishes.

I hear the sound of plastic dishes and cheap silverware banging in the metal sink. Carl is on to a new song, a singing and humming a howling version of "Mr. Tambourine Man." Soon he'll come stomping into our bedroom ready to talk literature. He reads voraciously—mostly non-fiction, often politics or philosophy—and he likes to discuss what he reads.

"Theroux is dark!" he says. He's been reading Paul Theroux books, one after the other. He's waving a copy of one of them at me, grinning.

"The world can't be as bad as all that," I answer from under the sheets.

I'm trying to keep up with Carl's reading, so I've read some Theroux as well. He's subtle, but to me Theroux seems to push the pessimism a little far for the sake of drama. I tell Carl this. "Ha!" Carl answers, "Honesty is all he cares about. And writing—and writing honestly." With that he climbs into his bed and falls asleep.

Carl is utterly self-assured. A fancy outfit is a clean tee-shirt, khakis and running shoes.

"I am fashion exempt," he says.

Tell him he can't do something, he smiles and says very quietly, "Well, works for me," and then does it.

Carl has endless motivation. Normally, *that* is what I would say his secret is—what *the secret* is. But I think it is Carl's determination to *do* what he believes will work for him that is his real secret.

Success demands faith in what you are doing; and faith, does not hold up well under reason. You just have to know. There is no way Carl could have known, other than by faith in himself and his plan, that he was on the right track.

Scientific-based training theory does not allow for successfully racing all year round. The experience of coaches the world over does not admit the possibility of racing successfully all year round. So there were many in the skiing community eager to challenge Carl's faith in his ability to race successfully all year round. There certainly is wisdom in listening to others, but there is equal wisdom in tuning them out. Carl could nod his head and smile at any advice, turn around and keep doing what he had faith would work for him.

I wish I had followed Carl's lead while living with him in Sweden. It might have made all the difference. Carl got faster, while I lost momentum. My faith in what I was doing and how I wanted to do it grew weak. I started to see myself not as the first-tier skier I grew up believing myself to be, but as the second-tier skier I was becoming. I got slower, felt flatter, became depressed, burned out. Carl pushed on.

Trusting myself was a lesson I'd learned and lived by only four years earlier at the end of my first year in Sweden. In a single race, in Kuusamo, Finland, I was passed by every single one of the world's best ski racers, and from that experience I learned both to find inspiration in defeat and to design my own path to success. It was a lesson I put to good use—and then forgot too soon.

It was the spring of 1991. Cory Custer and I embarked on the last racing series of the season across northern Finland, Sweden, and Norway called the Polar Cup. Every race in the three-week trip took place above the Arctic Circle.

This was the end of our first year out of high school, our first year as genuine ski racers. Cory had spent the fall and winter living in Norway, and I in Sweden. As a junior racing in Sweden I found some success. I won a few races and placed well in many. I fancied myself fast and on the rise. The trip to the Polar Cup wasn't that far, but it opened our eyes to the real world of elite ski racing.

We had arranged a ride on the Polar Cup bus from race site to race site, starting in Helsinki, Finland. At the airport in Helsinki a Russian man held a cardboard sign with our names misspelled on it. We hopped on the bus and sped through the endless snow and pine forest of Finland. The bus, though full of skiers, was silent except for me and Cory rattling on about our latest adventure.

Though juniors, we registered as senior racers for the Polar Cup so we could race the big boys—the very best in the world.

The first race was held in Kuusamo, Finland. It was an individual start, classic-style race. Cory Custer and I held early (rookie) seeded start positions. We warmed up on a portion of the course and could not believe the hills. There was no skiing them at an easy pace. Just to get up them we had to ski hard or walk.

The starter took his hand off my shoulder and I took off on a fifty-minute epic. Every hill was brutal. I poled hard to maintain my momentum up the bottom of a hill, and then skied a few hard strides before the steep pitch forced me into a fast run and finally to a grueling herringbone out of the tracks. Eventually, the length of the hill forced me into a quick shuffle or scamper. As I scurried up the outside of the track, the world's best poured past me skiing up the tracks with big, powerful gliding strides.

Though I was well out of his way, many-time Olympic medalist Vladimir Smirnov whacked me in the leg with his pole as he powered past. Cory reported receiving a similar blow when the huge Kazak passed him. We couldn't decide if it was meant as punishment—the Alpha wolf scolding the pups—or as encouragement. In any case it stung.

Double-poling along the flats, I was passed by skiers whose poles whipped with a deep *whoop* as they swung forward and then kicked up a spray of snow with each push.

But it was really the steep uphills where they buried me. They had springs in their legs. Taking springing strides, they caught and passed me and disappeared over the hill, leaving me gawking and scurrying along.

I lived many little lives in that race and thought many thoughts—too many thoughts. I marveled at the skiers flying past me. I knew I was too weak to ski as they did, but I raced as hard as I could. In the end I was beat by almost eight minutes in just fifteen kilometers.

On the train home from northern Norway, after the whole of the Polar Cup was over, I spent a long time staring out the window at the snow-covered landscape. Among the juniors I had some good races, but after Kuusamo I knew they meant little. Racing the seniors had a tremendous impact on me, but I was not disheartened.

My young age enabled me to look at the distance I had to travel with excitement. As the snowbound villages clacked past the train's window I began to plot and steel myself for the voyage. *In ten years*, I thought, *I can win.*

I determined that explosive strength was the area where I could make the biggest gains. Specifically, I had to be able to bound up those hills on legs like coiled steel. I needed to develop explosive power in my lower body and huge strength in my upper-body.

Being beat that badly in Kuusamo became an inspiration.

I flipped ahead months in my training log and wrote reminders to myself about the experience.

"Remember Kuusamo."

"Build explosive power!"

"Strength!"

"Eight minutes in Kuusamo!"

And I set out a plan I devised myself on a train from northern Norway to middle Sweden.

Like a mountain climber at base camp, I had seen the peak and now understood what lay before me. There was no mystery in what had to be done. As in mountain climbing, where the mountain looks huge and unconquerable until the task is broken down into the details of climbing it, my plan relied on the details of training.

I thought there were many reasons that American skiers at the time weren't as good as their competitors from abroad. But the solution could be distilled down to one thing: training.

I started my new training regimen the day after I arrived home from the Polar Cup. I didn't take one day off from the end of that season to the beginning of the next, but set upon following my plan with utter determination and desire.

Not fewer than twice a week, sometimes as often as four times a week all summer I did a routine of plyometric exercises on the trails below the National Center for Atmospheric Research, in Boulder, Colorado. I ran half an hour to NCAR with my ski poles in hand. Once there I set upon a system of *spenst* training. "Spenst" is a Norwegian word for explosiveness, and explosiveness is what I was after.

My routine of spenst began with one-legged jumps. One-legged jumps imitate the animation and motion of a one-legged man in rabid pursuit of the rat-bastard who stole his prosthetic and cane. With great vigor I would jump with one leg and land a good distance up the steep dirt trail on the same leg, only to immediately explode forward again from the same leg. The point was to make as much distance as possible with each jump and to go as far as possible in the fifteen jumps per leg I'd take up the hill. I would repeat that process three times per leg, and it would never fail that someone out walking the dog would find me performing this mad one-legged assault on the hill, and stop abruptly, consider the scene and turn hurriedly around and disappear down the trail. I tried to set a distance record each time up the hill, on each leg, every time I went out to NCAR, two or more times a week, every week, all summer. The stronger I got, the further I flew with each leap and, I hoped, the faster I would ski. Three sets of one-legged jumps were followed by three sets of sideways, skate-like jumps. These are more refined and unlike the one-legged jumps actually look like training for some kind of sport. Again, the point was covering huge ground with each explosive jump. That was followed by three sets of two-legged hops, and these without fail would inspire either awe or fright in passersby. I started in a low crouch, bobbing, swinging my arms and peering intently up the hill prior to take off. When ready I unleashed a mighty hop and, like a frog, I leapt forward from my crouching position, and sailed forward in a near horizontal position, outleaping in distance and style even Mark Twain's celebrated jumping frog from Calaveras County. In mid-air I had time to pull my legs up to and past my chest, and then stick them out in front of me like landing gear, before coming down again in a low crouch with a grunt.

This I performed up the hill non-stop for fifteen jumps, and I didn't care who was there to see it.

As I jumped I was seldom aware of anyone approaching. I had just reached the end of my fifteen jumps when I heard a slurred, "Jesus!"

I looked up and there stood one of Boulder's homeless. He was squinting at me from a wrinkled, hairy face that was matted and dark with grime. His mouth hung agape showing few remaining teeth and an otherwise dark maw. His bare legs were planted wide to improve balance and in his hand was a brown bag twisted to the bottle it concealed.

"Holy Jesus," he went on, taking a few staggering steps toward me, "what in the hell is the matter with you?"

"Bunny hops," I told him.

"Bunny hops, hell," he answered, staggering and swaying, squinting at me hard, and then, swirling his finger in a circle at his temple shouted what sounded like, "Loco, hopping man!"

And he wandered off swearing and muttering, looking back over his shoulder at me every few feet.

I often heard guffaws and nervous laughter from dog walkers and joggers as they passed. I generally smiled casually to assure them of my sanity. And generally to no avail, but being called crazy by this dusty old man was proof enough that indeed it was crazy, and that felt just right. If it was crazy, others were less likely to do it, and doing what others would not, was what I needed to do. I had to go a little further, do a little more, for I believed I could be the best, but I had no illusion about accomplishing that with ease. Spenst was followed by ten to fifteen repeats of ski-bounding with my ski poles, twenty seconds each. This also was a dynamic activity, done with the power I thought necessary to ski the hills of Kuusamo. The motion is exactly like classical skiing, making it a perfect form of summer training. After that I performed a series of longer, but less-explosive ski-walking intervals, after which I ran home on wobbly legs.

I did the work alone. I did it without fail, and I did it with utter focus and confidence.

In addition, I roller-skied, ran, biked, and lifted weights. I did not record a lot of training hours on paper, because though I hiked and biked quite a bit, I did not count much of it as training. If I ran up a mountain but had to walk or even jog down, I didn't count coming down. I didn't count the downhills on my bike, and unless it was ski-walking I seldom counted walking up even a steep hill. To me, walking didn't seem directly enough related to what I wanted to do on skis to be considered training. I didn't log games, like soccer, or stretching or the time it took to rest between sets in the weight room.

If an activity wasn't directly related to my plan, it didn't count.

This wasn't exactly fair to my body, as my muscles endured more than I gave them credit for. And while it wasn't the best way to record my work, it focused my effort on what I thought was important. I had great confidence in my training and knew with certainty that what I was doing and recording as training was exactly what I needed to do.

In a single race in Kuusamo, Finland, every elite ski racer in the world passed me, and from that race I learned what I lacked as a skier and what I would need to get it—crazy or not.

I went from placing only once in the Top 25 even in U.S. events to making the 1992 Olympic team after a single summer and fall of training. After many years I narrowed my time behind the very best in the world from eight minutes to a minute and forty-five seconds for fifteen kilometers.

It is the struggle, it is each day's effort that I look back on with the most satisfaction. It is fun to say I've raced in the Olympics, but it is each day's work that I look back on with pride. That I chased my dream with such conviction that I could inspire a staggering homeless man to call me crazy, gives me great pleasure.

During that second year in Sweden, living with Carl at the young age of 25, I lost my desire, my confidence, and all my momentum. I'm not sure which I lost first. The closer I got to the mountain the bigger it looked.

Doing spent training on the trails below NCAR in '92 was the manifestation of my belief in my methods, my ability to succeed, and in my desire. I discovered my weakness, devised a way to overcome it, and followed through on it. That is the struggle, and the struggle is the important part.

But in '95 while Carl carried on with confidence and determination, I began to look around, wait for someone else to help me achieve the next step. I forgot about Kuusamo when I needed to remember it most.

 After racing all winter in Sweden with the U.S. Team and living with Carl, I returned to the U.S. and drove to Baja, Mexico, with two of my teammates who also had suffered through a long winter in Sweden.

Escapees and Stingrays

Drive a long way down the Baja peninsula and turn down an unmarked dirt road and keep going until that road ends. The gringos you find camped in the sand at the end of that road, at edge of the green Sea of Cortez can be categorized as either escapees or expatriates. Escapees are down there to discover or recover, while expatriates are down there for the duration.

Baja, Mexico, is about as far away as you can get from ski racing. My teammates Justin Wadsworth, Ben Husaby, and I drove to Baja from Bend, Oregon, in Justin's '82 Subaru hatchback to escape the snow and cold, the training and racing, the pressure and lifestyle of a cross-country ski racer. We didn't cross in category from escapee to expatriate, from half-mad visitor to perma-tan lunatic, but we came close.

Mexican Mermaids

"Mermaids, Abraham," Rocky says to me, knowing my name isn't Abraham. "Naked, sweet, and salty. Slippery as hell."

"Easy, Rock—you're gonna tip the damn boat over, man."

"She ain't gonna tip. I need a cigarette."

I flip my piece of hooked squid over the rail and watch it disappear into the green sea.

"Let's catch some fish, eh, Rocky?"

"Soon enough. I've got a pack around here somewhere..." his voice trails off.

I watch him search around the stern of the boat for another cigarette. Captain Rocky is agile for his size, but even so, the ten-foot long wooden craft tips and sways with his searching. Finally his search is rewarded.

"Listen," he says, reclined and relaxed, casually drawing on a bent and crumpled cigarette, "if the fishing ain't too good, I know a place where we can find us some mermaids."

"Yeah."

Justin, Ben, and I glance at one another.

With a flip of the wrist he sends his bait zipping over the water where it falls with a kerplunk and sinks. There is a moment of silence as Rocky concentrates on his smoking.

Just feet away, pelicans skim the water's surface in close-staggered lines, gliding and watching for schools of small fish. To the west the sun-baked and jagged desert mountains back a bright white sand beach. Cactus is the vegetation of choice here, and if it's not cactus it's a plant trying to be cactus. Everything is spiny, pokey, rough. Rattlers, scorpions, small rodents and lizards hide among the rocks. Small birds flit in the shade of cactus or the prickly branches of small trees. Above soar the vultures, waiting and watching. Many things die in the desert, but nothing dies unnoticed or unappreciated. Baja is a good place to be a vulture.

It is also a good place to sit quietly and do some serious fishing, but that is not what Rocky has in mind.

"I'm a two-time-divorced Wyoming jack-Mormon," Rocky says in a voice loud enough to startle a far-distant rodent, lizard, or rattler. "Do you know what that means? Means I like guns more than I like women, and trucks more than I like church—and, Abraham, I like women a whole helluva lot."

An un-puffed puffer fish took the bait. Rocky looks on. (Justin, Rocky, Pete—R to L.)

Rocky is our newest friend. We met him only yesterday. He was then, as now, clad in mismatched flip-flops and a pair of brown cotton gym shorts. A blue ship-captain's cap complete with gold piping is pulled over his bowling ball head, and a shock of blond hair curls from beneath the cap. At the shoulder Rocky must be three feet across. From back to belly he can't be less than four feet thick. And all that bulk rests on two thin legs. His enormous belly pushes his shorts down from above, and gravity tugs from below. His butt, too small for the rest of the show, does nothing to support the shorts—which are just south of halfway down his rear. Rocky is an overall, sun-ripened reddish brown the color of the surrounding mountains, exactly.

"Abraham"—he has invented this name for me—"there's hot springs over yonder that come right outta the sea. A fella can sit on these slimy rocks up to his eyeballs in hot salt water and watch naked sea women frolic and splash."

"Shit."

Again the three of us skiers share a glance.

"You'll see, Abraham. Just wait."

He leans toward Justin as if he has a secret to reveal. "You know what, Moses?" He calls Justin Moses. "My wife was kinda melancholy. —Head like a melon, face like a collie." I grab onto both sides of the boat as Rocky builds to his full laugh. The boat shakes violently while Rocky, with head tilted back, sends laughter across the water against the mountains and echoing back. Then his fishing pole jerks, and his eyes grow wide.

"Shit almighty. Fish on, boys, fish on."

It isn't long before our dinner is flopping in the diesel, saltwater, cigarette butts and fish guts in the bottom of the boat. I dispatch the big grouper with a hard stomp to the head. Rocky notices this, and I can see him weighing the meaning of this action—judging me by my show of mercy.

The thought passes.

Rocky yanks the cord, and the engine sputters to life. I can't hear him over the engine and the water slapping the bow, but he is talking and pointing ahead of us as we chug along. A huge grin holds his cigarette in its corner; smoke whips over his shoulder with each word he mouths.

We slow as we near a small island.

"That's right, boys. Mermaids, honest to God." He's pointing beyond me, over my shoulder. I'm not sure what I'm going to see, but I turn around, and there they are. Sitting up to their waists in water are three young women, their bare breasts buoyant on the water. They are as brown as the land beyond them. Mermaids.

There they were. They wave at us. Rocky waves back. We are a long way from anywhere. We have not seen a woman in a week. Where could they have come from if not the sea? I believe absolutely that these women are mermaids.

When mermaids are real the whole world changes and all things become possible. When mermaids are real the world grows huge and the possibilities are beyond imagination. I spend a long minute wandering through this new world. How sweet it is. But it simply can't be. These brown creatures with their long, tangled, wet hair *are* women, not mermaids.

Rocky is laughing again. The boat rocks with his booming.

We anchor the boat a little way off the seagull-stained island. Rocky, Justin, Ben, and I strip down and set off swimming. Sputtering with the saltwater slapping him in the mouth, and with a drenched cigarette clinging to his chin, swimming, Rocky is narrow-eyed and agitated.

"Damn cold water—shrinks my pod."

As quickly as possible we pull ourselves from the sea, up over the rock ring containing the hot spring water, and sink into the warmth next to the mermaids.

"Meet my buddies, Abraham, Moses, and Mohammed." Polite smiles all around, and nods of greeting.

"Should have seen the kid," he nods toward me, "when he saw what he never thought he'd see." Rocky has a huge open-mouth toothy smile and is on the verge of uproarious noise. "*Mermaids*, I told him!"

False Prophets

Avocado is the Incan word for testicle. Jimmy told me that while the group of us—Jimmy, Cranston, Justin, Ben, and I—peeled their leathery skins off and dropped the ripe mush into a large metal bowl. We skiers had just arrived and it is before we had even met Rocky. We had the first case of beer Jimmy and crew had seen in two weeks. Pacifico Ballena—the big ones, a liter in every bottle, and we had twenty-four of them. They had avocados, bought ten for a dollar, all in the peak of ripeness. We had limes, salsa, and a bulk bag of greasy corn chips. We were off to a good start.

Mexico Highway 1 is one of the very few paved roads in Baja. It runs north-south, from the southern tip to the U.S. border. It's a narrow two-lane road used by everything from speed freaks to donkey-carts. Driving its length you develop a terrible thirst as well as a hankering for avocado dip.

Justin's '82 Subie was named Butt-fur—I thought because of the furry sensation your butt got from the road vibration conveyed through the car's old shocks. But the name came from an old clothing company sticker—Butt Fur—adorning the car's ski rack.

Following a tip, Justin steered Butt-fur off of Highway 1 and guided us down one of a million dirt roads winding into the cactus. We bounced and rolled east, cut through a gap in the mountains, and dove in a spiral toward the Sea of Cortez. Before descending the miles of washed-out, rutted switchbacks, Justin pointed the sandblasted Subaru toward the edge of the road and ground to a stop in the gravel. Off the main road now for an hour, we were deep in Baja. The scene before us was the reason we had come: jagged mountains leading into hidden coves with real trees—not just cactus—shining beaches and a spattering of small islands in green water.

The village cove was hidden from view, but we descended the road, turned a corner and there it was. It wasn't a village so much as a collection of trailers, buses, and shacks.

"Jesus," Ben said as we laid eyes upon the ragtag village and its inhabitants. "We have reached the upper region of the river," he said, mocking "Apocalypse Now." "It's the heart of darkness, and Kurtz is waiting. He is a great man, Captain Kurtz."

We sat around sharing beer and food with the locals. Cranston didn't have a normal Adam's apple; he had a entire Washington Red Delicious. When he swallowed it bobbed, when he spoke it yo-yoed, when he laughed, I stared.

He was tall and skinny with big joints. He had a thin face with a long nose, wire legs with knobs for knees, toes like fingers, fingers like sticks, and knuckles like stones. He looked through eyes set five inches back from the tip of his nose. He was a blue heron hungry for avocado and thirsty for beer.

Jimmy's retired school bus was next to the tree we sat under. It was meticulously clean, inside and out. So was Jimmy. He wore nice slacks, a clean T-shirt, new flip-flops, and a Princeton Review ball cap. He spoke like a surfer and laughed like a hissing lizard.

"Thisss tree is spf fiffteen, man."

"Huh?"

"This tree, man, SPF 15. Sun block, dude. Solar radiation protection is vital here."

"See what he means?" said Cranston pointing over my shoulder. We all turned to see a man in brown shorts, flattened flip-flops, and a ship captain's hat striding toward us. There was a lot of him and it was all a deep reddish-brown.

Rocky approached rapidly. He sat down beside me, and had his mouth full of chips and avocado in no time.

Ben offered him a beer.

"Don't drink...*munch, munch, munch*...but thanks." He extended his hand all around.

"I'm Rocky. You're Abraham," and he burst into laughter while vigorously shaking my hand. "And you'd be Moses," he said to Justin. Ben, he embraced. "You are Mohammed. The prophets have arrived."

"Cranston"—he called Cranston by his real name—"how's it going? And Jimmy? Thanks for the snack. So Abe, what do you do?"

I popped a chip and considered the question as I chewed.

"I'm a ski racer."

"You're a who?" asked Rocky again.

"We're ski racers," Ben told him. "Cross-country ski racers." Ben meets people easily.

Justin fished a U.S. Ski Team pin from his bag and handed it to Rocky.

"Well, I'll be," Rocky said, turning the little pin in his sausage-sized fingers. He removed his hat and stuck the pin to the crown. "So am I!"

Rocky bellowed at his own joke. Jimmy hissed. Cranston's Adam's apple bounced. And we three prophets sat smiling, wondering what this guy was all about.

"What are you Prophets down here to achieve?" questioned Rocky.

"Just down for some sun and..."

"Bullshit! There's sun elsewhere," interrupted Rocky, "and not half the drive and with twice the amenities."

"Good point," Ben said with a smile.

"You're seeking the great Mexican dream," Rocky went on.

"The Baja Dream," Cranston said.

"A voyage of indeterminable duration to the Sea of Cortez," Jimmy said. "Crack me a fresh one, dude."

"Let's see," Cranston spoke thoughtfully. "Take Claus from down the beach there. He and his one-armed friend, ah, Weber, have traveled around the world in that old German military truck. They've been through Africa, Europe, South America, up Central America, the mainland Mexico, and it took them three years to get here. And now they've been here, right here on this beach, for almost a year." He pauses to pour beer down his blue heron gullet.

"Now, as he told me, before he—I mean Claus—started traveling, he was some kind of high-paid photographer. Had a wife, kids, house, money, and gave it all up. What he said was, 'I have vaisted za best of za moments peering from behind za camera.' "

"His perspective man..." Jimmy made the rough shape of a square with his hands "...mucho limitido, dude. And that is so not bueno."

Jimmy continued, "He doesn't even have a camera anymore."

"Or a wife, and I ain't casting no stones or anything," blurted Rocky.

There was a mumble of agreeable *uh-huhs* followed by a lull in the conversation. We concentrated on the chips. Jimmy sat smiling like a lizard, leaning back, lost in taste-bud delight. Rocky was not reclined. He was in a frenzy of eating. I watched Ben load a chip with creamy avocado, spicy salsa, and tangy lime into his mouth and chew with his eyes closed. The sight sent me back to the chip bowl.

A man and a woman walked past us with their arms around each other, ghost-like under loose clothing. They seemed to float and weave in the breeze. They moved slowly enough and were close enough to us that I could see them clearly. The skin on the left half of the man's body was twisted and pulled as if it had been heated, stretched like rubber, and cooled in its contorted shape.

They drifted by giggling. Cranston waved, said hello. They waved back vacantly and kept going. There was silence around the avocado dip for a few minutes. Rocky, who had been meticulously rolling a joint, stuck it behind his ear. Jimmy concentrated on his beer.

"So, that was Carlo and Wendy," Jimmy said, reaching forward with a hand, for emphasis. "And, dude, that's kind of the reality, or some real perspective anyway, on the Baja Dream."

Cranston swallowed dryly. "Carlo is a Vet. As he tells it, he was sitting up on a tank in Vietnam with his buddy, and they were passing a canteen full of water back and forth and smoking cigarettes when this Vietnamese kid stands up out of the grass with a rocket launcher. Carlo spent the next five years in and out of VA hospitals having pieces of his friend surgically removed from his back."

"Dude," broke in Jimmy, "we're all residents. I mean ten-year extendo-vacation residents maybe, but Carlo is a real resident here, permanently permanent." He continues, "Permanently checked out, or checked in, passed out, turned on or tripping out. I mean we're all residents. It's just that some of us have more to escape from than others."

"Man, whatever the story, it takes some serious avocados to live it."

Much head-nodding around the chips, and contemplative slurping of beer.

Justin Wadsworth and me paddling in Baja, Mexico.

Who Has More Fun Than People?

The Baja trip was cleansing, an exorcism. I was haunted by the past winter in Sweden, the sensation of my dream slipping away. Ski racing is a good lifestyle, but it is a hard one, and a cold one. In the winter it is one spent mostly on the road traveling from race to race, and for me each race was a test: *How fast am I, how fast can I be?* The ghost that haunted me was the answer to both those questions I'd gotten over the winter in Sweden: *Not nearly as fast as I wanted to be.*

And so the bones had to be laid out just right, sacrifices had to be made. Balance was restored, but blood was shed in the process.

Before we met Rocky and the other escapees, we suffered, and Justin took the brunt of it.

Justin was helping me tighten the knot holding a size ten fishhook to my line. As he pulled on the line with one hand, and the hook with the other, he slipped, and before he knew to let go he sunk the hook into his index finger. He made a sound like *Zzzzzsss* and held his finger before his eyes. The hook was buried in his flesh past the barb. We tried to pull it back out—no luck—and then tried to cut it out—too painful. The hook was going to have to go all the way through. While Ben held his arm still, Justin, sweating and swearing, pushed the tip of the hook deeper into his own finger until the point was pushing up and against the underside of his ski-pole callused fingertip. The tough skin of his finger tented and turned white under the pressure. Justin fought the strong natural aversion to pushing sharp objects into your own flesh. His hand fought itself, half pushing, half resisting. For a good half hour the three of us huddled on a point of rock sticking into the Sea of Cortez, focused on the hook in Justin's finger. Finally, with a prolonged grunt of pain the steel tip broke through and slid up out of his skin like a metallic parasite emerging from his finger. The hook completely pierced his finger—in the side, out the top. Ben cut the hook at the barb with a pair of wire-cutters and slid it back out.

A few hours later a greater agony made his fishhook episode look like a pretty good time.

As the sun was setting, Justin waded offshore to do some fly-fishing and, as it turned out, to redefine pain. He stepped on a stingray. The ray's tail whipped up and its spine punched a hole through Justin's shoe and into his foot. The spine deposited a poisonous protein into his foot, said by the locals to be more painful than the venom of a rattlesnake.

"Cascabel, you know? Serpiente? The rattlesnake, is nothing my friend. This…it's gonna hurt."

The gash was painful enough, but as the man told Justin, the real pain would come soon.

We were hours from any town, let alone a hospital. The bush-cure for a ray's sting is ugly, but there was no choice. As Justin writhed in agony we applied rags soaked with boiling fresh water and pieces of hot, fried cactus to his shaking foot.

The heat is said to neutralize the protein, and the cactus sucks it from the tissue. Rather than screaming at the application of burning hot cactus and boiling water, these things came as a relief compaired to the pain of the ray's sting. Upon application of the water or cactus, Justin was able to relax his clenched jaw as the venom's pain would momentarily subside. It was when we took away the heat that he yowled and shook. Justin endured four hours of this until the full effect of the sting faded and he was able to pass out in a cold, shaky sweat. He woke up at dawn covered in vomit, and feeling much better.

While Justin endured the most severe pain, my injury would last the rest of my life. It was our second day in Mexico—well before we met up with Rocky or the other ex-pats and before Justin's day of agony. The sun had just sunk behind a wall of tall, dark cliffs, and though it was just late afternoon, the beach fell under a dusk-like shadow. It was windy and cool.

After searching for a place to set our tents up out of the wind, we got out our kayaks and prepared to launch from the top of a steeply sloping, black-gravel beach.

I looked at the crashing waves and was scared. Ben and Justin got in their kayaks and slid down the gravel like seals into the surf. I was next. The waves seemed to get higher and higher as my boat slid toward them. I was not sure if I was breathing.

I was new to the sport of kayaking, and being from Colorado, new to playing in the sea. The waves rose and broke before me. I repeated the slogan taught to me by Justin: "Keep paddling, keep paddling, keep paddling…" My kayak was popped nose up and felt near vertical as a wave surged under me, but I stayed upright and alive—which bolstered my confidence considerably. Every wave pulled me back, but I kept paddling. Before long I found myself beyond the break. I watched as Justin turned himself toward shore in front of what at first seemed like a slight roll in the water. The roll grew and rose until Justin disappeared on its far side and was gone from sight. Then, in an explosion of water, he became a helmeted head and a windmilling paddle lost in the white froth of the tumbling wave. He emerged from the chaos shouting with triumphant glee.

"Oh, shit," I muttered, and turned myself toward shore. The water surged under me, and I dug with the paddle. *Keep paddling, keep paddling.* The wave and I moved together, gaining speed and rising. The roll turned into a wave, and the wave to a precipitous wall. I sat small in a small boat at the tip of the leading edge of the ocean and felt the full weight and force of it behind me. The precipitous wall gave in to gravity and began to fall in a graceful sheet. Before me, the nose of my boat rode only air. Leaning back and screaming—in what I describe now as utter joy but what was at the time absolute terror—I rode the mother all the way in.

Completely in the wave's embrace, I had no thoughts. The experience engulfed me. I hit the beach alive and raised my paddle over my head in victory. I was a lion, a sea lion. Without hesitation I turned around and headed out for more.

It was a new sensation, joining the surge of the ocean, riding it. Then a wave pushed me sideways and before I could react overturned my boat. I managed to grab a big gulp of air, and then went under. I found myself upside down in my boat looking at a swirl of bubbling rinse-cycle water. For no good reason I felt no fear, and I didn't struggle. As the liquid world swirled around me, I attempted a roll, just as Justin had taught me. I wasn't able to do it, but I grabbed a fresh breath of air before going back under. My second roll failed as well, and I was losing my calm. To roll the kayak you reach toward the sky with your arms holding the paddle at the surface of the water. My right arm was braced against my boat. I heaved on my paddle, twisting with my hips to try and bring my body up out of the water. A bolt of pain shot through me strong enough to make me retch and gulp saltwater. Without even trying I knew my arm wouldn't work. It hung awkwardly from its socket. I lost all remaining calm. I was consumed by panic and fought to escape my boat at all costs. "Never let go of the paddle" was a piece of advice given me, and "Never panic." I panicked. I let go of the paddle with my remaining good arm and pulled the spray-skirt cord, releasing me from the boat. The pain in my arm was receding, but I still didn't have any control over it; it dangled freely from my shoulder. Something was very wrong. Sputtering, I was washed ashore, holding my right arm with my left. Justin and Ben gathered my floating boat and paddle and came ashore. Ben helped strip off my wetsuit top, and we could see that my arm was no longer connected to my body except by skin and loose tissue. In more shock than pain, I sat down on the beach.

"Oh, yeah," said Justin, "that arm is dislocated. Here..." He put his foot in my armpit and grasped my dangling arm. With fair force he tugged it smoothly up and out, and with a solid pop it found its place back in my shoulder socket.

I sat panting, cradling my sore arm and blinking. Justin wiped the sweat from his forehead and said, "Who has more fun than people?"

Three amigos. Justin Wadsworth, Ben Husaby and me (right to left), above the Sea of Cortez.

Balance

"Beer?"

Shakes his head.

"Sorry, forgot."

Rocky is sunken. He quit drinking years ago, a decision he seems to regret, but doesn't regret enough to give up on. His eyes are nearly swollen shut with dope and the late night. The pulsating embers of our tired fire have us all hypnotized. I look away only to scan the ground around me for scorpions.

"Turn off that damn flashlight, Abraham."

"Scorpions."

He grunts and waves a lazy arm, dismissing my concern. I had seen a scorpion earlier—they're attracted to the fire—but I have a feeling they aren't worth pissing off Rocky for. The embers pull me in again and I feel my eyes lose their focus and my body sag. The Sea of Cortez is so calm it hardly licks the shore. There are few noises, and there's no breeze. Rocky and I, Justin, Cranston, Jimmy, Ben, the mermaids, and a few others lost in shadow around the coals all slip further toward unconsciousness. Scorpions crawl as they please, over me or nowhere near me. I am oblivious, half asleep, wholly detached. All of us sit unmoving, not speaking. Time passes. An hour...or was it only ten minutes?

"Boys."

Rocky yanks us back to Baja and the present.

"You prophets!"

He's alive again and shouting into the night. I flip on the flashlight and whip the beam around searching for tan translucent scorpions. Nothing but sand.

"I ever tell you about Charlie?" The embers cast a red glow on Rocky's rotund body and his dancing eyes.

"Old Charlie was unshakable. Quiet though, not unlike yourselves there.

One-armed fisherman, post shoulder dislocation,
Sea of Cortez. "I'll kill any man says the trigger
ain't a good eatin' fish."—Rocky.

Well, Charlie used to live down the beach a few miles, he and a buddy, and these guys would harvest from the sea everything and anything fit to eat.

"Well anyway, Charlie dives for lobster by night 'cause that's when they come out of the rocks. Well, this one time he and his buddy—a real stick, skinny as all hell, beef jerky looking guy..." Rocky says nodding in my direction, indicating that I, too, am a skinny type.

"...Anyway, Charlie and this guy, they take this Zodiac out to their secret lobstering spots late at night, and Charlie'll go down for lobster with a flashlight, weight belt, fins, mask, snorkel, and nothing else, and come up with dinner."

Rocky has both hands on his knees and is leaning forward precariously over the fire. His red and yellow skin wavers and twitches with the moving light. There is nothing but glowing coals and a flickering red Rocky belting out his tale.

"Well, this one time, going down without air, except what's in his lungs and his blood, old Charlie runs into something other than lobster.

"You see at the edge of his beam—can you picture the beam? I mean it's dark down there. All dark. Up dark, down dark, all around dark, except for this little cone of light that's his flashlight beam. And at the edge of his beam he sees a lobster, he thinks, pull back into its cave. So he swims over there like some kind of nocturnal merman," he says winking at me and nodding at the women we thought were mermaids.

"Now you know he's down like twenty or thirty feet, down with a weight belt and no air but that in his lungs, and sticks his hand into this crack after this lobster, but instead of grabbing it, something grabs him!" Teeth bared, Rocky makes a grabbing motion with his mouth.

"Well now, old Charlie is deep, his lungs squirming, with his hand caught tight in something's mouth. Me? Well, I'd a started yanking, like most people, and I would've kept yanking until I had to take a big, full breath of salt water, and that would have been good night." Rocky inhales, standing, filling his chest and gut, and then he sits down with a thud beyond the edge of the coals' glow where I can hardly see him.

"Yep, that would've been it for me, but..." says Rocky leaning in again slowly, coming back into view. "But not Charlie. Ol' Charlie turns the flashlight off, lets his whole body go limp, relaxes his hand, and shuts his eyes—like he was settling in for a snooze."

And Rocky is standing again, leaning full over the coals, almost over me, shining, flickering, with his eyes closed and his own limp arm held out before him, the great rolls of fat and muscle limp and swaying off his arm in the light.

"And the grip on his hand slowly loosens, and ever so slowly he pulls his arm out of that cave." With closed eyes, Rocky retracts his limp arm to demonstrate. "And Charlie flips on the light, and as he does the head of a moray eel as big around as the torso of a child follows his hand outta that cave. He gives a casual-like kick of his fins—and exhales all the way up."

With that Rocky rises, as if from in front of the TV, walks to his trailer, yanks open the door with a bang, steps inside, and slams it shut.

I rise from my seat, scorpions long forgotten, and wander barefoot to the obsidian-black sea. I was thinking of Charlie...swimming around way down deep in the dark. *People really do that kind of thing? Jeee-sus!* Like a person contemplating a jump from a high cliff I stand hesitant, with my toes at the edge. Thinking about old Charlie and that kind of control over fear, that kind of life, and wondering where he is now, I edge into the liquid black. Toes, feet, knees. Shuffling my feet so as to avoid Justin's stingray fate—a lesson well learned. Submersion is easy until the water level is even with my crotch. I can't see into the black water, thinking of Charlie calm as a clam, with his hand in the mouth of a moray eel.

Aiggggh! I propel myself forward with a yawlp and plunge, then thick silence. I scramble upwards in a mild panic, make the surface, open my eyes and see that I am glowing green. Shit, this can't be right. Pollution? Radioactivity? I don't feel right about this, but only momentarily. *Oh, yeah,* I have heard of this; it's phosphorescence. It's little animals or plants, very little bioluminescent creatures that emit a glow like a firefly when the water they are suspended in is disturbed. There are so many that they are like the water itself.

When I move my hand around in the water it is immediately surrounded by a green glow. It's as if I were the Norse god of the northern lights. Wherever I sweep my hand, the dark sky shimmers a cellophane-green, and after I remove my hand, the glow slowly fades to black.

I swim around glowing and spreading northern lights at will. As I swim I leave a frothy green trail of radiant foot-kicked water. I can see fish that swim close enough to the surface. Electric-green blobs moving through cool black velvet.

I climb from the water and pad awkwardly across the wave-rounded pebbles to the fire. Behind me a light green trail of water fades.

We decide to move on—to escape the lure of an extended stay of, say, the next twenty years. Around the fire we bid our friends good-bye and then step up to Rocky's trailer. Justin pounds on the closed aluminum door, and after the second bang, Rocky's bulk fills the doorway. He's blinking at us, squinting.

"We're off to see the next beach, Rocky," says Ben. "Wanted to say good-bye and thanks for taking us fishing."

"And thanks for the Mermaids," I add.

Rocky blinks in surprise at us for a few more seconds, and then stretches his hand to each of us.

"Via con huevos, muchachos," he's smiling broadly, "and see you on the other side."

We strode by the light of the just rising moon out to Butt-fur in silence.

The moon was pregnant, and there were no clouds. Justin left Butt-fur's headlights off and we began the long climb, motoring through the colorless moonlit night. Cactuses cast dim shadows across the road. The mountains, which mark the top of the high backbone of the Baja Peninsula, were a dark outline separating a sky defined by stars from a desert illuminated only by moonlight. It occurred to me that this is what perspective is—it is seeing something in a new light. In this case it was seeing my life as a skier in the light of my experiences in Baja.

Behind the Subaru, above the winding road hung a long, twisted cloud of silver dust. Butt-fur rattled over the washboard. Jackrabbits dodged out of our way and sprinted into the brush. The car entered the shadow of the mountains, and we had to slow. It didn't occur to us to turn the lights on. As we passed between the two mountains at the top of the climb, Justin ground the car to a stop. Butt-fur's tail of moonlit silver dust caught us, wrapped around the car, and settled. I could see the Sea of Cortez shining a thousand feet below, at the bottom of the road, where Rocky lived.

Balance can be achieved in many ways. You can pile everything in the middle or you can evenly load both sides. After the past year in Sweden, the scales were tipped so overwhelmingly to skiing, I felt trapped by the sport. I lost my perspective. I had nothing to view skiing against. I was a white rabbit running through a snowstorm, so self-absorbed that I couldn't see past the end of my nose.

We stopped in the same place we stopped mid-day on our way in. In a way, I could see the landscape and the sea more clearly without the sun. I was like a blind person with an extraordinary sense of hearing, keenly aware of the tone, rather than the hue. Color would have been a distraction. The sky had a tangible depth, as though I could reach into it. There was no emptiness, no space. Looking over the valley and the sea I felt I could touch it all.

We drove the thousand-mile return trip from Baja to Bend, Oregon, in two days. Bend was where the final portion of my spring adventure was to start.

I called a girl. She picked up the phone, and I hung up. When I got my courage back I called again. She answered not with a hello, but with a gruff, "It's your quarter."

I'd met Rachael at the Spring Series ski races a month prior. Her lesbian lover introduced us. Rachael was an ex-kick-boxer, a Californian, tan, blond, long, and beautiful. She bragged that her first car was a Porsche.

"Yeah," she said, "come on down." I couldn't afford a plane ticket and didn't have a car, so I bought a Volkswagen Rabbit pickup that cost less than a plane ticket. It seemed like a good idea since I could have used the plane ticket only once. The bad idea was buying it without a test drive or having it checked out. A day and a half after driving to Bend from Mexico, I was on the road to California.

I drove at top speed to Mills College in Oakland, California. Mills College, I learned, was an all-girls school, and I was the only boy around. One afternoon while attending class with Rachael, the professor asked me jokingly if I'd considered any other colleges.

Mills seemed a lot like heaven. I soon discovered it wasn't. The friend who introduced me to Rachael wasn't her real lover, and of course neither was I, but I didn't know that when I drove down. *Besides*, I thought, *I have nothing to lose.*

Rachael's true lover found and cornered me. She was the captain of the school volleyball team and towered over me. I do not know if schools like Mills attract confident, outgoing women or if they are simply produced in such places, but the Mills student body contained more secure, strong women than I'd ever encountered before.

"How would you like it," she asked me, bending her face within an inch of mine, "if *I* was trying to ruin *your* life?" I didn't think she was looking for an answer.

The lecture went on and was long and loud. People steered around us on the sidewalk, gawking. A few paused to watch, some glaring at me. *How the hell did I get here?*

How surreal to have come from a winter racing trip in Europe, an epic journey in Mexico, and to now be standing on this sunny all-girl's campus in California, receiving a horrendous verbal beat-down. I couldn't follow or accept every detail of her argument, but there were tears running down her cheeks and her fists were clenched white. I loaded my truck and departed.

The Rabbit took me from Oakland all the way to Lovelock, Nevada, where it overheated and died in a puff of smoke. The cost of repair would have cost me more than the car, " 'Sides," pointed out the tow truck driver, "the hell you want with this foreign piece of shit, anyways?"

My mom wired me some money for a train ticket to Denver. In two overloaded hikes I carried a bodybag-sized tote of skis, two huge duffel bags, the car's ski racks and radio, and my backpack, from the garage, where the car sat, to the tracks a mile away where the train stopped. There was no train station, so I sat on the tracks and waited.

Being an elite cross-country ski racer in America can be compared to going through medical school while being homeless. There are extremely high performance expectations but no support system to help you reach them. All the motivation is self-supplied. After the last racing season it was becoming a struggle for me to maintain my enthusiasm. The spring trip with Justin and Ben to Mexico and my solo trip to see Rachael in California were not intended to be anything but an escape. At a cost, I'd salvaged something important besides balance: I regained perspective on my life, and that helped remove a lot of the pressure I'd put on myself, which had been doing nothing for my skiing besides make me uptight.

I had made some sacrifices, and when the bones fell, they pointed toward home. I was ready. In the desert and the ocean of Baja, I regained confidence and conviction, like the train I rode toward home, began to build momentum on the way out of Nevada.

A Clear Electric Moment

It took two more dislocations before I realized my shoulder had to be repaired surgically. The operation changed my direction a bit, but didn't slow me down. Four days post-op and I was training again, on a stationary bike with one arm in a sling. After three weeks I could hike with the arm still in the sling.

My old LERT teammate, Nathan Schultz, called me up eight weeks post surgery. "I hear you'll be back in business soon," he said.

For six weeks I had been training steadily at about fourteen hours a week, doing more and more as my shoulder would allow.

"I'm back in business," I told him.

"Well then, I'll see you on Monday."

Up until that Monday, the entries in my training log looked more like the entries in the diary of a weekend racer, a ski enthusiast training for the local winter showdown, not someone training for the Olympics. *Easy run, forty-five minutes. Hike three hours. Fairly easy run, feel okay.*

Nathan lived about two miles down the hill from my parents' house in Boulder, where I was staying while my shoulder recovered. That Monday morning he ran up to my house, ran with me for two hours, then ran home. I could tell right away that this kid was working and that I had not been. Later that afternoon he showed up on his roller-skis. We roller-skied for an hour and a half on the city streets of Boulder. He didn't give a damn about the traffic, the cops, or what people thought of a couple of skiers roller-skiing around town. We were moving out, me behind him. As we zipped down hills and hung tight corners to avoid traffic, I held onto my boots with my toenails, and on the uphills I hung onto Nathan by will-power alone. Nathan was on a mission. He hadn't always been a good skier but, like Cory, he had always been a workhouse of a trainer and, as it had for Cory, the work had paid off. We had been friends since high school, but this was a new Nathan. Always strong, and abnormally bumpy with muscles from rock climbing, he had reached a new level on skis. In college he had proven himself to be among the best collegiate skiers in the country, but until that Monday I had no idea he had any real interest in pursuing the sport beyond that.

At a stoplight in downtown Boulder we stood, two skiers on wheeled skis, poles in hand, alongside the rest of the traffic.

"Nathan, what the hell is going on?"

"I'm going to the Olympics, man." The light turned green, and we set off in a blast of honking amid the rush of traffic.

Every Tuesday morning we met for intervals on the Mesa Trail above Boulder. The protocol was five intervals in which we bounded, using ski poles, up a steep gravel grade for four minutes each time. Once on top, at the fire lookout, we turned around, jogged down, and did it again. For fifteen seconds the interval was fine. Each step was an explosive bound, and we pushed hard off our poles. After a minute, Nathan and I were breathing hard, and already had to work to maintain our speed and the explosiveness of our bounding. After two minutes we were in outright pain. And still there were two more minutes to endure. The thing was, even though it hurt, even though I anxiously wished to reach the fire lookout as quickly as possible, even though I dreaded the next interval, I simply loved it. I loved the sensation of effort and pain and my ability to thrive in the face of it. I loved working with Nathan because he wouldn't let me get a step on him, and I loved sharing the intense, emotional effort. Each interval was a little test of commitment and a battle of willpower. At any point either of us could have relinquished the lead, cut back on the pace just a little, but if we had, the love would have fallen right out of it.

The previous winter in Sweden I had cut myself too much slack, second-guessing everything I did, and giving myself a foot when I shouldn't have given an inch. Though I didn't admit it to myself at the time, every time I let go I was letting go of the essence of my dream—the work. As I let the work slip I was losing not only any chance I had at realizing the dream, but also the reason I was chasing it.

At the fire lookout Nathan and I would stand, hunkered over with hands on our knees or leaning on our poles, but only for a few seconds, then one of us would pick up and start down the hill again.

For eight weeks we trained together. By the time snow fell I could even push the pace. And though I could never break Nathan, sometimes I felt like I could get him up against the ropes.

Nathan and I were skiers for the Factory Team, a professional cross-country ski team sponsored primarily by Fischer Skis, Salomon Boots, Swix wax and poles and Subaru of America.

But sponsorship alone is never enough. Throughout a cross-country skier's career he is forced to find ways to support himself to stay in the sport. I had worked summers at a grocery store in Bend, Oregon, and I worked a summer and fall at a hotel in Åsarna, Sweden, and for many summers built hiking trails in Boulder. For many years I survived off my college scholarship combined with about three grand a year in funding from the U.S. Olympic Committee. This funding was typical of anyone on the U.S. Ski Team. And for a while I was supported as a resident athlete at the Olympic Education Center in Marquette, Michigan.

Nathan was a computer programmer, Cory worked odd jobs, and Carl Swenson raced mountain bikes for money. We did whatever we could, whatever it took, just to keep skiing. None of us were rich, and most of us were in debt. We were propelled by a love of the sport.

The Factory Team enabled us to survive as skiers. The pay was slight, but coupled with some free plane tickets, lodging at races, and the best equipment available, it was a huge boost to the athletes, as well as to the sport itself.

On the Factory Team's ticket, Nathan and I headed to West Yellowstone for the winter's first snow.

West Yellowstone, Montana, is two towns. In summer, heat rises from the asphalt. It bustles with eager tourists dressed in bright colors. Its streets are clogged with motor homes mashed headlight to taillight, all part of Yellowstone's parade of gawkers and gas-guzzlers.

In winter the streets fill with snow and the city does not plow it, but packs it down. Snowmobiles sit coughing in hotel parking lots. There are few cars, few tourists, and, in winter, no motor homes. The wind blows and twisters of snow spiral down Main Street. This is the West Yellowstone I know. At town's edge begins a wonderful network of ski trails. Skiers push through the blowing snow right from their hotel, down the otherwise-empty street, and into the woods.

It's not even ten degrees out and there's a sharp wind. From the comfort of the Holiday Inn it looks forbidding, but when we get out the door and get moving, the weather loses its ferocity. Ice forms on the hat and on the ski jacket, but under it you are warm, even hot.

Deep and rhythmic inhalations bring crisp air into the lungs. Exhalations expel moist clouds that disappear behind the chugging human locomotive. Nathan and I ski together, two engines, no cargo, just energy.

*This is the essence of ski training. Long days in the wind and snow. Nothing better.
West Yellowstone, Montana.*

The trails pitch and wind, and we climb and dive with them. Skiing lets
you escape—you can get lost in the rhythmic, repetitive motion. The terrain would demand constant attention from a recreational skier, but we
can negotiate it without a thought. Negotiating it, however, is not the goal—
negotiating it as quickly and easily as possible is. For this reason it is important while training to not get lost in the act, but to be fully present and
aware.

For this reason in almost every workout I focus on a few specific things.
It isn't enough to simply do the training. Skiing demands attention because every time you are out skiing you are teaching yourself to ski. So
every time you are out, you must teach yourself to ski well—to negotiate
the terrain as quickly and easily as possible.

Just like we did as kids in LERT, we ski one behind the other. We engage in technique battles. We work on exploding forward and gliding, on
skiing faster, easier. We work on very specific aspects of technique, but also
on the general feel of it, the rhythm and how that translates into our gaining speed and maintaining momentum over the snow. We are still kids
learning to ski fast by playing, by imagining ourselves as the champions we
work to become. And just like in LERT, we always race the downhills. We
lean into each other, grab at each other's poles, and launch ourselves off
jumps. It is play, but it is also practice, for in play we learn balance and

coordination. And then we climb again.

West Yellowstone's Windy Ridge Loop is the outer perimeter of the trail system, and has its longest climb. Nathan and I are together at the bottom of the hill. I am working on keeping my hips in a forward position, and struggling to do so. Nathan pulls away slightly as I experiment with ways to maintain a forward position. Skiing with Nathan I have immediate feedback. If I do it well it not only feels right, but I find myself riding up on him. If I do it poorly it feels wrong, and I fall behind. It feels wrong now. My hips fall back with each kick and I fight simply to regain my forward position. That won't do. All my strength has to be dedicated to driving me forward, and right now it isn't. I'm working harder and going slower than I should be. I'm fighting gravity. Nathan is ten feet in front. *Damn it. Up! Hips up!* And then, *Whoa, got it!* and suddenly it feels as if I'm falling up the hill, *Now that's how it should feel*, as if I'm being tugged by my head up and forward. Each kick is more powerful and I'm in position to ride the ski. *This is right.* I'm back on Nathan again, clipping his tails. My whole outlook changes, the frustration is gone, I'm no longer fighting it. I scoot past him. "Hips up, Schultz!"

He is behind me now and trying to match my rhythm, perhaps thinking, *Hips up, hips up!* We improve together, play and train hard together, no different than being back in LERT, still kids more than ten years later.

For hours a day we ski this way on these trails we know so well. It's snowing hard, and the wind is fierce and cold. We're heading into wind-driven squalls. It feels like something wild and alive is clawing at our clothes, sucking away our warmth, biting our chins and noses. Our faces are raw, and the rims of our jackets are coated with ice, frozen breath, and crusted snot. We seldom talk and stop only occasionally to drink. It is easy to fall fully into the act and joy of skiing. In this harsh environment we are at home.

Hours later we emerge from the woods as if from a trance, and we walk from this cold, hard, perfect world into the hot and stuffy hotel lobby. We are visitors from a better place. We nod, wind-blown and red-faced, at the gray people huddled around the TV who've turned to look us over. Our clothing is caked with ice, evidence of our efforts outside. It sloughs off our clothes onto the floor. I pick it from my beard, and smile.

After lunch and a little nap we head back out—into our true home.

After the training camp in West Yellowstone, where Nathan and I skied four to five hours a day, I started to feel unbelievably strong. Skiing, while I was in such shape, with power and strength and seemingly limitless endurance, filled me with a kind of happy pride I hadn't experienced since training at Trout Lake or racing for Northern Michigan. I could not go too fast; there were no hills too long.

The next series of races were in Canmore, Canada, and after the West Yellowstone camp I was in shape and psyched up for them. The first race was a disappointment. I waxed my skis poorly for the conditions and so knew my bad race result did not mean I was out of shape, but still, I felt a twinge of panic.

After the previous season's fiasco, my self-confidence was vulnerable. The bad result was a ghost from the past season. That afternoon I returned to the racecourse for an easy ski. I had the place to myself. I cruised around alone and regained a feeling of well-being. Canmore was the site of the 1988 Olympics, and I skied the trails imagining myself winning an Olympic race. The '88 Olympics were the first I watched knowing that one day I would be in the Olympics myself—or at least knowing I wanted to be. The Swedes were the dominant country at the time, but the Russians stole most of the races. Very little of the racing was televised, but I watched all I could and recorded all they showed. On TV the venue looked so big, so grand. In person it was small. Without the crowds or the racers, it was dead. But in my mind I returned to the '88 Olympics and to the dreams of my youth.

The next morning in the skate race, when the starter took his hand off my shoulder, I blasted forward with a surge of animal joy. This is what racing was all about. While Nathan had reintroduced me to a love of work,

Snow Mountain Ranch, Granby, Colorado.

this race reintroduced me to a love of competition. A charged current began in my chest, rose up, passed through my face like a shiver, and rammed the roof of my head. I was electrified from within, and there was no stopping me. Every skate was an attack on my competitors. I ate chunks of trail with each plant of my poles.

I knew I was tasting it, that clear electric moment—that is momentum. Nothing escapes your attention, yet nothing is capable of distracting you. Extreme effort comes easily; is a pleasure. It is like being back in Baja in my kayak. It is the moment the ocean really takes you, and you surge forward with all the power of the sea behind you with the nose of your boat suspended between sky and water. Freeze yourself in that stage where you are grimacing happily, separate from earth and everything else except the experience.

For me that is the essence not only of competition, but of life. The moment. While the end goal lies kilometers, days, weeks, years away, it is today that counts. It is what you do today, right now, this moment, on this day that you will look back on with pride, from which you will derive immediate joy and in the end satisfaction, regardless of how it turns out.

In Canmore I was engrossed in an experience as exhilaratingly intense as that moment in my kayak in the waves of Baja. For me that race was an elastic moment stretching up each hill, across all the flats and descents between the hills, waves, all the way from *Go!* for fifteen kilometers, to the finish line. The moment snapped when I crossed the line. It was over. I filed it away as a step forward and a joy in itself. Second place ended up nearly a minute behind me.

For five more weeks Nathan and I traveled all over the western U.S. and Canada, racing and training together. I was in shape, placing at worst among North America's top five or six skiers; and Nathan, who had also raced well, burst into the country's Top 10. With the '98 Olympics only two seasons away I did indeed seem to be back in business.

I spent the rest of the season racing well for the Factory Team, winning some major U.S. marathons and contending for the win in nearly every race I entered. I finished the '95-'96 season feeling strong and went into the '96-'97 season with high hopes.

Smiling Fred

My Grandpa Fred E. Vordenberg was a Chevy dealer known as "Smiling Fred the Walking Man's Friend." Fred had the fleshy red nose and full lips I recognized as my dad's but did not inherit myself. He was tall and hunch-shouldered, a lumbering, smiling man. On a Christmas trip to visit Grandpa Fred and Grandma Helen in Cincinnati when I was eight, Fred bought me a Cincinnati Reds baseball shirt and matching cap. The back of the shirt said Pete Rose.

We boated around Cincinnati in Fred's big Chevrolet, rolling as if over waves. Fred pointed things out, and in the too-warm car I fought to stay awake. We ate hot dogs dripping with Cincinnati chili. We stopped for slammers at White Castle. Grandma Helen, thin with a great puff of soft blond hair atop her narrow face, warmed store-bought cinnamon rolls for our breakfast and worried over me in a high, wavering voice. Cincinnati was a foreign place. Its citizens seemed like a foreign race compared to the people of Boulder. Even among my own family, I felt like I was from a different planet. Then there was the fact that my Grandpa Fred's bad heart valve had been replaced by a good one taken from a living pig.

Lloyd, who was prone to telling tall tales, related the story of my Grandpa's heart to me while sitting in a roadside diner in St. Louis en route to Cincinnati. It was snowing and we were looking out huge diner windows at the highway. Two cars spun past performing simultaneous slow-motion 360s down the Interstate. Not crashing, just spinning, silently, gracefully. It was an auto ballet. It was while I watched this slow motion dance that Lloyd told me about Grandpa's heart. It seemed like a fairy tale, like an amusing fabrication of the sort adults tell children. It *couldn't* be true. The world I knew was orderly, perfect. Everything had a purpose, and everything fit. The pieces had specific roles, and parts were defined by their purpose. And, obviously, pig parts were not interchangeable with people parts.

But the pig valve story was true. I put my head against Smiling Fred's chest and I could hear his heart beating. I looked up and he looked down at me smiling.

The pig valve was put in after his original heart valve gave out. The valve worked, but pigs do not live as long as humans and neither do their valves.

In late December of 1996, a season before the '98 Olympics, my friend Patrick Weaver and I raced in the North American Cup Series near Quebec City. I skied well, placing among the top four in each of the races. This was encouraging because the National Championships, in Lake Placid that year, were only a week away. Somewhere between Canada and New York I got a sore throat. We drove to the nearest grocery where I bought a head of garlic. It is said that garlic can stave off a cold so long as it's fresh, eaten raw, and chewed thoroughly. I peeled a clove and chomped down on it. It felt like fire, and it spread from my mouth to my nose and throat. I danced madly as I chewed. Tears ran from my spastically blinking eyes, and I clenched and unclenched my fists rapidly, as if in a seizure. The second clove was just as bad. I drank half a gallon of orange juice, took a handful of echinacea pills, rested as best I could, and came down with a cold anyway.

My making the World Championship team was on the line. I had to qualify for the team at nationals and I was in shape to do it, but the best-laid plans can be quickly and unceremoniously undone by something as common as a cold. I raced among the Top 10 in the first two races at Nationals, which wasn't nearly as well as I wanted or needed to do, but for having been sick it wasn't too bad. In the third race I chose my ski wax poorly and so was pushing slow skis around the course—my fault completely, and a stupid mistake. I ended up fourteenth. There was one race remaining, the fifty kilometer skate. After my performance in the first races, making the team was unlikely, but the 50k was my last shot at proving to myself that I was really on the rise, that the dream had been resurrected.

That night word came to me that Smiling Fred the Walking Man's Friend passed away. The pig heart valve had given out.

Feeling glum, I joined several skiers the day before the race on a ski around the racecourse, a very tough 16.8 kilometer loop that we completed three times the following day. After the ski we jumped in a pickup and started the drive home. I sat wedged behind the front seat on a little drop-down jump seat. My friend Marcus Nash, the driver, was talking with

Patrick, who was screwing around with the radio. The sky was clear and
the roads were dry, but it was very windy. The trees lining the two-lane
road protected it from the wind-blown snow, and so the roadway was clear
and the driving seemed safe. Marcus pulled out to pass a car and as we were
on the left side of the road we entered a clearing in the trees. Where moments before our vision had been clear, as we came into the clearing a gust
of wind sent a white wall of snow over us. We all stared into the snow but
couldn't see any farther than the end of the hood. From out of the whit-
eout a pair of headlights suddenly materialized, and Marcus jerked the
wheel. I flinched, clenching my muscles involuntarily. There was an instant of extreme violence and the sound of grinding metal and breaking
glass. We came to a stop. Then, amidst the wind-whipped white-out, another car slammed into the tangle. Stunned, I inspected myself for injury.
Except for the sound of wind-driven snow against steel, and the hissing of
spewing car fluid, it was calm and after the wreck seemed very quiet.

There were voices, some moaning. Patrick clambered from the car. I
piled out after him, sick and uncoordinated, but giddy, somehow energetic
realizing my luck. I was hurt, I was limping, but alive. Marcus was still
sitting behind the crumpled wheel; I helped him out of the cab. We stumbled
away from the vehicle just as another car slammed into the side of the
truck where we had just been standing. We were lucky not to have been
crushed.

In the wreck Marcus broke his ankle and was knocked momentarily
unconscious. Patrick compressed one of his vertebrae, and the friction of
his body against the seatbelt burned a patch of his jacket to his skin. No
one was killed and all I did was badly twist an ankle and break the rear
window of the truck with my head. I was scratched, bruised, and sore—and
happy.

Lake Placid, New York, is beautiful and picturesque. And I hate it. In
Placid I sleep poorly, get sick, get hassled by anyone with authority—and
even those without it. I race slower in Placid than anywhere else I've raced.

In Placid I've been in a car wreck, been passed over for the Junior World
team, showed up to races that had been cancelled, and raced in races that
should have been cancelled. I have never had a good race in Lake Placid, or
even a good time. But despite all that, Lake Placid bestowed upon me one
great blessing.

The night of the wreck Patrick Weaver and I were commiserating in
the cafeteria at the Olympic Training Center. Patrick sat awkwardly, half
stiff and half slumped because of his crushed vertebrae; me lumpy-headed,
sucking a huge fat lip and fingering a cut across my nose. From across the

cafeteria Barb Jones, a girl neither of us had ever seen before, came toward the sorry two of us, strutting and skipping, brown-faced, bouncy-boobed, and smiling.

"Jesus, Patrick," I said elbowing him and nodding at her.

"Sissy Hankshaw," he responded.

We had both just read Tom Robbins' book, "Even Cowgirls Get the Blues," and in this glowing, happy woman skipping toward and then past us we thought we saw the embodiment of Tom Robbins' heroine—the cowgirl, Sissy Hankshaw.

Barb Jones beamed, bounced, and smiled; and through my gloom I gawked, and without hesitation, developed an infatuation. My lack of courage was finally over-ridden by my crush, and I limped over to sit at her table. Through my fat lip I said dumb things at the wrong times and then self-consciously bought her an ice cream cone in the hope that it would make her forget everything else about me. I could have guessed then that I would fall in love with Barb Jones, but I wouldn't have guessed she would ever fall in love with me. It was half a year before I saw her again.

The next day, as I continued into the last of three laps in the National Championship 50k, I was in pain and in nearly last place, almost forty-five minutes behind the leader. I slowly skied by Patrick, who was standing along the course watching, listing to one side because of his back.

"Should I keep going?" I asked him.

"Yeah," he answered. "Do it 'cause you're still alive."

It was the week after Smiling Fred passed away, a week of illness, less-than-stellar racing, and a head-on car crash. I was low and unsure what my next move should be. I asked the head U.S. coach which races I could do next. I hadn't qualified to race in Europe, and there wasn't much on the U.S. schedule, but I knew I had some good races in me. He shrugged and turned away. I was shocked. Even though I was on the U.S. Ski Team, the coaches would not pay my way. And there was only one set of races remotely within my financial reach—the Canadian National Championships held in Prince George, British Columbia.

For the first time in my skiing career a coach, any coach, and in this case the head U.S. Ski Team coach, showed a complete lack of interest in me, a complete lack of faith or respect in my ability as a skier. The message was clear: according to the U.S. Ski Team, my career was over.

Over the years I had suffered more losses—by far—than wins, but my coaches, every one of them—from the first, a guy named Andy Aiken, to Bjorn Sæteroy, Aage Schaanning, Kristian Næss, and of course Sten Fjeldheim—showed confidence in me, even when I lost—especially when

I lost—and that confidence took me beyond my losses. Their confidence and belief in my abilities took me to two Olympics by the age of 22, won me the NCAA title, and many other races big and small. Their confidence had always given me momentum.

Now, I was in dummy math all over again. I gathered my books and marched out of the regular classroom and headed back down to the basement where they hold the special classes. Cut and bruised, ankle swollen and sore, I paid my own way to Prince George, determined to taste once again the sensation of my hard-earned speed.

As the plane touched down in Canada, the pilot came over the loud-speaker and said, "I hope you folks got your winter parkas, 'cause it's a cold one out there today—minus thirty centigrade, not counting the wind chill."

I caught a cab to a hotel, checked in, and counted my pennies when I should have been counting my marbles. In the morning I headed out into the wind-blown and snow-stung little paper-mill city with all its brick and concrete buildings to hunt for a place to buy breakfast. Afterwards I returned to the room, changed, and walked to a small park behind the hotel. There was no ski trail, so I made my own tracks. I skied around slowly and tenderly on my still swollen ankle, wearing everything I brought. The park was small and overlooked an endless expanse of frozen pine forest and clear-cut patchwork surrounding the town and its stinking paper mill smoke stacks. The sky was pale and the sun weak. I skied for an hour, stopping to rub warmth into my cheeks and nose, swinging my hands to bring the blood into my fingers. Then I returned to the room, changed, and headed out for lunch. After lunch, I went to the library and read or poked around town until dinner, after which I walked back to the hotel room and watched TV alone.

I've trained alone a good deal of my life. I've traveled alone often. I was an only child and a latchkey kid, and growing up I spent a lot of time entertaining myself. I've never been comfortable in large groups, and I've always enjoyed being by myself, especially skiing, but here I felt the loneliness as clearly and bitterly as the cold. I struggled to hold myself together and focus on skiing. Feeling sorry for myself was uncharacteristic. I didn't feel like me, and the sensation was frustrating. I couldn't figure out how to pull myself out of this slump.

When temperatures are low enough, snow-crystals become small and sharp, creating a lot of friction between the ski base and the snow. This friction makes skiing slow and difficult.

It warmed up to minus twenty, which is warm enough to race, but just barely. The snow was sandpaper slow, and the constant pressure I had to exert against the unyielding snow was tough on my tender ankle. But every day it got better. The little skiing and the walking kept it from getting stiff, and I was stretching it many times daily.

The first race was held in minus twenty-degree temperatures. I raced hard and finished tenth, which wasn't good, but after the race I felt fresh, and my ankle—luckily—had survived the beating. I had four more races to improve in, and I thought by the last few I'd ski my way back into racing shape. I yearned for the clear moment I had experienced in Canmore only weeks before. I yearned to put a race together that fed my desire, that put me to sleep at night confident of what I was doing.

That night the temperature sank to minus fifty, and the next day's race was postponed. The temperature didn't rise, and the race was postponed again. When the temperature still didn't rise, the Canadian Nationals were postponed until March, and everyone flew home...but me. My ticket was non-refundable and, according to the ticketing agent on the phone, not changeable. I'd have to buy a new ticket if I wanted to get out of Prince George before I was scheduled to. Though I desperately wanted to, I simply couldn't afford it.

I was getting to know Prince George very well, its streets, the library, the librarians, and my hotel room. I read, watched TV, and called the airline to check on airfares. I thought of Sissy Hankshaw incarnate, Barb Jones, a girl I hardly knew, but who strutted and smiled in my mind.

I walked from my room to the ski trails every morning and skied as best I could in the fifty-below temperatures. I once put a banana in my jacket pocket on the way out the door, and after skiing I pulled it out to find it as hard as if it had been dipped in liquid nitrogen. In frustration I threw it on the sidewalk, where it broke with a sharp *crack*.

I was a long way from anywhere I cared to be, a long way from friends, and an impossible distance from the realization of my dream which I couldn't help but picture as cracked as that frozen banana.

Smiling Fred, I thought, *what the hell am I doing? I'm a modern day Don Quixote, a Don Skixote, chasing the impossible. No matter the purity of my intentions, all I'm doing is tilting at windmills.*

To my dad's family, the Vordenberg clan, I was an oddity. When I was in junior high, Lloyd and I attended Tom Brown's school for tracking and wilderness survival in the Pine Barrens of New Jersey. Tom Brown was an author and world-renowned tracker. His book, "The Tracker," was one of the first books I ever read without being forced to. It was on a topic I could get into, and without it I'm not sure I would ever have learned to enjoy reading.

For a week Lloyd and I spent our days on hands and knees following the tracks of deer, rabbits, and any creature that touched down, walked around, or dropped turds. We built shelters without plastic, fire without matches, and traps without a prayer of catching anything. We sat in sweat lodges and emerged soaked with perspiration, choking with smoke, and dizzy with heat. We exited the Pine Barrens with a new appreciation for wilderness that we wore on our clothes, hands, skin, hair, fingernails, toes, shoes, ears, and even our teeth.

Lloyd and I landed in Cincinnati for a short visit after our week in the woods. When we got off the plane, all my Grandma Helen could say was, "Oh Lloyd, *ohhhh Lloyd.*"

Early in my high school years I was enthusiastically taking kendo lessons . Practitioners of the Japanese art of sword fencing wear long, pleated pants so baggy they look like a dress. I stomped around in the grass behind my grandparent's apartment in my kendo dress swinging a wooden sword overhead and yelling with each cutting stroke. Inside the Reds were on TV.

"Pete Rose is up," Grandpa Fred yelled out the screen door, but I didn't come in. I probably should have.

In Prince George I suffered for my sin of forsaking the national pastime to pursue swordsmanship, wilderness adventure, ski racing and general weirdness. There is more comfort to be had in the world than that provided by ski racing, and certainly more security. There are many pre-packaged lifestyles available. Role models can be found in every home and in droves on the freeway. Lifestyle blueprints can be picked up at any school. They are advertised on TV shows, and on every street corner. "Everything I learned," jokes a friend, "about interacting with other humans, I learned from watching prime-time sitcoms."

For accountant, lawyer, fry chef, teacher, homeowner, and responsible pet owner, the path is well trodden. Not so for the American cross-country ski racer. There is a risk in rejecting the standard blueprint, for then you are left to not only build but first design your own life, and there are few design guidelines to go by.

Prince George was not on any plan. The stagnation and the frustration I was experiencing was never evident on NBC's "Up Close and Personal" Olympic features. Alone in my hotel room in Prince George, I was on the verge of violence. I was frustrated and angry. I didn't know what to do next. I itched and squirmed. I wanted to rip things to pieces. Maybe it was chemical; I wasn't eating the right food or something. What was my problem? Did I even have one? It could have been that my expectations were somewhat fantastic to begin with. But why should I settle for anything less? So I stewed: stagnant, itching, and irritable, wondering what I should do. Violence and self-destruction offer immediate gratification and a way off the plateau. Prince George certainly offered a sizeable quantity of drinking buddies. But that option stank of sloth and stagnation. I didn't see smiles on the lips of my potential partners in debauchery. Drinking myself silly would have been too easy and undisciplined. And the solution would have been temporary, necessitating indefinite repetition.

On the other hand, I felt I could have chosen violence with great satisfaction. Grab the phone by its cradle and launch it against the wall. The idea appealed to me and I actually grabbed the phone. I pictured the joyous destruction. With any luck it would have shattered and bounced about the room with a loud *brinngggggg*. The imagined scene offered some relief. But the phone looked pretty durable. Probably it would have just dented the wall.

Shit. What kind of pessimism had I sunk to? I couldn't imagine destroying a phone with success. So what other options were there? If not violence, then what? I calmed down, took a few breaths—and felt suddenly itchy. Maybe the maids had played a joke on me. No, it was internal itching. Mental. I turned on the TV. That's what I should have thrown the phone at. There would have been no failure there, plenty of destruction, and total satisfaction guaranteed.

Pitiful. I lacked the courage. My time in the hotel room had my heart pumping pink froth; the beats were hollow, irregular, and insubstantial.

I said out loud, "I quit," and a feeling of utter relief poured though me, but it was the kind of relief you get when no one answers a call you dread making. The situation had not been remedied. Eventually you have to pick up the phone and dial again. Failure lurks, but I would not quit.

I needed a replacement part, swine or otherwise. My heart was broken, but I had come to understand that it could be fixed—even if only temporarily, even if only for the life-span of a pig. *Cut me open.* I was ready for the knife.

The day for my departure arrived and I felt like a freed jailbird must feel. I smiled at the taxi driver, the ticket agent, the flight attendant, the pilot, the other passengers. I was not well, but I was free.

I performed poorly for the remainder of the season. In the spring I bought myself a snowboard, and though I trained and raced all the while, I was more interested in going out at night and snowboarding during the day. Riding a snowboard through powder and bleary nights spent dancing and rough housing were the closest thing I could get to a good ski race.

During a time that I could not earn it on cross-country skis, snowboarding was a substitute for the Clear Electric Moment, the sensation I believed to be the root of living well and which I'd experienced in so many ski races.

Oftentimes I'd head out with a group of other cross-country skiers burnt-out from the season, we tele-skied or snowboarded whenever the opportunity presented itself. And at night we went out looking for trouble, and seldom failed to find it.

That spring, in Sun Valley, Idaho, sometime after two in the morning, on the walk home from Whisky Jacques, where we had been doing some dancing, Nathan bought a box of doughnuts at a Circle K convenience store. For no good reason I grabbed the box from his hands and gave it a mighty punt. Powdered mini-donuts exploded like firecrackers, and Nathan screamed, "Doughnut abuse, doughnut abuse! You bastard!" And, as if ready for just such a situation, three Sun Valley squad cars pulled up with their lights flashing. I was cited for littering and released with the stipulation that I pick up all the doughnut pieces, which I did.

The second time I punted Nathan's box of doughnuts, the law was not as lenient. The warrant for my arrest showed up at my house in Boulder a month later. To this day my father refers to me as a common criminal—affectionately, I think. Anytime he and I are together and we see a police car, he says, "Over here, officer. I got one right here next to me. Doughnut abuse. Despicable."

Me and Scott Loomis, 2002. (Bob Allen photo.)

No Excuses

I was starting to wonder if I was afraid to really do it: to work without excuses, without hiding behind nonchalance, false modesty, or some other mechanism of self-defense. Those things are meant to shield you from shame in case of failure. If you failed, you could say you weren't really trying anyway. And if you can say that, then what was the point? To really go for it is to grant the world an intimate view of who you are. And that can be scary, because what if you are not all that you dream?

Attempting to realize a dream is personal, creative work. It's like reading your poetry at open mic night down at the coffee shop, or sharing a painted self-portrait with your art class. It's passing out your story in Composition 102 without apology. Most of all it's allowing yourself an honest look in the mirror. It is saying: This is me, and what I have done is the best I can do.

Long ago I told myself I would be pleased with the outcome of my life as a skier so long as I did what I believed it would take to succeed. At the time I had no intention of failing.

The summer leading into the 1997-1998 season it was a different matter. Failure was now something I could see as easily as success, but I decided that if I were to continue the chase, then I would own up to my dream and not be afraid to say that I was going for it—that I was trying as hard as I could. I would put it on the line and accept the outcome, whatever it turned out to be. I would go for it, without excuses and have no regrets regardless of the outcome. From the start, training had always been the only way. It was what hooked me, and what fed my dream. And so I trained and intended to succeed. The next two pages show excerpts from my log during this period.

Training log: Week 11. Month 3. June, 1997. Bend, Oregon

Day	Dist.	Interval	Strength	Comments
Mon. AM	RClassic 2:10			Roller-ski. Feel good. Tired at work mid-day. Morning hr: 40
PM	Run :15 Swim :15		lift :50	Warm-up run. Weights went well. Swim was good.
Tues. AM	Rskate 2 hours			AM heart rate: 43. Felt tired at first but got better. Good technique.
PM	Run 1:20	Level 3 run :10	Spenst :30	Started to feel good in the run and spenst was very good.
Wed. AM	Run 1 hr	Level 4 Run :20		AM heart rate: 36. Felt great. Rolling terrain.
PM	Rclassic 1 hr		Specific strength 1	Very good specific strength. D-pole was not so great though.
Thur. AM	Rskate 3 hrs			Felt good. Got tired at the end. Good technique.
PM	Run :15 Swim :15		Lift :50	Feel great. Strong today.
Fri. AM	Run 1 hr Ski 2:05			Don' t feel too great today. Real skiing on snow though. AM hr. 39
PM	Run 1:35	Level 3 Run :10		Sweet run. Felt great.
Sat. AM	RClassic 2:15		d-pole	Long double-pole session.
PM	Run 40 hr	Level 3-4 Bound :20	Spenst :35	Good spenst, but knee hurt during the warm-down. It' s an issue. Bounding felt strong.
Sun. AM	RClassic 2:30			Feel strong. AM hr 42
PM	Rskate 1:30			Don' t feel as good, but okay. Very good week of training. Knee is my only problem.
Week Total	28 hours			

Training log: Week 30. Month 8. Nov., 1997. West Yellowstone, Mont.

Day	Dist.	Interval	Strength	Comments
Mon. AM	Classical ski 2:20			Feel the altitude. AM hr 35. Technique is good/okay. Need be more forward
PM	Skate ski 1:40			Feel a bit off, little awkward. Came together better at the end. Hr, under 150.
Tues. AM	Classic 2	Speed :30+	Specific :30+	AM heart rate: 38. Good strength and specific strength. Technique is only okay (!)
PM	Skate 2		Spenst :30	Easy. Technique feeling more natural. Still not 100%. Feel tired after last week's training.
Wed. AM	Classic 2:25			AM heart rate: 40. very easy.
PM	Skate 2:30			Very easy.
Thur. AM	Classic 2			Again easy distance. Miles and miles. Hard snowstorm
PM	Skate 2		Lift :30	Easy. Good lift, not long, but good.
Fri. AM	Classic 1:15			Am heart rate 40, but feel tired. Called it quits before I wanted to.
PM	Off			Didn't want to rest..but
Sat. AM	Classic 2			Easy!
PM	Skate 2			Feeling great. Technique was much better, not so tired. Good.
Sun. AM	Classical 3	Natural int. :45 mins		AM hr 41. Technique seems close. Need to have quicker kick. More down on poles.
PM	Skate 2:30			Again nice and easy and long. Storming like hell. Tech coming. Confident now.
Week Total	30 hours			

I increased my training volume by 100 hours that year. It is generally unwise to increase it by more than 50 per year. Sometimes I was concerned because I would slump into periods of fatigue, but at other times I felt incredible. Increasing the training volume so much was a risk. But, I thought, success demands risk.

Mode of propulsion.

The Perfect One

Barb Jones has been on my mind since the U.S. Team Trials in Lake Placid in 1996. For the season prior to the '98 Games Eli and I are resident athletes at the Olympic Training Center in Marquette Michigan, prodigies again of Sten Fjeldheim; and after a few years away from the books, we were students again as well. Barb Jones is temporarily a student and a ski racer at Northern Michigan University before she transfers to Dartmouth. And she is Eli's girlfriend.

Eli's girlfriend! Why does she have to be *Eli's* girlfriend? I'm so jealous it hurts. I fantasize about breaking them up somehow, and feel guilty about even thinking it. Eli and I have lived together off and on as close friends since we were freshmen in college. I tell myself to forget it and it works—for a while. Then I see Barb and my infatuation for her re-ignites as she skips past, smiling, always smiling, always bright. She says hello, smiles at me...and I start scheming reflexively, *God, I like her. How can I win her?* More guilt. *How could I do that to one of my best friends? I'm a selfish schmuck.* What's as disturbing is that I'd be willing to return to my third grade romance with Penny: I'd be willing to fight for her. I'd be happy to fight for her. *What a fool*, but I can't help it.

We'd had a hard day of training, and I was surprised when Eli asked me to join him for some beer drinking. We are sitting in the sand watching small waves roll up on the sandy shore of Lake Superior. "She likes you," says Eli.

"Barb Jones likes me?"

"We broke up," continues Eli.

"Sorry, man," I say.

"Naw," says Eli, "I know you like her." I thought I'd hidden my feelings well.

"I don't know how to feel about this," I lie. I am ecstatic and feel guilty for it.

"It's OK, it was mutual," he tells me. I feel like dancing circles, jumping around. I want to give him gifts, but instead I try to hide my smile, and to think of the right thing to say.

"I…"

"Don't worry about it," says Eli.

It's a week after I get the good news and a blessing from Eli but I'm pacing around the dorm wondering how Barb will respond when I ask her to the concert. She's nineteen; I'm twenty-five. It's like junior high all over again. *Should I ask her? Oh man, I don't know!* Her legs are maple yogurt, sweet, brown and smooth. She laughs quick and easy. She smiles at strangers, free of cynicism. She's genuine and honest enough to be mistaken for naïve. She has a bounce in her stride, and it's almost the best thing about her. This bounce, from muscled calf, through thigh, butt, boob and brain. Brain? Yes. I see it in the eager inquisitiveness of her face and the concentration she pours into drawing and painting. She's like a kid, absorbed in the wonder. She *is* smart. She's pre-med and philosophy, and, for what it's worth, gets all A's. Her eyes glow, full of energy and cheerfulness. She skips, whistles, and plays the piano. She studies like a fiend and dances with glee.

Butterflies are for amateurs. She's gonna laugh, then say something like "You're kidding right?" Ferrets frolic in my stomach. I pick up the phone anyway, and hop around like a fool when she says, "Sure!"

After the concert, standing under a crisp half moon, I felt her breath on my cheek, and then her warm lips on mine. And she was as soft and perfect as my first kiss on the pitcher's mound in third grade. And I floated as I floated then. We've been together ever since.

The school year of our first year together had ended. Barb's parents came to help drag her belongings back to Minnesota, and I got the chance to meet the Jones family. For reasons I don't recall, I'd shaved my head bald. My face was not. My beard grows fast and I can't be bothered with daily, or even weekly, shaving. I have other things to do—like shave my head. So when Barb and I walked out to her folk's car, holding hands, she skipping merrily, me trying to look pleasant in spite of my appearance, I could feel their disapproving eyes on us, on me. They knew I was more than five years older. That was a strike against me. And I thought I sensed their fear: *Let's hope she's just going through a phase.*

I was relieved when our conversation was easy and pleasant. Though it was hard to imagine I got an enthusiastic thumbs-up, I knew I didn't get a complete thumbs-down either.

After school we both flew to the Northwest, where I was planning to train all summer. Barb would return home after ten days.

We are pressed on all sides by fellow travelers, moving from airplane to terminal by bus. There are huge doors at the back, like those at the back of a cattle truck. There is cell phone chatter and general conversation. We stand placidly, waiting for the big doors to open and spill us into the terminal. "What's for dinner?" a man asks into his cellular.

"What if," Barb says to me, "these doors don't open into the terminal?" I just look at her.

"What if, instead—see all these people crowded in here, talking and shuffling their feet and staring at the exit, assuming the best?" Barb relishes putting together strange scenarios, and carefully crafts them like stories. "Picture the doors opening not into a terminal filled with other travelers, newspaper stands, Cinnabons and McDonald's, but a stench of wet hay, urine, blood, and panic. What if those doors opened into a slaughterhouse? Picture the fear and confusion, the press of unaware people in back pushing forward and those in front bracing backward all choked with terror, and screaming, trying to escape but being forced forward toward the man, or maybe even a man-like cow standing on hind legs, wearing a dark, bloody rubber apron holding a giant, stained sledgehammer."

I've caught on. "People," I say. "They're what's for dinner."

We laugh and start pushing forward. "*Mmmmmmm!!!*" moos Barb as the big doors open and the bus disgorges us into…the terminal.

Barb was an exotic mix of twisted imagination and bubbly beauty. As we walked through the terminal, her eyes alert, she pointed out the *really* odd ones. The question I wrestled with was: how do you fall in love for sure, if not forever? How do you *know*? I didn't expect an answer. I was happy just to be asking myself this particular question about this particular girl. Barb Jones.

Training and racing is sort of a miniature life, with everything crammed into the distance of ten kilometers, or thirteen years, or even a single snow-covered hill—agony and victory and joy and defeat. I am accustomed to both failure and success, and I find them almost equally valuable. You can prepare with great seriousness and no joy, as some do, or with seriousness *and* joy, and either way you can never be absolutely certain of anything, and that mystery is the beauty of it. You could be blessed with courage but lack lungs, or brains but weak legs, or with all these things and no luck (and you thought the Wizard of Oz was about a little girl and her dog). At the race's end, if not sooner, you'll know, but never before the start, never before you push mightily and with conviction onto the course. The only thing to do is go for it, the only thing ever to do was go for it. Be it a single 10k race, 13 years, or one snowy hill. How many chances do you get?

Hope you get one, and don't count on two.

Just as my parents failed to supply me with predigested dreams and regurgitated fears, so had the world failed to supply me with meaning. And how great is that? It *is* great, because I am free to grant meaning to those things I determine for myself as worthy. I chose ski racing. Is it important? Of course not, not on a grand scale. It's meaningful to me and a handful of other people around the world, and that's really about it.

Meanwhile I read of 300 Cambodian refugees escaping war in a forty-foot wooden boat, surviving a hundred-day voyage by eating raw fish and drinking rainwater, to finally find peace and freedom. Skiing doesn't carry that kind of meaning—thankfully. It's just ski racing, and that is enough.

What are the things that are most important to me? My friends, my family, ski racing… And what makes me so sure any of it is worthy of meaning? Nothing. What will enable me to *know*? Nothing.

Barb and I are standing at curbside. There is a man standing next to us. His nose is bent, and gray hair swoops from his temples. He is standing on the curb waiting for the long-term parking shuttle, as we are. He reaches into his jacket, pulls a pack of cigarettes out, eyes it with disdain and shakes one loose. He finds a book of matches in his other pocket. I eye him with disgust. Barb pays no attention. I zoom in. The flame leaps to life, the match rises, the cigarette lowers. The flame touches the end. Cheeks collapse as lungs suck, the flame pulls into the cylinder, paper burns, tobacco ignites, glows. There is no smoke, but there is fire. The eyes close with the inhalation, there is a pause and then two fingers pluck the cigarette from between the lips in an easy motion and a damp *pop*. Smoke oozes from the nostrils, floats upward and then, *whoooo*, shoots from the mouth in a long sigh. It rises and disappears, and the man watches it with a curiously sublime look on his face.

"Every once in a while you get the perfect one." He says absently, indicating the cigarette. *Has he seen me watching him? Is he talking to me?*

"Most of them suck," he says, making eye contact with me to express his point. His lids are half shut. "Most aren't worth shit, but every now and then…" He closes his eyes and inhales, looking as though he were sucking on joy itself.

"…Every now and then you get the perfect one. Sometimes it's after a cup of coffee in the morning, or watching a sunset. Sometimes it's, I don't know, it's not about the time or the place. Maybe it is—I don't know—but sometimes you get the perfect one." He smiles at me, a man with the perfect one between his fingers.

I'm just nodding to get rid of him, not really listening, and thinking, *It's my air too, asshole. —But who's the asshole?*

"Racing is like that," says Barb. I glance at her, surprised. The man gives her his attention, interested. "Racing?" he asks.

"Races are mostly okay, sometimes great, often they just suck."

"Mmmm," the man says nodding, sucking. He pulls the cigarette out. "Yeah, and it's the perfect one that keeps you lightin' up." *Whooooo.* The smoke leaves his mouth, swirling inside itself, rising.

"So," he starts, "is it an addiction, racing?"

"Probably," says Barb. "In skiing it's the perfect races that are addictive. Most of them are good, a lot are OK, some of them suck, but you do it for the perfect ones."

"Hmmm," the smoker says. "Keeps you ripping into new packs. It does for me."

The shuttle pulls up and the man drops the perfect one in the gutter sorrowfully. Still smoking, it rolls a short distance, stops, and smolders like a dud firecracker. He grinds it with his loafer, looks at Barb with a shrug, and steps onto the shuttle.

"You know," Barb says as we search the long-term parking lot for my Subaru, which has been left for us there, "I don't like smoking, but you got to sympathize with the smokers."

A wind-driven ruckus of crows and dry leaves squawked and shuffled. The clouds lifted and revealed Mt. Rainer in the distance. The last of the day's sun peeked above the horizon putting a spotlight on the snow-covered mountain. It blushed a bright reddish-pink in the waning minutes before the sun set. The parking lot turned gray, the crows took up their noisy fight, and the leaves scratched along the concrete. Then the leaves and crows took flight with a strong gust, like the choice was theirs, and Barb and I were left behind, standing still and stupid, weary travelers looking for their car.

I have always pretended to make choices, but secretly I think I am more like those crows, deciding to fly after the wind has already bore them up. In spite of this, I seldom feel out of control. I fool myself necessarily well.

A perfect example of this is my decision to become an Olympic champion. You could say I was sitting on a tree branch bickering and clowning with my buddies when all of a sudden a strong gust of wind took me half-way to where I then wisely and promptly decided I wanted to go—the top podium at the Olympic Games. That wind has faded, and my momentum with it. I was dropped within sight of my destination, but not there.

Is racing an addiction? Maybe it's something like it. Decisions, it seems to me, besides not being chosen at all are not just a matter of random acts of nature but are set up by a complex series of events that conspire toward a specific choice. Am I a skier by choice? Am I training for the '98 Games because I choose to? I'm not sure I do. I share this thought with Barb.

"You don't believe in free will?" she asks.

"Oh, God. I was just talking. I'm not saying anything."

Barb is a philosophy major. I have a minor, but I've only skimmed what she's actually read and understood.

"You don't believe in free will." She's not really asking, so, hell, I take that stand and decide to defend it. It's how we explore ideas, or at least how Barb explores ideas...I just like to argue.

"Nope, I don't. Why would anyone choose to do this? No money, no glory. It was a conspiracy of upbringing, genetics, and an ever-increasing collection of experiences."

"Ha!" she takes up the fight, "and you're trying to drag me into it, get me to train for the next Games. Unbelievable."

"Like you have a *choice*. Anyway, the experiences must have been positive. I must have tasted the perfect one at least once. I wouldn't try to talk you into it otherwise, besides, there's no reason for me to...you won't be able to help it," I say.

"There is no way to prove or disprove free will," continues Barb, ignoring my stab.

"Everything you do, you do for a reason based on your background," I butt in.

"You can't prove that, and I can't prove you wrong. The thing is you, we, have to function as if we were capable of making choices. We have to be able to hold ourselves and others accountable. Society demands it and functions by it. Do you hold people responsible for what they do? Do you treat people as if they were in control of their actions? Having no free will is an easy philosophy to defend because you can point to certain things that led you to a specific outcome, but there may have been a decision behind that. Your background may have narrowed your choices, but not down to one. Who knows? It's probably a mix, but the thing is, if you don't live by the philosophy of determinism, which you don't, then 'no decisions' is a bad philosophy to hold."

Damn, just when you find a really unpopular, fatalistic and mean-spirited belief to hold, there is Barb.

"So why should I be sympathetic toward a smoker who doesn't quit?" I ask.

"Look," she says, "In essence you've told me you're having a hard time lately pulling the perfect ones from skiing. Why don't *you* quit?"

"I don't want to." My tone was thin, but Barb was nice enough to ignore that. In reality, some days when I don't train, I turn sour with withdrawal. It took a long time for me to recognize the

Barb Jones.

connection between a few days without training and this depression, but it is real.

"Well, even if our smoker wanted to, decided to, that doesn't mean he will be able to. It may not be the choice to *do* that we have, but the choice to try."

"There's the car." I felt thankful for a respite from having my smug self humbled.

It is getting dark as we load up and start south toward our goal, Bend, Oregon, my summer home. I have *chosen* it as the best site for a last stand. There, I can wedge my back against the wall and bare my teeth with honest intent. With two of my best friends, training partners, and rivals—Justin Wadsworth and Patrick Weaver—living there, I will have no escape.

"There is a race I promised myself to remember," I say, breaking the silence. "It was the 1993 NCAA National Championships. I won. Few Americans win the NCAAs because of all the Euro skiers recruited to ski for colleges here. But I did, and I don't mind bragging."

"Gawd."

As we drove I relived the race in my mind as Barb looked out the window. It was a 20k race, mass start skate race, on two hard loops at altitude in Steamboat Springs, Colorado. The race broke apart, and I was among the first group, even while holding off a side-ache. Skiers kept dropping off the front pack, but I stayed calm and tried to ski as easily as I could. Eventually I drifted off the back as my side-ache worsened and tied me up.

We're on the second lap now and there's a series of long climbs ahead. If I lose the leaders before the climbs, there won't be any more chances. But I stay calm and try to ski relaxed so my side-ache goes away. I could have just hacked away at the back of the pack until my gut was totally tied up, but I let off. The spectators and coaches thought I was quitting. They were yelling at me, telling me to get back up to the group, but I kind of stood up, skied a little slower and let my gut work itself out. And it did. And when it did it was like I was starting fresh. No one had caught up to me, and the lead group, which had six or seven guys, had only gained twenty seconds on me. I still had to be careful, so I stayed calm and seriously *flew*. To keep my side-ache away I focused on my exhalations. I was a breathing machine. I must have sounded like a steam train pulling out of the station, *WHEW* inhale, *WHEW*, inhale, *WHEW*, *WHEW*, sweet and steady. And I *was* a train. I chugged over those twenty seconds in what felt like ten, and whoever was on the end of the lead group, some Euro skier, looked back at me with wonder as I chugged up to him. My eyes were wide and focused and my face relaxed. He sees me.

When I slipped off the back I'm sure he thought, "Well, that guy's gone," and now I'm back and sounding like a locomotive. His head whipped forward again like he didn't want to see me back with the pack.

I could feel my legs strain as we hit the first climbs, but I knew everyone was feeling the race now, so I just bore it, took it, and kept breathing. *Whew, Whew, Whew.* Anytime someone tried to attack and get away, I was there. The group got smaller, but my attention was only on the lead. *Whew, Whew, Whew.* I could feel the cramp lingering in my side, waiting for me to tense up. It wasn't one of those races where you think, *Oh yeah, I'm going to win.* I kept on hoping I could do it when the time came, but I never knew. We gained the top of the course, which went along a ridge and then dropped steeply back toward the ski stadium. There were four skiers left in the lead. I was fourth in line.

The descent was crazy. From the top of the ridge you gain top speed in about five seconds and then there are two switchback turns where you need to get low and throw the skis sideways—no way you're going to carve around these corners—and slide like hell to the outside of the turn. You drop down into the second turn, muscle your skis around the other way, and hope you've scrubbed off enough speed to make it. Then it was a straight ride, tears-running-out-the-corner-of-your-eyes kind of fast, over these little jumps, where you have to pre-jump them or get launched. The first guy in line sucked up, like his legs were taken out from under him as he tops the roll. Then the second guy and the third, like a roller coaster going over the top. You know the roll is coming even though you can't see it because the guy in front of you absorbs the thing with his whole body and, boom, he's gone. You're on it, your knees at your chin, then a moment of floating and, *slap*, you're back on the snow about a foot behind him. It was sweet just to be a part of this synchronized battle, fighting up the hill and then jamming full throttle down off the ridge.

We reach the bottom and it's simply all out for the finish. I just kept my head down, as one person after the other tried to escape. I wish I could have watched it. The coaches were going crazy. What could they have done? They screamed and yelled and hoped their horse had what it took. With a kilometer to go, the course came up over a hill and into the stadium before heading back out and around a little knoll. I don't know what happened, I just punched it. I swear it took me by as much surprise as anyone. I came from third around two guys in what felt like two skates and gained ten yards in ten seconds. Once I was at the front a reserve of hidden energy just poured into my blood. I didn't need to breathe, I couldn't think—didn't *try* to think—I just hammered. I gained ten more yards before the track ducked around another knoll. I didn't look back, but I heard the coaches yelling for their skiers. I knew someone was close, but I didn't look. I was fully committed; knowing where the other racers were wouldn't have done me any good. A hill led back up into the stadium, then there were 100 meters left. The terrain was flat and wide enough that I could get passed by three people if they had the gas. I was seriously delirious with pain all of a sudden, but it was time to really fight. I was stiff from the effort. My lungs seared, and I could hardly see. I burst into the stadium and pounded toward home, feeling like I was going to pop. But I knew I had it and chanced a glance back. Instant relief. I was well clear and raised my arms spastically, jumped into the air again and again as my speed carried me over the finish line.

"Jesus, Barb," I blurt out, and she looks at me as if to say *Jesus what?* "That race, it was one of those moments. I had a bad side-ache in that race, and won anyway. It wasn't the perfect one, but it was. In spite of the side-ache, or maybe because if it, *that race was one of the perfect ones.* And the thing is, right now in my career is like the point in the race when I had the side-ache. I can quit—which crosses my mind—I can hang on at all costs, or I can hang back and hope I don't lose too much time until I'm ready to go full bore again. I thought to hang back when I had the side-ache and it paid off. I didn't think at all when I attacked, and it paid off. Now, not only do I not know what to do, but I don't know how to even start figuring out what to do. How many dud packs do you rip into before you go looking elsewhere for the perfect one?"

Driving to Bend that night I recalled the comfort and safety of childhood. I remember the light from an oncoming car illuminating the faces of my parents. Lloyd is at the wheel, Sue in the passenger seat. I am lying in the back, maybe ten years old. One of our dogs stands in the very back and hangs his head over me with his tongue hanging. Occasional drops of saliva fall, hitting the seat and roll toward me. I smear them into the seat with a finger. The lights brighten. Lloyd and Sue squint as the oncoming car draws near. The lights race up the ceiling and zoom overhead. It's like I lay face up in a copy machine. Then it's dark. There was never a moment of fear. My parents' faces are calm in the mellow green glow of the instrument panel. We hurtle down the road following a small patch of light held in front of the car like a blind man's cane. We won't know what lies ahead until we are upon it, but we all pretend it isn't so and push on full speed ahead. The radio is on. *There's the pitch. Swing and a miss. There's the pitch. High and outside.* I'm awake and day-dreaming watching the lights, and mindful of dog slobber but lost in my dreams I am able to become a samurai, a cowboy, a Marine, a medalist.

Barb and I hurtle through the dark behind beams of light that only see so far. I'm in charge, at the wheel, and comfortable enough with that, but now there is no escaping into fantasy. We squint at the beams of oncoming cars, which illuminate our car's interior and flash past. What dangers lay beyond the beams of our headlights? Deer? Shredded retreads? I've seen a logging truck overturn its load. There were cars scattered like toys. Whole trees lay splintered across both lanes, as well as in the median and the ditch. For some there had been no escape. Long patches of burnt rubber show the only choice they had: hit the breaks, clench their jaws and hold on. Could we be the first upon such a scene tonight? What will our beams swing onto around the next corner?

It is ignorant faith that makes possible the comfort I felt while laying in the backseat of a car piloted by my parents, and which even now allows me to sit in the driver's seat, mashing pedal to floor.

Onward.

Driving is a huge part of ski racing. In winter we drive long hours from race to race, often through blizzards, and often at great speed. In the summer we drive to training camps and running races and bike races. In the fall we drive across country to school and in the spring we drive back again. So much of this time on the road is spent in conversation, with music playing and the miles ticking by.

Barb Jones and me, high in the Colorado Rockies.

"Why don't you go for it?" I ask Barb. "You know you're talented enough."

"I'm in school."

She is in school, but she's also skiing for the college team, and has ski raced all her life. In fact, she has placed among the Top 10 at the National Championships.

"I don't mean this Olympics, but in four years. 2002. Salt Lake." She doesn't answer right away. Barb is en route to medical school. Though she's very good and loves the sport, she hasn't considered taking skiing to the next level.

"What good would I be doing anyone?" Barb asks good questions.

"You'd be doing yourself some good. Think about what racing has already given you in general—direction, discipline, good times, good friends."

"Pragmatism. It helps you learn to be pragmatic." Barb is way beyond me in most things.

"Sure, but more importantly by dreaming and skiing and living the way you want to live, you'll help other people do the same," I tell her.

"You're just trying to justify doing what you want to do. If you can convince me, it'll just help justify it for you," she says.

"*What?*" I say with indignation. Barb's at least partly right, but I go on. "Are you crazy? Sure, I don't ski for charity's sake, but I know from my own experience that it's not a useless pastime. My heroes gave me dreams and hopes and ambitions and confidence. And I'm not even talking about big, faraway guys, but close-to-home heroes who gave me their old boots, or went skiing with me when I was a kid. Or even Bill Koch just saying, 'Man, you skied one hell of a race.' Bill Koch, saying that to me, it meant something to my life."

We're both quiet for some time.

"Ever watch a video of Jimi Hendrix playing guitar?" I ask. "I want to be able to do something with that same feeling. The guy has a look on his face that's all ecstasy. To do anything like that…

"These local heroes," I go on, "they give you confidence, like maybe you can ski—if not like Jimi Hendrix played guitar, at least with some kind of perfection. Does that make any sense?"

She reaches and scoops my hand off my thigh and holds it in her lap. We sit holding hands in the dark, driving. With one finger she caresses my thumb as if to calm me down. I can tell she wants to change topics. I get going on something and have a hard time backing off.

I look at Barb illuminated by the dash. Here's my girlfriend, for God's sake. Snap out of it, man. What's this talk all about? Shiny, dark almond hair falls straight down her back, swings across her face as she shifts her head. She pulls errant strands from her mouth with a quick, practiced swipe of the hand. She has cheeks that grandmas of the world dream of pinching, a sharp little chin, even a beauty mark in the corner of her smile—always this smile and those white teeth. She leans over against me, doesn't so much lay her head on my shoulder, as nuzzles up against it. Who cares about ski racing?

"Anyway," I continue against all reason, "the skills you learn—um, pragmatism and all that—it'll make you a better doctor. Plus, if you don't do it you'll always wonder if you could have." Now I have her, I can tell when she tunes in: *a better doctor?*

My argument style relies on bombardment and volume, exactly what I hate in others: the conservative-talk-show-host technique. It makes me want to kick my own ass.

"Listen, there is plenty of time to be a doctor. You've got a summa cumi-lumi from Dartmouth. They'll let you into any med school."

"I got a what? Anyway, not necessarily," she says. "I still have to…"

"Oh, come on, I know that's just your driven attitude speaking. You know you can get into med school when you're twenty-six or thirty. This," I pause, sweeping my hand to somehow indicate skiing. "This, you can only do now. You're twenty-one. The Olympics—you can only do that now." Ha-ha, I think, victory.

"It's a different world," she says. "Skiing—any sport—is a totally self-centered activity. All we're doing is working to improve ourselves. When I talk to Sten it's always I, I, I. 'I'm feeling good this morning,' 'My heart rate is high today,' 'I need to do more strength.' Most people—people in the real world—do this for other people. It's not about me. It's about others."

"Bullshit"—a good word, I believe, to start a defense with. "Well, maybe, but besides the fact that improving yourself is underrated, don't tell me you don't *want* to be a doctor, but feel you owe it to the world. You want to be a doctor for your own reasons, and it's handy that doctors happen to help other people."

"Yep, I want to be a doctor for my own reasons, one of which is that I like to help people. It's a human need, to feel like I'm contributing to society."

"Living well is a grand contribution to society, being a hometown Hendrix to someone, or likely several someones. Maybe like that little Houghton reggae band we saw together," I say.

"The Houghton reggae band travels in a beat-up van. Doctors are paid a lot because society values what they do. Skiers are paid nothing because society doesn't."

"Gandhi and Martin Luther King they killed, and Kennedy too. By your argument the world needs more football players, more evangelists and more TV talk show hosts."

"Well, I don't mean to say all the values our society has are right."

"What *I'm* saying is that you can come down off your high horse any time it suits you." Whoops, I've gone too far and now she's getting pissed. Barb's eyes are a swirl of green and brown—little tornadoes.

Backtrack. I try again, "Many of the important people in my life have been ski racers. Skiers have helped me better myself both in and outside of skiing. My coaches and my Uncle Mike, and even racers like Gunde who I've never met all made a positive impact on my life. And I'm just one person in whose life such people have made a difference."

"No doubt they are great people. But did they really make a positive influence in your life because they were cross-country skiers? Doctors *help people*. It is part of their job description. It's a service. What do athletes do?"

"We only need doctors when we're sick. We need heroes all the time."

She makes a *pshaw* noise and rolls her eyes, "Corny."

"Okay, so you might not ski race in the future, but you have up till now.

Why?" I ask.

"Because it's fun. And ultimately it will make me better in my career."

"Is there any value in the simple fact that it's fun?" I press on.

"Well, alcohol is fun—does that make it valuable?"

"If you think fun has value, it is. Anyway we're not arguing the merits of getting drunk. Are you afraid?" Here a little pause, which I consider a small victory.

"Sure, but that's not playing a role in my decision-making." Funny thing, I argue for victory, she for the exploration of ideas.

"Are *you* afraid?" she asks. *Damn!*

"Yeah, well, no. I mean, I'm beyond that, I think,"

"Ohhhh, big man,"

"Really, I am not afraid to go for it," I say. "I am afraid I'll fail—just a little bit anyway. And I think that plays a role in any success I may have had. But, no, I like trying."

"Okay, I'll give you this," Barb says. "Potential has received too great an emphasis. It's almost as if having potential is more important than doing anything with it. I mean, I was tested in the lab and told I had great potential as a skier. I left there thinking, *cool*, like that's all I needed to know. With the discovery of my potential, there was success, now I can go on to something with a little more mystery. Like, 'I can be a skier, but can I be a doctor?' "

"But—" I try to interrupt.

"—But I realize that's not true. Potential is just that, and it has no value beyond its actualization."

"So can you actualize a potential without ignoring all the others? Like Edward Abbey says, 'How can you be true to one, and not be untrue to all the others?' I mean can you be a great doctor and a great mom at the same time? Can you ski first and then be a doctor?"

"Abbey is a chauvinist and a hypocrite."

"I like him!"

"Sure, he's a good writer, but the other things, too. You know what was a pivotal time? When I decided to go to Dartmouth instead of Harvard. That was my biggest moment of decision-making ever—so far. I went to Dartmouth because I went on a run on the Charles in Boston and then went running in the woods around Dartmouth. No contest. One can be at the supposedly most exciting institution in the world, and that's not everything. At Dartmouth there was less conflict between activities. One thing didn't have to suffer just to do the other."

"So you're going to go for it?"

"Damn you."

"Well?"

"I don't know yet. Jeez. You know it's not really an arguable thing. You might be right, on some things. Wait, this isn't even an argument! And you're trying to win?"

She's laughing at me.

"Maybe it's not, but I *did* win."

"Idiot."

I give her my best Sten impression: "You have to want it, Jones! It's no use otherwise. You just have to want it!"

Grit

I met a woman one summer at a running race near Trout Lake. I'd seen her before. She came to all the local races to watch her husband run. While he was as skinny as grass, she was huge. She was very outgoing and struck up a conversation with me. She told me that she used to run a lot, but that even in her running days she weighed more than three hundred pounds. Her mood darkened as she told me how her knees had given out, and that she couldn't run anymore.

She lit up then and told me about a half-marathon she ran in. For her, just running down the block was a challenge, and running thirteen miles seemed like an impossible goal, but she had done a few half-marathons before and had been considering a whole marathon before her knees quit.

She was the last runner, she told me—further than last. Everyone else had run, finished, and gone home except her husband, who she knew was waiting at the finish line. Meanwhile, she was still chugging along. The race was rolling, open, and lonely as it cut through the endless eastern Washington wheat fields.

Gradually, she became aware of a hum. The hum grew and the air vibrated with it. It was hot, and thirteen miles is a long way to run, especially, she said, carrying three hundred pounds. At first she paid the sound no mind. She chugged along, coaxing herself down the road. She was alone on a long road, running at a death-march pace. Her clothes were sticky with sweat, twisted, and pinching uncomfortably. They just don't make— and she stood up to show me—running clothes in her size. Her inner thighs and underarms were raw from the constant rubbing, but she kept running.

The sound had become a growl, a metallic roar, and she kept running. It was deafening now and she knew without having to look that it was the sound of motorcycles. Hogs, Harleys, and lots of them.

Against her better judgment she sneaked a peek over her shoulder and saw a massive wave of steel and leather, noise and exhaust. *Hells Angels!*

Her eyes were wide now as she told me her tale. Not knowing what else to do, she kept running. They slowed up behind her. A solitary fat woman running uncomfortably down a long, lonely road, followed by a coughing roar of chrome, steel, black leather, goggles, bandanas, beards, and road dust. The leader pulled up slowly alongside her. Her pace was so slow he had to work to keep the monster bike upright. She glanced over at him, smiled weakly and returned her gaze straight-ahead. She could tell he was looking at her, his face tan and smudged with oil and grease, wrinkled, dusty, and hairy. He gave nothing away.

His eyes were behind mirrored glasses. The roar of a hundred Harleys at her heels was overwhelming. This was a long—she reminded me—a long way to run, and at her pace, a long time to be running. Tears built up at her eyes, but she held them back. Whatever happened next, she realized, was out of her hands. She was at their mercy, and the realization was strangely relaxing, because—and she shrugged her shoulders at me—what could she do? So she just kept running, sure they would stop her soon enough. They would stop her, and when they did they would do whatever they wanted with her. The leader leaned his bike closer. This is it, she thought. In a voice like the growl of his bike he said,

"Way to fucking go, lady!"

True Inheritance

This could be it—I wrote in my 1997-1998 training log—*the last summer of ski training. The last fall. The final season. If I succeed in making the '98 Olympic team, I will go on.*
   I didn't need to write anymore. I knew that if I didn't make the team that would be it. The dream would be over.

   I crossed the finish line knowing it wasn't enough. *So, this is what it is like to finally lose, to see my dream escape me—this time for good.* I was sitting in the snow, across the finish line, done, and well out of the way. *How can this be happening? It is not real. But it is. I am smaller than I dreamed of being. Whatever comes along now can only be less than the dream. It is clear, I will not strive whole-heartedly for anything ever again. I'll become a Taoist and dispel desire. The ache will be less.* I have picked myself up now, and I am walking, carrying my skis. *Then again, so too would the glory have been less—had I won. But I didn't. It's over.* I stopped to look at the scoreboard, just to be sure. Fourth place: Pete Vordenberg. It isn't enough. I was second in the first race, and fourth in the last. I beat two of the five skiers who made the team two out of three times, but it wasn't enough, because I blew it in the middle race in which I placed sixteenth.
   Just then I had a very clear vision of my dream watching me in the rear-view mirror as I fell behind. Its eyes framed in the mirror are curious. They ask *Why don't you keep up? I am, after all, your dream. Why don't you keep up?* My image grows small in its wake. *Come on*, it beckons, but it does not wait.

   ***

   "Come on, Pete. Let's go home." Barb had me by the arm and was trying to pull me out of a snow bank. "Pete." She sat down in the snow next to me. "Pete, you can't stay here." It was early morning, dark and raining. Mist hovered in illuminated triangles under the streetlights. I lay still, face down in stubborn, stupid self-pity, snuffling in a snow bank. Barb had given up trying to drag me home, but wouldn't leave me there as I asked her to. And I'm glad she didn't. It was the night after the last '98 Trials race—my last race, I told myself, ever. I was thinking about my Grandpa Steve.

When I was young we would go backpacking, and I would try to match his long strides. I envisioned myself as big as he was, as great as Grandpa Steve was.

"Grandpa Steve was raised in Oklahoma," I told Barb. "While working his way through college he earned food and rent money from an oil company by walking along a pipeline, checking gauges, just to make sure all was well. On the first day he walked fourteen miles. On the second day, eleven miles. On both days he walked through the Oklahoma prairie." Barb was staring down the street through the mist toward the Olympic Training Center where we were staying for the Trials. I kept talking to her anyway. "Both days earned him the total of a dollar twenty-five. Dirt poor—and in Oklahoma that means something—he paid his way through and graduated from college. He fought in World War II, survived, became a professor and then the dean of education at Colorado University."

I related the story as she looked down the street, away from me, but I had the feeling she was at least half-listening.

"He climbed mountains all over Europe, Asia, and North America. He helped my Grandma raise four kids. He helped his son start the cross-country ski area in Steamboat, and then he gave lessons there. You know how many things he accomplished? He and my grandma built the house I grew up in. Listen to this," and I tugged at her arm, until she was looking at me, not showing much interest, but playing along. "He is eighty-five years old." My volume was rising. "And he still roller-skis! Eighty-five and he still skis!"

"The first Olympic team I made was 1992, in Albertville, and my grandpa came to watch me race," I said. Barb was listening now. "You know how the Olympics are all about glory?" I started snuffling, my throat was yoyoing, my chin wobbling. "But I didn't find glory there. Not until my Grandpa told me that watching me race in those Olympic Games was one of the proudest moments of his life."

I let Barb pull me out of the snow. With our arms wrapped around each other we wandered off down the street toward the Training Center weaving around the puddles we could see and sloshing through the ones we couldn't.

Grandpa Steve is my Mom's dad. When her brother, Mike, took up cross-country skiing as a teenager, my grandpa took it up along with him. My mom, who was an alpine ski racer, was happy to go along. My dad inherited the sport from her. I inherited it from them. From the youngest, who is not even a year old and rides in a backpack, to the oldest, who is still skiing at eighty-five, we are a cross-country ski family.

My grandpa took my cousin Perrin cross-country skiing several winters prior to the '98 Trials. I skied along with them for a time. I followed the two of them slowly, a bowlegged and lanky eighty-five-year-old man skiing side-by-side with his four-year old granddaughter. I'm sure he was dying to give her all the advice his fifty years of skiing had to offer, but he knew it was best to just let her ski as she wished. She was probably frustrated going so slow. Kids, like dogs, like to sprint, jump, fall, zoom down hills, and charge up them. My Grandpa, spry though he was at eighty-five, didn't. So we stuck together and skied at an easy, sauntering pace.

For fifteen of my then twenty-six years I had completely devoted my life to ski racing. I sacrificed a lot to the sport, but it didn't feel like a sacrifice because I loved doing it. It was pure love. In 1998 I missed the Olympic team by less than thirty seconds after three days and two and a half hours of racing.

After the last race, I quit the sport. The thing I had once loved and which had defined me, I now hated. So I swore to give it up—totally and forever.

Only three weeks later I went skiing with my mom and dad just to keep them company. The day was gray, windy, and cold, and I wasn't interested in going skiing, but I had committed myself. Putting on my skis sickened me. I should have been laying the final preparations on my training for the Olympic Games in Japan. Instead I was going skiing with my parents.

As we skied off together, I grumbled under my breath about the stupid sport. My mom led down the trail, I followed, with my dad at the tail. It had been a long time since I'd skied with my parents. I was surprised at how well these old timers could move along. We were a smooth train rolling rhythmically under snow-laden trees, skiing briskly and comfortably.

I took up my inheritance again that day, and I will not put it down again.

"You know, Barb, there's only four years until 2002."
"I don't know. Should I do it?"

"Without a doubt."

"How can you say that? I just pulled you out of a snow-bank."

"You could do it. You could be great."

"If I didn't make it—I don't need that kind of agony."

"If you don't make it, would it put you in that kind of agony?"

"After four years, don't you think?"

"I know."

"Yeah, and what a way to waste four years."

"Are you shitting me? I'm not even talking about making it. Last summer, you should have seen it. I remember this one day…"

"Spare me."

"I never trained more than for these Olympics."

"Yeah, and…"

"It was great."

"Yeah, but you didn't—this time you didn't go."

"I wanted to win, not just go. If you make the team or not, the work is still yours. The friends you get to keep. And if you genuinely do it with all you can muster, the satisfaction will be real regardless of the outcome.

"Take the dopers and cheaters," I continue, "many of them win, but their having won is far less than your having tried…even if you lose, provided you give it everything you have."

"Would you do it again?"

Barb Jones. 2002 Olympic Games, Salt Lake City.   *(photo courtesy Patty Morrissey)*

We stopped in the street, shivering in the damp chill.
  "Yes."
"Come on."
"I would do it starting all over. Right now."
She gives me a look of disbelief.
"Well," I say, "but now it has to be something new."
"See."
"I don't want it bad enough anymore. But we were talking about you."
"I don't know."
"It's not something you can be talked into."
We walk on—she, thinking.
Finally she says, "I'll do it."
We stood looking at each other.
  "All right!" I say, full of excitement. The dream wasn't dead. "Listen," I said, "the trick is to leap out of bed as soon as you are aware of consciousness. Up, into motion, no questions asked."

I Always Wanted to be a Cowboy

Picture the Hollywood cowboy. He's alone on his horse trotting around sage, between juniper. His hat is tipped back. There's a sandstone cliff above him and a trail of dust behind. He's a dark outline against a fading sunset, with a long shadow resembling Picasso's Don Quixote.

Ignore that he is riding into the sun, for all cowboys know to keep it at their back. Ignore too the realities of the cowboy life, for it is this moving image that I wanted to be—this snapshot in motion, self-sufficient and confident and heroic. And surrounded by wild country, wild animals, and wild people.

The fact that cowboys ride all day in the dust kicked up by cows is not relevant and never was. What I wanted was the Hollywood perfection and the ideal I sometimes glimpsed in the Colorado Rockies. The image wasn't so much a perfect lifestyle as a perfect moment.

Like the realities of being a cowboy, the few unpleasant realities of a ski racer's lifestyle are easy to ignore while in motion—while doing the actual thing that defines you.

In a fraction of a second a skier applies his weight to the center of a single ski, and in an instant presses the grip wax to the snow, and is gone. The skier propels himself forward and onto the other ski and rides it down the trail, gliding, free, flying. And before the momentum dies he sets the wax into the snow again, applies his weight and strength and power and is gone again, fast and seamless. Broken down, the technique is intricate. The skier propels himself down the trail, using poles and legs working in timed coordination. The skier's weight must be perfectly balanced on a ski for the wax to stick to the snow. One arm swings, the other pushes, one leg swings, the other propels you forward. The whole body is engaged in the act, but it is so practiced as to be mindlessly fluid and simple, subtle and lithe, and beautiful to see and much more beautiful to do.

It's the whole thing that makes the snapshot, the moment. It's not each individual movement but the collaboration of all the motions combined to create movement, momentum, and perfection.

The image of cowboy-at-sunset is a moment captured. The image of my ski hero, Gunde Svan in the '84 Games is a moment captured. So, too, is a tape of Jimmy Hendrix on guitar or Janis Joplin shaking and yowling, or even a shot of Ansel Adams focusing on his subject from behind the lens—in all cases it is the artist at work, involved in a moment of perfection, and in these images and sounds I find inspiration.

The gold medal, the music, and Ansel's photograph are only products of the moment. These things represent it, but it is the moment itself that matters.

I raced all the way through the 2002 season. At the U.S. National Championships in 2002, I finished fourth in the 50k classic, a good result, but by then I had come to define a great race in a new way. Results were one thing, but for a race to be great it had to fit my description of a perfect moment. My last great race, great as I'd come to define it anyway—was at the 2000 Nationals in Soldier Hollow, Utah, on the courses used for the 2002 Olympics. I was a ski coach and a student at the University of New Mexico, and I was racing for the pure enjoyment of it. I had no expectations and, as at the 1992 Olympic 30k, I wanted only to ski as well as I could.

It was my last perfect moment as a ski racer. It was not perfect because of how I finished, though I took second, but because of how I skied and how I felt doing it.

The moment. It's like being in love for the first time: total immersion in a feeling of helpless bliss. It hurts, too, but just right, with a sort of subconscious yearning, a longing, because it won't last forever, and you miss it already. Like writing or painting, *doing* anything with inspiration delivered by lightning, a muse who might escape. And so you sink fully into it, the act, and you do not let go, do not come up for air, you cannot press *pause*, because it will be gone—this moment.

And it's fun. Above all else it's fun. And for all the thousands of words given it by Zen masters and pop psychologists, war historians and Little League coaches, the final word is fun.

To get there takes effort, but once there it becomes effortless. At first glance it seems all Ansel did was push a button—*click*—to make a pretty picture. But it isn't so.

Many years of training and hard work took me a long way and enabled me to enjoy the sport at its fullest, to taste the perfect moment—in this case for the last time as a racer.

It was warm and the waxing conditions were tricky. I prepared my skis with a unique combination of waxes and ran to the start confident that they were as good as they could be and that so was I.

I left the stadium heading uphill. Ski racing is so much uphill. On this day I sprang forward and gained the top of the first hill smiling. I was intent on a few things. I wanted to ski as perfectly as possible, and I wanted to stay in control of my effort. To go out too fast on the Soldier Hollow course is to die a horrible death on skis. The course goes up and up, and when it comes time to go down, it zips you down so fast that seconds later you're going uphill again.

Perfection is not being perfect, but being completely *there*. In the race I was not perfect, but I was as perfect as I could have been, as perfectly present as it was possible for me to be.

Skiing takes me there, as does writing, drawing, snowboarding, hiking, and woodcarving. With skiing I am so practiced that it takes me there often. It's my sure ticket *to being right there—right here*. Skiing does this for me. And Barb Jones does, too.

With Barb I can taste the same sensation as can be found racing. Driving and talking, my hand held by hers in her lap, or walking and exploring southern Utah's sandstone wilderness, Barb enables me to be perfectly present, enjoying the moment.

In all cases experiencing this perfection is active, it's a matter of gaining and maintaining momentum. Skiing takes energy and effort, but returns your energy investment twofold. And so does dreaming.

I crossed the finish line at the 2000 Nationals, in love again with the sport of ski racing. When a guy named Kris Freeman crossed the line with a time one second better than my own, it didn't get me down. I didn't win, but how I felt about my race remained unfazed. I had done what I came to do. I came to ski as well as I could, and I was happy.

As a younger skier I would not have found the same satisfaction in having raced as well as I could if I didn't achieve my goal. That's a good thing, too, for to be great not only by your own measure, but also on the results page, you have to want to win. That desire—the thing a racer needs most— is what I lost, and is why I quit racing. With that I'll call the 2000 National 30k my sunset event, the moving image I want playing as the curtain closes on a career that was not everything I dreamed it would be, but which was, as I've come to measure it, still great.

I told Barb that I would do it all over again, and in writing this book I feel that I have.

Both living and writing the ski racer's life were fun, and they are both over for me now, but riding into the sunset is not the end. When the movie cowboy disappeared over the horizon and the audience got to their feet, my imagination always went on. To me a movie was only a chapter in a life that continues off-screen, a segment worthy of putting between opening and closing credits, and of spending five bucks to see, but that cannot tell the whole story.

You should count on getting only one chance to be great, for that is the only way to chase a dream, but catch it or not, you'd also better count on the sun coming up the next morning and a new adventure with it. So keep the sun at your back and make sure you have all six pills in your pistol, because tomorrow is a new day. No time for doubt. Game on.

Skiing into the future...as coach. New Zealand, (August, 2002).

Afterward

After making the 2002 Olympic Team and placing thirty-fifth in the Olympic 30k at Salt Lake City, Barb Jones started medical school at the University of Washington.

That same year I became the assistant coach for the U.S. Cross-Country Ski Team.

Barb and I are still together.

Cory Custer is a financial consultant, a husband and a father, in Bozeman, Montana. Sten Fjeldheim still rules Northern Michigan and continues to turn out fast skiers. The Black-Grigsby clan still lives in Trout Lake, Washington, and still takes in skiers. (Give them a call if you need a place to stay.) Eli is the head coach for the Maine Winter Sports Center. Kurt's fiancé had their first baby in 2002; they live in Norway. Nathan is married. He lives in Boulder and runs his own programming business. He still skis fast, and he is also coaching.

Many of my ex-teammates are still racing, including Carl, Patrick and Justin; and they can now place among the top fifteen best skiers in the world and are still improving. As members of the U.S. team they are on their way to the medal I still dream of today—as a coach.

It has been many years since anyone has seen, or heard from Rocky, or, come to think of it, since I've heard from Dan Ray.

Thanks

Thanks to Sue for proofreading this thing so many times, as well as everything else I've ever written, and to Lloyd for telling me stories, and to both for enabling me to dream and chase my dreams.

Thanks to Barb for her constant smile.

Thanks to Grandma for support and love, for putting my paintings on the wall, and for biscuits, and gravy like you read about.

Thanks to Grandpa Steve for untangling ten miles of my fishing line, always while the trout were rising. A kid never had a better old coot to explore with.

Thanks to Grandma and Grandpa V for their long-distance love and support, in spite of my weird pursuits.

Thanks to my whole family for always being there.

Thanks to all my friends for being the story. I wish there had been room to include you all in this telling of it.

Thanks to Jeff Potter for his hard work in publishing this.

Out Your Backdoor Catalog of Books

Topics

- **Outdoor Culture:**

  Momentum: Chasing the Olympic Dream—Pete Vordenberg
  A Dirt Road Rider's Trek Epic—Victor Vincente of America
  The Recumbent Bicycle—Gunnar Fehlau
  Fold-It! –The Folding Bicycle—Gunnar Fehlau
  DreamBoats: 3rd World Boating for Everyone—Richard Carsen
  The Cross Country Look, Cook & Pleasure Book—Hal Painter
  The Captain Nemo Cookbook Papers—Hal Painter

- **Fiction**—*Jack Saunders, Wild Bill Blackolive, Jack Rudloe*

- **Philosophy (Fifth Way Press)**—*Ronald E. Puhek, Vince L. Lombardi*

- **Local Culture Ruminations**—*Jeff Potter*

- **OYB Anthologies Vols. I/II**—*The Magazine of Cultural Rescue, Modern Folkways and Homemade Adventure (OYB #1-8; #9; 10)*

How to Order

Publisher: Jeff Potter   Email: jp@outyourbackdoor.com
Mail to: OYB Press, 4686 Meridian Rd., Williamston MI 48895
Send cash, check, or MO. Shipping included.
Or order with a credit card from OutYourBackdoor.com.
All titles available via Amazon, Barnes&Noble, and Borders, who take more than half the
  proceeds. Best to order from me directly! All titles in Books-In-Print for special orders.

What is OYB?

What is OYB? It's a resource for otherwise unobtainable books at a high level of cultural development on socially relevant topics and in various genres.

These titles have an integrity which is hard to find. So if you don't usually like bike books, novels, or religious books, don't fret. These ain't like that. OYB books are cross-training for the brain, often in multi-genre format. They're crossovers. They combine several areas of distinction. So even when they're about specific topics, they're general interest because they build from the roots of life, working against fragmentation and alienation. With OYB you don't get just a bike book, or just a ski book, or just a novel. As a result, perhaps you'll be inspired to set aside your usual subject biases, if you have any.

I've read most of what's been done in these areas, found something lacking, backtracked to the writer who fills that need (often suppressed, unknown or out-of-print)...and publish them for you. A few years ago this could *not* have happened. Thank you, Internet, for breaking down barriers set up by the establishment. Thank you, DocuTech and short-run printing innovations. Thank you zining and underground publishing for just being who you are. You're getting bigger, because the big-guys are neglecting more and more of life.

Get your hands on an OYB First Edition and you have something worth reading. Be the first on your block. If you know of similar books that need help, let me know. —*Jeff Potter*

Outdoor Culture

Momentum: Chasing the Olympic Dream

AUTHOR: Pete Vordenberg ISBN:1892590565 PAGES: 200 LISTPRICE: $17.95
DESCRIPTION: An inside look into life as an elite XC skier. Vordenberg is a 2X-Olympian, Natl Champ and a current US Team Coach. The most interesting picture to date on what it's like to ski...and live...really fast. (With dozens of black&white photos.) Vordenberg says: "We have seen the Olympics through the filter of mass media. But at the edge of the screen there is another figure. When the camera zooms out you can see him, almost too small to recognize. This is the story of the figure at the edge of your screen. It's a voyage following the pursuit of my dream to win an Olympic gold medal. It travels the world, crossing from childhood to the precipitous edge of adulthood. It shares the quixotic humor, excitement, and poignancy inherent in the pursuit of dreams. It is not a retelling of the little engine that could. Rather, it is about why the little engine even tried." REVIEW: "The marvel of Vordenberg's book is that it appeals to the non-skier as well as to ski racers past and present. Healthy doses of self-revelation, touches of *On The Road*, and remarkable insights make this a unique book. It's supposedly about skiing—but it's more about life and seizing it." —Bob Woodward, veteran XC ski journalist.

The Recumbent Bicycle

AUTHOR: Gunnar Fehlau ISBN:1892590530 PAGES: 180 LISTPRICE: $19.95
DESCRIPTION: There haven't been any general books about a whole amazing, creative side of bicycling: recumbents and HPVs. Finally, here's one! Enjoy. This book covers History, Racing, Touring, Construction and much more, as regards the colorful, diverse world of recumbents and HPVs. Many great black&white photos, full color 12-pg center spread. REVIEWS: 5-star ratings at Amazon.com. "A most informative Recumbenteer's handbook. Its coverage from grass roots right up to current standards is a "must" for anyone interested in building or improving a recumbent."—L. Morse. "This is a fantastic history of recumbents, along with lots of technical information. It has everything you need to know to get started, if you're thinking about buying a recumbent. If you're experienced with recumbents, it has a lot to offer as well."—a reader "No other book that I know of deals with recumbent bicycles in this breadth and depth. It also helps that it is extremely readable and full of cool pictures. Lots of interesting stuff here, from the history of these odd vehicles to the latest speed records and excellent tips on how to get one for yourself. Very well written and well-suited to anyone who might be interested in these bikes, even if they have no previous knowledge. A bargain at twice the price."—P. Pancella.

A Dirt Road Rider's Trek Epic

AUTHOR: Victor Vicente of America ISBN:1892590506 PAGES: 100 LISTPRICE: $10
DESCRIPTION: If you're a bike buff, you know how rare bike literature is. Here's a bit of story-telling to savor, *A Dirt Road Rider's Trek Epic* by Victor Vincente of America, a bike cult guru hero. This book presents the many media offerings of a unique *victor*. The *Epic* is showcased in this volume along with media reprints from VVA's heyday as first US road racing champion, first modern-era Euro winner, first ultra-distance record holder, and early mountain-bike innovator, dirt guru, events host and then some. Illustrated with his own art from many projects, including bike-making, coin art, posters, and stamps. Sports today seem one-dimensional: why? Here's a fantastically different take: the world of a champ who explores widely. Among many surprises, you'll find that offroad riding offers a treasure of lore and insight. Our author has mined a wondrous chunk of life. His notorious So. Calif. newsletter was the first home of his prose-poem about days and nights in the natural and cultural outback.

Fold-It! —The World of the Folding Bicycle

AUTHOR: Gunnar Fehlau ISBN:1892590573 PAGES: 150 LISTPRICE: $19.95
DESCRIPTION: The world's only book with everything you need to know about folding bikes. Covers history, development, features and the various models offered, with pro's and

con's. With so much new technology readily available, the scene is booming, and the future of the folding bike never looked better! Elegant established models are still inspiring and holding their own, while gorgeous new models are coming out to challenge rigid bikes in every way— but especially in convenience! Find out for yourself. *(Due to be released April, 2003.)*

DreamBoats: A Rare Look at Small Boats in Light of the Heritage of Seafaring Peoples
Memories, Explanation and Innovation with Coastal Craft, Junks, Dhows, Outriggers & More...in the eyes of an old salt. AUTHOR: Richard Carsen ISBN:1892590549 PAGES: 80 LISTPRICE: $10 DESCRIPTION: There aren't any books about the exotic sailboats of sea-faring peoples for the lay reader. And there sure aren't any on how and why they do what they do and how their methods might help the average backyard boater. The anthropology of boats is fascinating and relevant: Western boating developed with expendable crews for maximum profit; 3rd World boating is about sustainability, family, and bringing 'em back alive with enough to live on. Whose heritage or reality seems better to you? Richard Carsen is in his 80's and has traveled the world working in indigenous boatyards. He first gave us his designs and ideas in the magazine *Messing About in Boats*. This book is a compilation of his columns.

The Cross Country Ski, Cook, Look & Pleasure Book
(Out of Print: some dealer copies available.) AUTHOR: Hal Painter ISBN:1892590514 PAGES: 154 LISTPRICE: $20 DESCRIPTION: Reprints and originals available of this 60's-style classic. A unique literary art book on cross country skiing capturing the spirit of the outdoor culture heyday in the US. Zen and the art of skiing. An antidote to consumerism in skiing and an energetic attempt to reconnect skiing with its roots in fluidity, friendship and just plain fun.

The Captain Nemo Cookbook Papers
Everyone's Guide to Zen and the Art of Boating in Hard Times Illustrated, A Nautical Fantasy (Out of Print: some dealer copies available.) AUTHOR: Hal Painter ISBN:18925905522 PAGES: 135 LISTPRICE: $20 DESCRIPTION: Reprints and originals available of this comic 60's look at boating through the eyes of a variety of escapees from the rat race. Zen nuggets, marina etiquette, boat fixer-uppers and an appearance by a wildly mythic hero of boating all combine for a rare literary addition to the boating bookshelf. A great period piece that offers wit and antidotes to the consumerism that's overwhelming modern boating.

Fiction: The Novels of Jack Saunders

General Description of Jack's Style...
In no-holds-barred "Florida writer" tradition, Jack Saunders writes stories about publishing, academia and everyday life, about what it's like to work and succeed while being true to oneself and one's family and culture. He writes honestly and creatively, and that's the understatement of the year--yet it's accessible, fits like a shoe. Tastes like coffee (being an acquired taste, a step up). He writes with encyclopedic insight about how this effort relates to the world around him, other authors, books, movies, music, Florida, cooking, his life, work, business, progress. In folk vernacular with local color that won't quit. Jack names names, uses cultural artifacts in his poetry so superbly you'll be spurred to rent movies, read books, listen to music that you never would've otherwise. Heck, you'll get new appreciation for boxing and baseball..and everything else. (Sailing? Farming?) Folky yet also a linguistic eye-opener. It's that big. It's all about someone trying to do their best in the modern world, to write honestly. Give it a try and see where it gets you, is one of his motifs. Each book is a slice of a larger ouevre (ahem, can you say forklift pallet?)--with letters, memoir, poetry and essay all playing off each other. In the end, though, "it's just stories." Jazz and the blues. In the mainstream of American outsiders: Whitman, Melville, Faulkner, Kerouac, Miller, Algren, Thompson, Bukowski, MacDonald, Willeford, Burke, Hiassen and Finster. As he says, the Cracker spirit lives on and a country boy will make do. Except for

insiders, he is entirely unknown. But he's been working close, prolific and giving it his all for 25 years now. Why haven't you heard of him? Find out...

General Reviews of Jack's Books...

In Jack Saunders our generation is extremely lucky to have a powerful and determined writer, an honest writer. A Diogenes not merely of words, but of provocative thoughts. From his hideaway in Florida, like a super-energized lobster, Saunders lashes out at the sickening hypocrisy which is deadening our senses and rotting our souls. It is Saunders' adamant, boneheaded, determined persistence that is his great strength, his great gift to a society staggering in its own materialistic greed. Saunders is America at its best. He spells out what spirit is all about. And humanity. How do we live? When do we really come ALIVE? As we should? And deserve? America needs writers with such strength and ferocity and independence and integrity, not all those greedy little wordmongers contemplating their private parts on every supermarket shelf. Saunders is more than a literary volcano. He is a live, writhing, crackling wire. Spewing sparks in all directions. Creating and developing a brighter, newer world. *--Raymond Barrio*

As exasperating and slippery a "read" as they come. This work is totally unpretentious (and thus honest) and yet its theme is the total unrelenting pretension of a life. That life is excruciating and unavoidable, unedited and ambiguous, squalling and scrawling, elegant and vulgar, ordinary and completely out of the ordinary. Read it; you'll never forget it. *--John M. Bennett*

I have a hunch your stuff is wild and terrific and keeps going off the rails. I have no better explanation for why you don't find publishers, since you certainly write well enough sentence for sentence and paragraph for paragraph. *--Norman Mailer*

This is some very clever writing...rings true to my own wars with the publishers--good luck! *--Theodore Roszak*

All fine hard hitting work. The works of Jack Saunders give us hope. Hope that our lives won't be horrible wasted foolishness. Even when it seems that hope is all we have left, if you feel you can live a fuller life and spend your days in a more profitable way for yourself AND MANKIND you should read Jack Saunders for a ray of hope and a great deal of enjoyment and amusement. OK it rings so true that you'll forget you're reading & think you're talking to yourself. *--Larry Schlueter*

Hey it broke me up--I imagined someone calling here and asking what I was crying about. I was not crying, kid. I was laughing at Jack Saunders' new movie. *--David Zack*

Screed

AUTHOR:Saunders,Jack,L ISBN: 0912824247 LISTPRICE: $15 DESCRIPTION: Stories about life and dealings with the fine arts scene, as world literature. REVIEWS: Thanks for the copy of Screed. I liked it very much. In fact, I've been reading it aloud to my wife in bed at night. You write in a kind of natural, organic, free-flowing and perfectly lucid style that I much admire. *--Edward Abbey* Dear Jack: Thanks for Screed. It's good diatribe. The reason I know is that diatribe makes me feel better. And I felt better reading it. *--Walker Percy* Thanks for Screed. Nicely done. He rolls on. *--Charles Bukowski*

Evil Genius

AUTHOR: Saunders, Jack L. ISBN: 1892590298 PAGES: 277 LISTPRICE: $15 DESCRIPTION: Mortgages house and gives self Evil Genius Award, first prize ever won. Many cultural reviews. Stories of his days in archeology and grad school, fun with The System, as world literature. REVIEWS: In my library the novels of Jack Saunders go right next to MOBY DICK, ISLANDIA, and THE RECOGNITIONS. EVIL GENIUS is an astonishing feat--like watching a man lay eight hundred miles of track single-handed, without ever once stopping, or faltering, or resorting to adjectives. *--Dr. Al Ackerman* Thank you for sending me EVIL GENIUS, which I read last night. I didn't really want to stay up so late, but the book moved forward with a momentum that was overpowering and almost tragic. Your fiction can also be very annoying--which is a virtue, I think. *--Richard Grayson* I am very pleased at the way you handled the tale of your life in EVIL GENIUS. It owes something to Henry Miller, but every writer owes a debt to those before them and those in turn were helped by their predecessors. No one is an absolute original, but you come close. *--William Eastlake* Words for Evil Genius? I took nearly a year out of my own writing time to work on SCREED, on its production, what more need to be said for how I feel about your worth? You're a diamond in the rough, Jack. You've got an intrinsic worth worth more than the realized worth of about 99% of the writers in this country lumped together. If you feel in your heart of hearts that what you're doing is what you must do, then that's settled. Settled with nothing further implied. I'd say your chances of being treated with any sort of kindness, your chances of being recognized for your intrinsic worth, are worse than mine, and mine are Virginia slim. *--John Bennett*

Open Book

AUTHOR: Saunders, Jack L. ISBN: 1892590301 PAGES: 250 LISTPRICE: $15 DE-SCRIPTION: Covers what happened to Evil Genius, how he goes from bad to worse: who would follow up EG with another book? None but a blockhead. Stories about working life after college, as world literature. REVIEW: Thanks for Evil Genius and Open Book; I enjoyed both of them, and asked my publisher to send you my new book, Sideswipe, when it comes out in Feb. In 1957, Theodore Pratt told me that Delray Beach was a better town than N. Y. for a writer. "If you stay in Florida," he told me, "you'll never run out of things to write about." He was right, of course; I never have, and you won't either. My most productive years were from age 50 to 55, and I'm sure that yours will be too. *--Charles Willeford*

Forty

AUTHOR:Saunders,Jack,L ISBN: 0945209010 LISTPRICE: $10 DESCRIPTION: Stories about Jack's efforts to enter "Stage 4" of writing, to give it up, then see what happens. Plenty of culture and bluegrass reviews and overview of life on the edge, with kids, as world literature.

Common Sense

AUTHOR: Saunders, Jack L. ISBN: 1892590263 PAGES: 137 LISTPRICE: $10 DE-SCRIPTION: Part 1 of a 2-part series, Jack Saunders writes stories about his efforts to acculturize IBM during the early days of the PC so they wouldn't get left behind by a competitor more in tune with the times...it didn't work. ("Full Plate", book 2.) An open discussion with his superiors asking how a committee system which rewards buck-passing could ever recognize innovation. "This is the only treaty I will make." World literature.

Full Plate

AUTHOR: Saunders, Jack L. ISBN: 1892590271 PAGES: 76 LISTPRICE: $10 DESCRIP-TION: Part 2 of a 2-part series, Jack Saunders writes stories about his efforts to acculturize IBM during the early days of the PC so they wouldn't get left behind by a competitor more in tune with the times...it didn't work. ("Common Sense", book 1.) "A Contract between Dem and I'Ashola." World literature.

Blue Darter

AUTHOR: Saunders, Jack L. ISBN: 1892590255 PAGES: 85 LISTPRICE: $10 DESCRIP-TION: An aggressive, tricky fast pitch: "Rare back and hurl your blue darter at their ear." Stories from Jack's youth. World literature.

Lost Writings

AUTHOR: Saunders, Jack ISBN: 189259028X PAGES: 158 LISTPRICE: $10 DESCRIP-TION: "Minor chord: Bigfoot sidles into the shadows." Fiesty writings, as world literature.

Other Fiction

Potluck

AUTHOR: Rudloe, Jack ISBN: 1892590375 PAGES: 228 LISTPRICE: $14.95
DESCRIPTION: Hard times and opportunity collide on the high seas. *Potluck* is a page-turning thriller about a decent captain who decides, in extremity, to take a big risk. It's the only realistic picture of small family commercial fishing on the Gulf Coast of Florida and the problems and temptations that confront it. Corrupt forces on all sides are pushing this stalwart breed of Americans into desperation or extinction. But they still do their best to feed us. If you've ever wondered what the lives are like behind the few fishing boats you still see along the coast, look no further. A rare look at the broad and surprising impacts of drug smuggling, misguided regulation and realtor greed along the coast. Author Rudloe is the pre-eminent conservationist of the Florida Gulf Coast, author of highly regarded naturalist books, and operator of the only independent (and thus frequently bureaucratically besieged) marine institute in the region. REVIEW: "Jack Rudloe's non-fiction account of living on the Gulf Coast, *The Living Dock at Panacea*, is a Florida classic that ranks with *Cross Creek*. In *Potluck*, Rudloe proves he can handle fiction with the same energy and insightful style."—Randy Wayne White (*Shark River, Sanibel Flats*)

Tales From the Texas Gang

AUTHOR: Blackolive, Bill ISBN: 1892590387 PAGES: 339 LISTPRICE: $19.95
DESCRIPTION: Wild Bill's writing is in the tradition of Melville...and Keroauc and Castenada and Abbey. It's a bit like Cormac McCarthy as well, only more realistic, authentic and candid. If you like the thrust of those other writers, you'll be thankful for *Tales From the Texas Gang*. It's one of the rare significant additions to American literature. And it's based on real life, and a real life gang. It's set in the late 1800's. It's an outlaw gang gunfighter novel...but so much more. (*Due out Winter 2003.*)

The Emeryville War

AUTHOR: Blackolive, Bill ISBN: 1892590395 PAGES: 109 LISTPRICE: $12.95
DESCRIPTION: If you liked *Confederacy of Dunces*, you'll like this. Only, remember, it's real. Life in the fringey, unhip edge of Berkeley in the 60's. You've never seen neighbors, cops and city officials like these, nor an observer like Wild Bill—dogs, barbels, wrecked cars and all. (*Due out Spring 2004.*)

Philosophy: Fifth Way Press

Author: Ron Puhek

Fifth Way Press is an imprint of OYB. It is sponsored by the MIEM, the Michigan Institute of Educational Metapsychology—a fancy way to say "workable religion, philosophy and psychology for living today, inspired by the best of the past". The institute has been represented for 30 years by weekly meetings of quiet, polite folk. Typically these have been people from the 'helping' professions who themselves see that their ways need help. Are in desparate straits. Due to modernism. The 'Fifth Way' concept comes from 'the fourth way' of Ouspensky and Gurdjieff. The previous three ways to attain contact with reality were: the emotional way of the monk, the intellectual way of the yogi, and the physical way of the fakir. These were unified and superceded by the fourth way of the householder, who lives normally in everyday life. The Fifth Way takes the best of all ways without leaving any behind, transcending them all: count your fingers: thumbs up!

If you like Simone Weil, St. Theresa and St. John of the Cross, you'll like Puhek. It's plainly written but maximumly intense philosophy for a modern age. His reflections integrate and build on many works, especially Plato, Sartre, Jung and Freud.

Analects of Wisdom

SERIES: The Art of Living, Book 1 AUTHOR: Puhek, Ronald E. ISBN: 1892590123 PAGES: 118 LISTPRICE: $10 DESCRIPTION: Analects are, literally, "cut readings." In this collection of verses and commentaries, not just the verses but even the commentaries are brief. They all use two devices of higher knowledge: *paradoxical logic* and experiential thinking. Representing the first phase of the soul's transformation in this life, the *Analects* provide instruction in how to live. They establish "rules" whose truth can be tested even by the mind still held captive by the senses. Anyone can understand them without a great development of faith. These stirrings of other-worldly wisdom can work effectively in guiding life in this world. We are of the opinion that the verses themselves may have had more than one author. This is almost certainly true of the commentaries. *Analects of Wisdom* is the first volume of the trilogy, *The Art of Living*. This trilogy is companion to its predecessor, *The Science of Life*, and it is recommended that each volume be read in tandem with its parallel in the other trilogy.

Descent into the World

SERIES: The Art of Living, Book 2 AUTHOR: Puhek, Ronald E. ISBN: 189259014X PAGES: 175 LISTPRICE: $10 DESCRIPTION: As the middle book of the *Art of Living* trilogy, the *Descent into the World* deals with the second phase of development. It is the one hardest to pass through. In the first phase as we launch on our inner journey, hope sustains our spirits. In the third phase, as we draw closer to our destination, we see it distinctly ahead and the joy of anticipation arises. The second phase, however, requires that we return to face the world where we will do our final work. The *Descent* describes this harshest and driest time. Now the comforts of inward meditation leave us. We meditate but return to the world where we must overcome severe tests and avoid deep traps if we are to find in the end the redemption of love.

The Redemption of Love

SERIES: The Art of Living, Book 3 AUTHOR: Puhek, Ronald E. ISBN: 1892590158 PAGES: 209 LISTPRICE: $15 DESCRIPTION: Love is the greatest, most enduring, most divine blessing on earth. But love is also suffering, and much of what is done in its name makes it appear to be a curse. The Greeks celebrated love in the form of gods such as Aphrodite and Eros; the ancient Christians said, "God is love." As both indicate, love is a powerful spiritual principle in our lives, but any spiritual principle can be corrupted and its power transformed into a malignant force. *The Redemption of Love* seeks to answer how love gets corrupted and how it can be purified and freed to serve its natural function of rescuing human life and redeeming the world.

A Special Note About the Triologies

All of Puhek's books stands on their own, but the previous 3 books listed are part of a trilogy called *"The Art of Living,"* which interacts with the next three books listed which are themselves part of a trilogy called *"The Science of Life."* Each of the three volumes in the two trilogies describes development in qualities of soul called hope, faith, and love. The first volume in each trilogy focuses on the inner and outer growth of hope; the second in each, on faith; and the third in each, on love. The twin trilogies are distinct in as much as one (*"The Science of Life"*) deals with the three-step movement to integrity in life by means of an upward and inward journey to knowledge of the integrating good that alone makes a life of integrity possible while the other (*"The Art of Living"*) deals with how actually to live in the world with integrity and meaning. But each volume in the *"Science"* trilogy parallels its like number in the *"Art"* trilogy. This is because the first volume in each represents the principle of *hope*. Hope is the virtue of memory. The first volumes represent how human, not individual, memory stimulates and guides hope's development first upward through group study under rules where the group represents human or universal wisdom (*Seminars*) and then downward through insightful sayings of inherited wisdom guiding life (*Analects*). The second volume in each trilogy represents the subsequent movement of *faith*. Similarly, this involves first an upward direction by losing illusory beliefs in the realm of visible goods and attending to the timeless or eternal good (*Meditations*) and then a downward direction in the practical world (*Descent*). Finally, the third volumes represent the movement in *love* upward to the ultimately indefinable Good (*Contemplation*) and downward to living divine love in the world (*Redemption of Love*). While each volume can be read independently, there are two additional reading strategies. First, the reader might well first follow the movement of understanding through the whole *"Science"* trilogy and then the movement of life in the world in the *"Art"* trilogy. Alternatively, the reader might even better follow the path of hope upward in the first book of *"Science"* and downward in the first book of *"Art,"* then the path of faith upward and downward in the second books of each trilogy, and finally the path of love upward and downward in the third books.

A Guide to the Nature & Practice of Seminars in Integrative Studies

SERIES: The Science of Life: Book 1 AUTHOR: Puhek, Ronald E. ISBN: 1892590093 PAGES: 145 LISTPRICE: $10 DESCRIPTION: *"Seminars in Integrative Studies"* is written to serve a distinct and special kind of learning. Integrative studies focus on searching for a principle of unity or integrity to hold together our knowledge and our life. These studies concern themselves with consciousness and conscience. Consciousness and conscience are different from mere knowledge and value judgments. Consciousness and conscience are comprehensive and integrating instead of single, narrow and analytical. Consciousness integrates your understanding and conscience integrates your sense of the good. We concentrate here not on offering a preliminary and superficial "exposure" to the concept and practice of integrated knowledge. Instead, we address those with a serious commitment to integrative research and to those working together as a permanent community dedicated to integrative studies. Thus, the idea of "seminars" in integrative studies refers not to classes in any ordinary sense of external enrollment but to personal intention, interest, and involvement. Seminars are regular gatherings of those devoted to pursuing integration in knowledge and life. These seminars have formal and informal rules. They require an inner commitment and a desire to grow to knowledge of life through investigating the nature of life using the only concrete and direct perspective we have: our own existence.

Spiritual Meditations

SERIES: The Science of Life: Book 2 AUTHOR: Puhek, Ronald E. ISBN: 1892590107 PAGES: 166 LISTPRICE: $10 DESCRIPTION: *Spiritual Meditations*, the second book in the trilogy *The Science of Life*, is an excursion into the second stage of human spiritual development. Its primary focus is on the practices that will allow us to elevate our understanding so we might better perceive the standard of value that can inwardly bring us peace and outwardly guide us to the best life possible. Integrative knowledge is essential to both and methods of pursuing such knowledge are essential if we are to gain it and live fuller, less violent, and more harmonious lives. None of the methods prevailing today is adequate to the task of arriving at integrative knowledge. This book presents part of the process of an effective response to life.

The Spirit of Contemplation

SERIES: The Science of Life: Book 3 AUTHOR: Puhek, Ronald E. ISBN: 1892590115 PAGES: 175 LISTPRICE: $10 DESCRIPTION: *The Spirit of Contemplation* is the final book in the trilogy *The Science of Life*. It explores the culminating phase of spiritual development and what needs to happen after the completion of the spiritual exercises associated with meditation. Meditation takes us out of the world; contemplation returns us to it. Meditation renders us unable to live in reality; contemplation realizes the redemption of reality. It is the highest peak of the mountain of spriutal growth. The entire trilogy, however, is only the first of two. *The Science of Life* concentrates on the development of spiritual understanding; the second trilogy, *The Art of Living*, will focus on the transformation of life.

Meaning & Creativity

SERIES: Blue Trilogy, Book 1 AUTHOR: Puhek, Ronald E. ISBN: 1892590069 PAGES: 118 LISTPRICE: $10 DESCRIPTION: *Meaning and Creativity*, first book of the Blue Trilogy, explores the illusions of meaning that dominate life today and how to break out of their chains-a vital first step in the process of reality. Life is not worth living if it is not meaningful. Most of the strategies for living today are, however, merely methods of enabling us to endure frightful meaninglessness. They are all mechanical and operate by encouraging us to flee from one meaningless activity as soon as we catch the scent of its decaying character and race to another, equally meaningless. Life becomes a continuous merry-go-round. We move in circles, getting nowhere, but are lost in the illusion that we are moving along a straight path to greater good-even when we try to use methods that are thought to counteract this. So long have we lived like this that if we would wake up and see our true state, we would be shattered. Nihilism would be our fate. To avoid this catastrophe, we need to prepare ourselves with some understanding of how to live a life of meaning. The only meaningful life is a creative life. This is easy to see once we realize what "creativity" consists of.

The Abyss Absolute

The Autobiography of a Suicide SERIES: Blue Trilogy, Book 2 AUTHOR: Puhek, Ronald E. ISBN: 1892590077 PAGES: 146 LISTPRICE: $10 DESCRIPTION: *The Abyss Absolute* is the second book of the Blue Trilogy. It is the heart and soul of this series. Realizing the meaning-lessness of most of contemporary life and even understanding how we must live if we are to find meaning are not enough. By themselves, these achievements may end in nothing but disillusion-disillusion of the meaninglessness and disillusion with the prospects of finding an alternative-even among those approaches typically thought to bring hope. This is because before we can find a way upward we must first allow ourselves to fall into an abyss so profound that it feels as if it will annihilate us. Courage to enter this abyss is the only hope of escaping the emptiness of contemporary life, but there are dangerous traps along the way.

Killer Competitiveness

SERIES: Blue Trilogy, Book 3 AUTHOR: Puhek, Ronald E. ISBN: 1892590085 PAGES: 130 LISTPRICE: $10 DESCRIPTION:*Killer Competitiveness* is the third and last book of the Blue Trilogy. We explored the meaninglessness that dominates life today in *Meaning and Creativity*, the first book of the series. Then we face a great challenge when we take up a path to meaning in the second book, *The Abyss Absolute*. This last book accounts for how it is possible for us today to exist so long under meaningless conditions without realizing it. So empty is life without meaning that it could continue only with the help of an extremely powerful illusion. This compelling illusion is generated by competitiveness in nearly everything we do-even in our supposed efforts to cooperate or function independently. Competitiveness generates the illusion of value. Therefore, we do not see the valuelessness of our lives even as we suffer from it.

Mind, Soul & Spirit

An Inquiry into the Spiritual Derailments of Modern Life AUTHOR: Puhek, Ronald E. ISBN: 1892590026 PAGES: 148 LISTPRICE: $10 DESCRIPTION:The prevailing styles of living today require the "derailment" of our energies. The spirit or energy that life grants us to fulfill our destiny is seized, imprisoned, and then turned away from its natural direction, usually to be amplified for ulterior motives. The various derailments of spirit operate unconsciously upon their victims. We today are particularly vulnerable to blindness here because of our ignorance of the dynamics of spiritual life-even as many of us pretend to spirituality and feel energy which we trust to be helpful. Spiritual knowledge is almost completely absent in all contemporary education, and, as a society, we are nearly bankrupt spiritually. This book maps out the many ways our spirit gets diverted without our knowing it. We must take back our spiritual birthright.

The Powers of Knowledge

SERIES: The Crisis in Modern Culture: Book 1 AUTHOR: Puhek, Ronald E. ISBN: 1892590042 PAGES: 83 LISTPRICE: $10 DESCRIPTION: Modern culture is the source of a crisis in civilization. This now world-wide culture is generating increasingly intolerable conditions of human life mostly because of the faulty assumptions built into it that concern our powers of knowledge. Because of these assumptions, we fail today to develop and use the whole range of our powers. Consequently, we find ourselves increasingly unable to perceive, let alone understand, the forces flowing into and out of our lives. We can see that things are bad but not why they are so. We do not see this because the very tools of perception we use are the flawed victims of a culture that renders them inadequate. *The Powers of Knowledge* (Book I of The Crisis of Modern Culture) explores our powers of knowledge-both those we only partly or wrongly develop and those we entirely neglect. It shows how we may expand our awareness by actualizing all of them in a more integrated way. It illustrates how we can turn aside the forces of destruction that today are reaching critical mass everywhere, even in places we thought were protected.

Violence

SERIES: The Crisis in Modern Culture: Book 2 AUTHOR: Puhek, Ronald E. ISBN: 1892590050 PAGES: 82 LISTPRICE: $10 DESCRIPTION:This book (Book II of The Crisis of Modern Culture) presents an approach to understanding the specific forms of violence particularly appropriate to contemporary life. It illustrates that most violence today is completely invisible both to those who do it and to those who suffer it. This is because the prevailing concept of violence is inadequate. If our concept of violence encompasses only its physical or sensible forms, we will not see it when it operates even when we think we fight against it in its emotional and especially in spiritual forms. Today the dominant form of violence is spiritual. Today we can even love violence because we suffer from it in ways we do not see. Today there is violence in our acts of love. We must be concerned, therefore, both about our love of violence and the violence of our love.

Stephen of the Holy Mountain

AUTHOR: Puhek, Ronald E. ISBN: 1892590018 PAGES: 94 LISTPRICE: $10 DESCRIPTION: An inner journey, outwardly masking itself as a sojourn up the side of a high mountain, *Stephen of the Holy Mountain* seeks answers to the most perplexing questions that come to those who have awakened from the sleep of ordinary existence. The mysterious figure of Stephen acts as a guide both to the author and to many others who climb Stephen's mountain to find him. His advice is often too harsh for many who think they seek it. Unfailingly kind, however, Stephen does his best to aid all who come to him.

The Metaphysical Imperative

A Critique of the Modern Approach to Science AUTHOR: Puhek, Ronald E. ISBN: 1892590034 PAGES: 135 LISTPRICE: $10 DESCRIPTION: Metaphysical assumptions are and have always been a necessary and unavoidable part of human life. Unfortunately, today we have fallen into the catastrophic belief that our basic perceptions of reality do not rest on metaphysical judgments but are purely "physical." If we use the term "metaphysics" at all, it is only to refer to abstract philosophical ideas or, worse, to half-crazed religious attitudes. Consequently, we have rendered ourselves unable to distinguish between the metaphysical and non-metaphysical aspects of any knowledge and are still less able to judge whether our hidden or flaunted metaphysical assumptions are faulty and, if so, how they might be corrected. *The Metaphysical Imperative* explores the nature of metaphysical assumptions, how they are all-pervasive, which ones dominate our attitudes today, what their flaws are, and how we might improve them.

Social Consciousness
Renewed Theory in the Social Sciences AUTHOR: Puhek, Ronald E. ISBN: 189259000X PAGES: 202 LISTPRICE: $10 DESCRIPTION:This is a unique study of the theoretical foundations of social science. In particular, it criticizes the practice of applying the methods of the physical sciences to the study of human life. Methods very appropriate to the study of "things" or objects are not appropriate to the study of the human self. When we use such inappropriate methods, we end in making the human self into a thing, and all the knowledge we gain affords us only more power to dominate and suppress the human. These methods violate human freedom and dignity in any use, let alone in their application in fields like psychology, advertising and politics. This study concludes by developing an alternative approach to explanation.

Matricide
AUTHOR: Lombardi, Vincent L. ISBN: 189259031X PAGES: 287 LISTPRICE: $15 DESCRIPTION: A novel about a crime that shook a small town and hurled a 12-year-old girl into the bizarre world of court-appointed professionals. As she grows up, she's driven to madness, torn between cultures, struggling at the crossroads of what comes next—will it be Brave New World or a new Renaissance?

Local Culture Ruminations

Making Somewhere from Nowhere: Growing Up in Freeway Exitville
AUTHOR: Potter, Jeff PAGES: 100 LISTPRICE: $10 DESCRIPTION: Contemporary essays written about the author's hometown—a faceless suburb of professors, professionals, mall-rats, and mini-malls. A rare look at 'here,' but perhaps it's important to break the aversion to looking at what's closest to home since everywhere is starting to look like 'here.' —It's a traffic-packed sector smashed out of the rural countryside in the last 30 years. But it's also a place with hidden natural and cultural distinctions. How can it survive the onslaught of speculation? That's the drama of it. Potter writes about Place versus Noplace and offers practical methods which can be used to rebuild somewhere out of the nowhere created by our best and brightest. A candid, polite, unpublishable point of view unseen before (the average view) intended to raise the level of discussion by taking it away from experts, specialists and those who hope to separate people from each other for their advantage.

"Out Your Backdoor" Zine Anthology, Vols. 1 & 2
OYB: the Magazine of Cultural Rescue, Modern Folkways and Homemade Adventure (*OYB* Issues #1-8 & #9)

OYB has been covering the neglected aspects of modern folk culture since 1990. The latest issue #9 is the Vol. 2 of the anthology, $5, 64 pages; earlier issues #1-8 are reproduced together as Vol.1., $20, 200+ pages.

OYB is the back porch of culture, where people hang out helping each other enjoy and endure the nifty things that people really do. (The front door being for salesmen and authorities.) *OYB* helps those who've 'been there, done that' to get to the next level. *OYB* is for all-rounders and generalists, like most people are. It works against the alienating specialties that society uses to split us from ourselves and each other. It explores all sorts of things: biking, books, boats, movies, zines, religion, skiing, fishing, hunting, garage sales, getting by, making do. Get the picture? (Big website at OutYourBackdoor.com.)

The magazine restarts Summer 2003 with #10, $3. Subscriptions $5 a year for two issues.